Phenomenology and the E: Sport Experience

Understanding the motivations behind those who partake in extreme sports can be difficult for some. If the popular conception holds that the incentive behind extreme sports participation is entirely to do with risking one's life, then this confusion will continue to exist. However, an in-depth examination of the phenomenology of the extreme sport experience yields a much more complex picture.

This book revisits the definition of extreme sports as those activities where a mismanaged mistake or accident would most likely result in death. Extreme sports are not necessarily synonymous with risk and participation may not be about risk-taking. Participants report deep inner transformations that influence world views and meaningfulness, feelings of coming home and authentic integration as well as a freedom beyond the everyday. Phenomenologically, these experiences have been interpreted as transcendent of time, other, space and body. Extreme sport participation therefore points to a more potent, life-enhancing endeavour worthy of further investigation. This book adopts a broad hermeneutic phenomenological approach to critique the assumed relationship to risk-taking, the death wish and the concept of 'No Fear' in extreme sports, and repositions the experience in a previously unexplored manner.

This is valuable reading for students and academics interested in Sports Psychology, Social Psychology, Health Psychology, Tourism, Leisure Studies and the practical applications of phenomenology.

Eric Brymer is a Reader in the Institute of Sport, Physical Activity and Leisure at Leeds Beckett University, Leeds, UK.

Robert Schweitzer is Professor of Psychology at the School of Psychology and Counselling at Queensland University of Technology, Brisbane, Australia.

Routledge Research in Sport, Culture and Society

Phenomenology and the Extreme Sport Experience

Eric Brymer and Robert Schweitzer

Routledge
Taylor & Francis Group

LONDON AND NEW YORK

First published 2017
by Routledge

2 Park Square, Milton Park, Abingdon, Oxfordshire OX14 4RN
52 Vanderbilt Avenue, New York, NY 10017

Routledge is an imprint of the Taylor & Francis Group, an informa business

First issued in paperback 2020

British Library Cataloguing in Publication Data
A catalogue record for this book is available from the British Library

Library of Congress Cataloging in Publication Data
Names: Ferraro, Gary P., author. | Briody, Elizabeth Kathleen, author.
Title: The cultural dimension of global business / Gary P. Ferraro,
Elizabeth K. Briody.
Description: Eighth edition. | Abingdon, Oxon ; New York, NY :
Routledge, 2017. | Includes bibliographical references and index.
Identifiers: LCCN 2016047798 (print) | LCCN 2017005696 (ebook) |
ISBN 9781138632455 (hardback : alk. paper) | ISBN 9781138202290
(pbk. : alk. paper) | ISBN 9781315411019 (e-book)
Subjects: LCSH: International business enterprises–Social aspects. |
Intercultural communication. | Technical assistance–Anthropological
aspects.
Classification: LCC HD2755.5 .F48 2017 (print) | LCC HD2755.5 (ebook)
| DDC 302.3/5–dc23
LC record available at https://lccn.loc.gov/2016047798

ISBN: 978-1-138-95761-9 (hbk)
ISBN: 978-0-367-37450-1 (pbk)

Typeset in Times New Roman
by Wearset Ltd, Boldon, Tyne and Wear

Printed in the United Kingdom
by Henry Ling Limited

Contents

Foreword

Extreme sports have emerged as a frontier of human experience. The reasons are not difficult to understand, the extreme sport person embodies, for many of us, the realisation of our greatest desires. At the same time extreme sport activities expose us to our most profound fears relating to risk, dread and even death. The current work has been inspired by our own association with extreme sport and the often inspiring people involved in these activities.

Extreme sports consistently evoke images of crazy people taking unnecessary risks, living out a death wish or walking the edge vigorously espousing the 'no fear' slogan. Traditional explanations about motivations for participating in extreme sports and viewpoints on extreme sports activities are most often disapproving and derogatory: 'Because some people are stone crazy. Or, because some people are addicted to adrenalin' (Bane, 1996, p. 23). These perspectives are reflected in the writings of theorists and researchers alike.

On the surface, the logic behind these preconceptions is undeniable; it would seem that to willingly participate in an activity, for fun, that has a strong chance of resulting in death, a person has got to be crazy! After all, why would anyone want to provoke physical, mental and emotional annihilation? We are not talking breaks, scratches and bruises; we are talking about the end of life. The extrapolation is clear. Extreme sport participants must be crazy to spend leisure time pursuing an activity characterised by inherent and unnecessary risks, or if participants are not crazy then they must be fearless with no respect for life. Not just any kind of fearlessness but an unhealthy one, one that means life for these people has no worth. There are even web-based discussions on whether society should ban these crazy, unnecessary activities. After all, a sane person would not be found hanging their toes over a 300 metre cliff getting ready to jump or balancing precariously on a board riding a wave the size of a house, would they?

Yet on closer inspection participants, whether men or women, teenagers or pensioners, come from all cultures and walks of life; doctors, carpenters, engineers, software programmers, and when pushed for an opinion, do not share the viewpoints outlined above. The image of the risk-taking adrenaline junky espousing a 'no fear' image projected on to extreme sport participants reveals interpretive difficulties when a non-participant attempts to understand an experience by metaphorically placing themselves in a participant's shoes. That is, the only way to understand the extreme sport experience is to live it. This is a point succinctly articulated by the immortal words of the great mountaineer, Edmund Hillary: 'if you have to ask the question you will never understand why' (Hillary cited in Ogilvie, 1974, p. 94). Yet ask we have.

Certain individuals have sought and developed unbelievable skills in activities that seem to have little purpose. Effective extreme sport participation requires an extraordinary level of technical expertise, environmental knowledge, self-awareness, hard work and commitment. Getting it wrong would most likely result in death. For a majority of participants, there is little if any material reward in the form of fame or fortune. The nature of an extreme sport means that the participant is subject to the whims of the natural world. No water in the rivers means no kayaking; the wind in the wrong direction means no BASE jumping. Yet despite these obvious hazards and constraints people still choose to participate.

This book is about the experiences of those who have chosen to walk the road less travelled, and traverses the edge of what is commonly conceived as being beyond normal risk-taking behaviour. It is about the experiences of those who continually extend known boundaries by participating at the extreme or outer limits of certain sports. Extreme sport participants are involved in a range of sports including extreme skiing, BASE jumping, waterfall kayaking, big wave surfing and free-solo climbing.

Extreme sports have been written about and explored before, so what makes this book different? First we have drawn from a multi-layered set of resource material, from face-to-face discussions with experienced extreme sports participants, from first-hand accounts, from biographies and from research papers across a variety of disciplines. The thread that ties them all together is that resources referred to focus on leisure activities with the potential to result in the death of the participants. For example, mountaineering and big wave surfing may not immediately strike one as being in accord but at the extreme level death is the likely result if something goes wrong. Our aim is to stay true to the lived experience and explicate an understanding of the extreme sports experience.

A second reason why this book is different derives from the philosophy and methodology that underpinned the exploration. We endeavoured to start afresh and look beyond the traditional and limiting risk-focused or cultural explanations to discover extreme sports as if they were new and unexplored, to minimise the influence of bias or assumptions based on theoretical standpoints and personal perspectives and consider participants from a purely experiential standpoint. Phenomenology provides the explorer with such a framework.

Phenomenology rejects Cartesian dualism that considers mind and body as two distinct things and objectivist assumptions that the world is filled with objects that exist independent of human experience. The phenomenological attitude requires the adoption of a different worldview, one that is more radical and comprehensive than any other. This is akin to observing the world in a state of wonder, as if the familiar is suddenly unfamiliar, to learn to see all over again. Thus, phenomenology is, in its simplest form, a method for exploring human experience and defining its nature from a stance requiring the transcendence of cultural conditioning and its consequent assumptions about self, consciousness and external objects. The ultimate aim of phenomenology is to return to immediate or primordial experience through intuition or insights.

A relatively new addition to the phenomenological family is transpersonal phenomenology. Traditional phenomenology is appropriate for exploration into those experiences that can be articulated in everyday language and are recognised by a reasonable number of people. Transpersonal phenomenology, on the other hand, aims to describe those experiences that are beyond the commonplace, but are shared by the few. The central point here is that some experiences (e.g. the extreme sport experience) are of an exceptional nature. Transpersonal perspectives recognise the relevance and legitimate experiences of those who have had extraordinary experiences. Transpersonal phenomenology steps out of the Western-oriented paradigm into a more inclusive paradigm by accepting and recognising parallels to the wisdom traditions such as indigenous spirituality, Taoism, Buddhism, Hinduism and Sufism as well as some of the mystical aspects from Judaism, Islam and Christianity. Essentially, transpersonal phenomenology is concerned with ultimate human experiences and the study of human potential.

The third reason this book is different to those previously considering extreme sports relates to the experiences that are described by participants. We have considered where appropriate how the findings as interpreted might be reflected in similar experiences as described by others, not so much as a means to explain but as a way of enhancing the descriptions offered by extreme sport participants. A fourth reason is that it has been written for anyone who may be interested in extreme sports in an accessible style which hopefully contrasts with the technical representations that fill so many library shelves. As a researcher interested in extreme sports or phenomenology this book presents a complete phenomenological study; as a participant in these activities you may well recognise yourself in these words. As a non-participant, you will get a glimpse into the world of the extreme participant. You may even get to learn something about what stops you from taking the plunge. As a 'wannabe' extreme athlete this book may help you formulate your next move.

The text is organised with each chapter exploring a concept or theme in-depth. The first chapter introduces extreme sports and provides boundaries for the sections and chapters which follow. Chapters 2, 3 and 4 present phenomenology as a principled and applied process lending itself to the study of human experience across the human sciences. Chapter 2 outlines what phenomenology is and the different ways in which phenomenology has been realised. We focus on the four phenomenological perspectives that influenced this study; transcendental phenomenology, hermeneutic phenomenology, existential phenomenology and transpersonal phenomenology. The argument presented is that for phenomenological research to be phenomenological there are certain essential principles that must be met. The third chapter describes the main ways that phenomenological research has been actualised from each of the four perspectives and how this knowledge may guide phenomenology in practice. The fourth chapter outlines our phenomenological method and shows how this method adheres to phenomenological principles. This chapter has been written to provide guidance for anyone interested in undertaking phenomenological research, with notes showing how the process guided our research project.

Chapters 5, 6 and 7 deconstruct the often-held notions about extreme sports and the relationship to risk, death and fear. It is not our intention to argue that these factors have never been part of some participants' extreme sport experience. After all, it is perhaps these qualities that attracted both media and marketing interest. Instead we aim to position these constructs in their proper place as for a majority of participants the 'extreme' notion as typically understood is just a reflection of marketing hype.

Perhaps risk-taking, death and fear are all part of the same identity; however, for ease of exploration the notions have been separated in the text in an attempt to do justice to each. Risk, death and fear are dealt with in that order as part of the journey towards revealing the extreme sports experience itself. This order has been chosen because out of the three constructs risk is arguably furthest away from the experience and fear more closely related to aspects of the experience.

Chapter 5, on risk, aims to place the extreme sports experience within a framework of current understandings by reviewing relevant scientific, technical and informal work on risk-taking. The view that extreme sport participation is purely about the notion of risk is questioned. The review highlights a limited and often inconclusive understanding of extreme sports and a potentially false assumption that the extreme sport experience is just further along a risk continuum.

The sixth chapter, on death, explores the assertion that the extreme sport experience is all about a desire for death. As the reader will find, fewer academic studies have theorised an explicit relationship with death than with risk, but this remains a common assumption. Once again this chapter draws upon the words of those who participate and other non-technical literature to support the arguments. The seventh chapter follows a pattern similar to the previous two but focuses on the notion of fear. Or to be more precise, it questions the belief that participants in extreme sports either have no fear or have some other inappropriate relationship with fear. Yet without the experience of fear and the potential of death the extreme sport experience may not even exist.

The next four chapters deal more directly with the experience as described by participants. It is assumed that the extreme sport experience is more than a moment in linear time and is better considered as a temporal journey or a stretched moment in time. Once again it may be that the subjects of these four chapters are as interwoven as string in a rope and that by attempting to unravel the mystery, we just end up with the rope reduced to three lengths of string. Still, as the reader will see, an effective understanding of the extreme sport experience requires us to gain an understanding of the components of the experience.

Chapter 8 considers the changes experienced by participants and asks the question 'what happens to me?'. The answer, it would seem, contradicts the often held assumption that the experience is just about being an 'extreme dude' or that extreme sports are about presenting a superficial face to the world in order to create an image of rebellion. The 'typical' perceptions about the 'extreme dude' identity are no more than a creation by non-participants or marketing hype. Chapter 9 is about identity. The aim of this chapter is to extend immediate or typical notions and show that the extreme sports participant describes a sense of self-understanding that goes beyond psychological and cultural notions of identity. Extreme sports are deeply rewarding and trigger feelings of truly being alive, excited and happy.

Chapter 10 is an exploration into how the experience enables, empowers and liberates participants and as such explores a theme of freedom, the argument being that freedom extends the typical notions of 'freedom-from' or 'freedom-to' and adds a third dimension, best described as 'freedom-as-letting-go'. Such freedom is about transcending abilities and limitations. As in the previous chapters the structure introduces relevant theoretical perceptions and discusses them against the perceptions of those who participate. Chapter 11 explores a theme we term the ineffable. That is, many of the experiences are not easily defined, and may best be understood in terms of something reaching beyond itself.

Throughout these chapters, theoretical and philosophical concepts seemingly describing similar notions are explored. Where appropriate, writings from the wisdom traditions as well as Western perspectives have been integrated to ensure a rounded and appropriately deep perspective on the issues highlighted. For, as even the great phenomenologist Heidegger reportedly confirmed, phenomenology might learn a great deal from those who espouse Eastern philosophical understandings.

All chapters have been written to support the aim of this text: a description of the fundamental nature of the extreme sport experience. The final chapter presents a full phenomenological description of the extreme sport experience in terms of lived body, lived other, lived space and lived time. So if the phenomenological account is your sole interest, then skip to the final chapter now. However, you may be missing something exciting: an understanding of something perhaps only experienced by a few but arguably wished for by many of us. A glimpse into human potential, a pointer to appreciating what it means to be human.

On our journeys we have had the privilege of meeting many extreme sport participants and have experienced them all as wonderfully inspiring people. Ordinary men and women who have answered the call to adventure often in the face of great adversity. The extreme sport participant, by accepting the challenge, embodies the realisation of human potential. Such experiences are not only those of the other, but if we could but stop for a while, listen and learn, we may all gain a greater appreciation of our own potential.

References

Bane, M. (1996). *Over the edge: a regular guy's odyssey in extreme sports*. New York: Macmillan.

Ogilvie, B. C. (1974). The sweet psychic jolt of danger. *Psychology Today*, 8(5), 88–94.

Acknowledgements

This project has inevitably engaged a number of people in numerous ways. Thus this section is a welcome opportunity to recognise those without whom this book would never have been written.

We acknowledge and thank our co-researchers who gave willingly of their time and lived experience to enable us to gain some understanding of the extreme sport experience as well as their motivation and aspirations allowing them to go where others fear to fly. They are ordinary men and women who exemplify the realisation of human potential. Wonderfully inspiring people who taught us a lot about what it means to be human. We felt privileged in our role as narrators; the task was both immensely rewarding and enjoyable and we trust that our readers will also experience some of the inspiration which has underpinned this work.

Beyond thanking those who directly participated we would not be writing this if it were not for the support, generosity and love of our families.

Eric Brymer: To my parents who provided the initial freedom to roam and inspiration for adventure all those years ago. And most importantly to three people for whom acknowledgements and recognition are not sufficient; this work is dedicated to them – Varuna, Surya and Vinathe.

Robert Schweitzer: To my family and mentors. My parents who through their unique parenting style, encouraged creativity, my mentors who introduced me to phenomenology in an African context, and, most important, Debbie, Daniel and Julian, you remain my inspiration. And Eric thanks mate for a wonderful journey.

We would also like to thank the publishers of *Annals of Leisure Research* for allowing us to reproduce some aspects of an article on risk.

1 An introduction to extreme sports

Extreme sports have developed into a significant worldwide phenomenon. While participant numbers in many traditional team and individual sports such as golf, basketball and racket sports have declined over the last decade or so, participant numbers in so-called extreme sports have surged. Extreme sports support a multi-billion dollar industry with millions of participants and the momentum seems to be intensifying. Explanations for why extreme sports have become so popular are varied and relatively superficial. For some, the popularity is explained as the desire to rebel against a society that is becoming too risk averse, for others it is about the spectacle and the merchandise that is associated with organised activities and athletes. For others it is just that there are a lot of people attracted by risk and danger or just want to show off. For others still it is about the desire to belong to sub-cultures and the glamour that goes with extreme sports.

Precise statistics about participation rates are hard to determine, partially because definitions are hard to pin down but also because extreme sports cross a variety of human activities. Extreme sports comprise tourist activities, therapeutic activities, recreation activities and sporting activities. They have become a sporting spectacle. They are discussed in medical literature by those interested in injury or other medical concepts, in psychology by those interested in motivations, performance and health, in physiology by those interested in how the body functions in extreme conditions and in the military as a means to enhance performance. Extreme sports are even discussed in marketing, management and policy literature as legitimate niches that require their own peculiar understanding or inappropriate activities that need to be banned.

There are four aims for this chapter. The first is to introduce extreme sports. The second is to show why extreme sports are an important area of study. The third is to introduce phenomenology as an appropriate methodology for investigating extreme sports. The fourth is to briefly outline how phenomenology is different from other seemingly similar research methodologies. The subsequent chapters will provide more detail on the principles of phenomenology and how to use phenomenology in a research context. Following these chapters the extreme sport experience will be explicated and a phenomenological structure described. The intention is to introduce phenomenology as a research methodology, explicate the extreme sport experiences and use the process as a means to exemplifying the phenomenological process.

While statistics that focus purely on extreme sports are difficult to separate from related sport activities, the popularity and impact of extreme sports can be approximated through an appreciation of the broader outdoor and adventure scene. A report published in 2016 by the physical activity council in the United States of America (USA) estimated that about 50 per cent of active people, that is, 22 million people in the USA, undertook adventurous outdoor activities. Participation rates published by Sport England in 2015 concluded that 50 per cent of people who were active in sport participated in outdoor sports. Similar results can be found throughout the Western world.

While extreme sports are still predominantly assumed to be a Western pastime there has been a considerable uptake in other parts of the world. For example, in 2016 approximately 130 million people undertook outdoor activities in China. The Chinese mountaineering association estimated that about 50 per cent of these participants undertake more intense adventure experiences. Outdoor adventure activities are also becoming increasingly popular in India. In December 2015 the Government of India even initiated a scheme to encourage central government employees to undertake adventure sports as a means to encourage risk-taking, environmental appreciation and a capacity to handle challenging situations. In June 2016 the Iran Surfing Federation (ISF) became the 100th member of the international surf association. In Iran women are the surfing pioneers.

The idea that adventure sports are only for the young is also changing as participation rates across the generations are growing. Baby boomers are enthusiastic participants in adventure sports more generally. A survey undertaken in the UK in 2015 suggested that more pensioners expressed an interest in undertaking adventure and extreme sports than those between the ages of eighteen and twenty-five years. Equally, while there is undoubtedly still a gender gap with regard to participation numbers, adventure and outdoor activities provide vast opportunities for women who participate on equal ground with men. For example, in June 2016 a British woman, Masha Gordon, completed the explorer's grand slam in seven months and nineteen days, breaking the previous record. The feat involves climbing the highest peaks on each continent as well as reaching the North and South poles. Masha joined only a handful of people who have completed the challenge in less than a year. At the time of writing less than 50 people have complete all nine challenges.

The impact of adventure and extreme sports on the international market is perhaps most obviously appreciated through its economic impact. At the time of writing the US outdoor industry supports 6.1 million jobs and the spending associated with the industry is approximately $646 billion annually. Therefore, how we understand extreme sport and extreme sport participation is important. If we understand participation as wrapped up in the personality structures of a few then this might suggest that the activities are not appropriate for all. This might also suggest that successful extreme sport participation is just about whether you have the right personality characteristics. Training will have very little influence on outcomes. A risk-based understanding might suggest the activities are only for a deviant few and as a consequence extreme sports should be banned in the same way that drugs are banned. There are many areas around the world where extreme sports are banned. An appreciation of extreme sports as valuable health enhancing activities will be more likely to develop into opportunities for the wider community.

The confusion over what constitutes an extreme sport has caused considerable ambiguity for researchers and theorists alike. Activities requiring high levels of training, commitment, personal skills and environmental knowledge such as BASE jumping and rope free climbing, are often categorised alongside activities such as commercial whitewater rafting and bungee jumping which require no participant skills or prior knowledge of the activity or environment. A similar confusion stems from an assumption that certain sport types are automatically extreme. For example, in whitewater kayaking gliding from rock to rock on grade two of the international classification system requires some skill and might be exciting but the activity can be undertaken by a relative novice and the most likely result of an accident or mistake is a swim. The result of an accident or mistake when on grade six, the highest grade on the international system, on the other hand, is far more serious. Similarly, a skier with a few weeks skiing and little knowledge of environmental factors can make their way down a well-manicured black run whereas skiing sheer cliffs in thick snow requires high level skills and expertise, and deep environmental knowledge.

In the context of this book extreme sports are those activities that lie on the outermost edges of independent adventurous leisure activities, where a mismanaged mistake or accident would most likely result in death. The term 'sport' in this context does not reflect the idea of sport in the modern sense where the term has become synonymous with competition and the idea of winning and losing. 'Sport' in this context reflects the original use of the term derived from the old French and means 'leisure' or 'pastime'. Extreme sports differ from traditional sports in other ways as well. For example, traditional sports have very tightly defined rules and regulations that govern how a sport is to be played whereas extreme sports are not governed by such rules or regulations. Traditional sports are also tightly constrained by fixed and well maintained environments that have been designed for the sole purpose of carrying out the sport. Extreme sports, on the other hand, are most often about adapting to the natural environment. Extreme sport activities are continually evolving: typical examples include BASE (an acronym for Buildings, Antennae, Span, Earth) jumping and related activities such as proximity flying, extreme skiing, big wave surfing, waterfall kayaking, rope free solo climbing and high-level mountaineering.

BASE jumping is a parachute sport where participants jump from solid structures such as buildings, cliffs or bridges that might be only a few hundred feet from the ground. While skydivers utilise safety devices such as warning technology and second parachutes, BASE jumpers do not have such mechanisms. The low altitude means that warning devices will not work and even if a participant did carry a spare parachute the likelihood is that the jumper would hit the solid structure or the ground before the parachute could be deployed. Whereas the first BASE jump has been traced back to the early 1700s the sport as currently defined began in the mid-1970s. In the early days BASE jumpers most often used equipment designed for skydiving from an aeroplane. However, this equipment was not ideal for the BASE jumping setting and technology was soon developed to suit the specific purpose of the modern BASE context.

Proximity flying is a version of BASE jumping whereby flyers or pilots wear a specially designed suit called a wingsuit that facilitates forward motion. A proximity flyer is able to travel forwards for a few kilometres, often at speeds of 200 miles per hour (over 300 kph).

Like many extreme sports extreme skiing also began in the 1970s. Extreme skiing requires that the skier descend long, dangerous and sheer mountain cliffs with gradients typically close to 50 or 60 degrees. The terrain is often littered with large boulders, trees or steep cliffs. A fall in this terrain results in the skier tumbling out of control. At times skiers will need to jump from cliffs. At the time of writing the record for a deliberate jump was set by a young skier named Jamie Pierre at 255 feet. Well-known names in this sport include Ingrid Backstrom and Seth Morrison.

Big wave surfing takes surfers into waves over 20 feet (6.2 metres) tall, where even renowned surfers have died. Surfers are often towed onto the wave by a jet ski because the speed and size of the wave are too great for the surfer to reach their destination unaided. If a surfer falls off their board they are forced deep underwater. To recover from this the surfer will have a matter of seconds to reorient and resurface before being hit by the next wave. At the time of writing the record for the biggest wave ever surfed is held by a 34-year-old British surfer named Andrew Cotton who successfully surfed a 24 metre wave off the coast of Portugal.

Waterfall kayaking involves kayaking over waterfalls often over 30 metres high. At this level it is not only the height of the waterfall that contributes to the sport's extreme nature but also the power of the water that comes with it. The record for the highest waterfall successfully descended by kayak is 57 metres. The current record holder, Tyler Bradt, eventually popped up away from the bottom of the fall with only a sprained wrist.

Free solo climbing involves climbing big walls without the aid of ropes or other safety equipment. Probably one of the most famous names in this sport is Alex Honnold who, amongst other feats, soloed the north-west face of the Half Dome in Yosemite National Park, United States in just under two and a half hours. This climb usually takes experienced, expert climbers a few days. Arguably, climbing moves are the same whether you are manoeuvring a few feet above the ground or few hundred feet above the ground. The challenge could therefore be seen as psychological. Most often the only equipment that a free solo climber has are a pair of climbing shoes and a bag of chalk.

Extreme mountaineering is harder to define as standing on the roof of the world has become a tourist quest. At its core it involves mountaineering over

8,000 metres. At this level, often called the death zone, the mount have the skills to manage the terrain and weather conditions ever oxygen levels are so low that normal breathing is mostly impo climbers at this level require oxygen bottles; however, a few moun climbed above this level successfully without oxygen. Rheinhold Messner is credited as the first person to solo Everest without oxygen, in 1980. Since this time, many mountaineering purists, for example, Lydia Bradey, Carla Perez and Melissa Arnot have been successful.

Phases of extreme sport activity

Becoming an extreme sport athlete requires a great deal of commitment and hard work. The notion that certain people just have the skills to participate does not reflect reality. The initial desire to begin the extreme sport journey is often complex and multidimensional. The idea that there is an inevitable process where those interested in kayaking, for example, automatically graduate to waterfall or extreme kayaking, is false. Technical skill does not determine extreme sport participation either as there are many very skilful climbers and skiers, for example, who do not participate at an extreme level. Geography does not seem to be a significant factor in choice of extreme sports as participants often report relocating to mountainous areas in order to climb or to the sea side for surfing as soon as they were able. Participants describe a deep affinity for particular areas and activities that does not reflect childhood location or adult occupations. These choices are often made years in advance and carefully planned. However, while it is difficult to pin down initial motivations for participation, our research reveals a number of phases that seem to encompass effective extreme sport participation. The details that exemplify these phases will be discussed throughout the book, however, for the purposes of this chapter we have summarised these as: preparation, approach, active, immediate post-activity and post-activity.

Preparation

It takes years for the participant to acquire the technical skills, environmental knowledge and self-awareness essential for successfully undertaking an extreme sport and minimising the potential of negative outcomes. Participants are committed to acquiring the requisite skills through study, practice and mentoring relationships. For some this is a deliberate process where a participant interested in an extreme sport might take years to build the knowledge, experience and expertise required for successful participation. For others participating in an extreme sport takes less time as the first sojourn might come after years of adventure sports participation without predetermined intention to try an extreme sport. However, whether the initial sojourn is planned years in advance or less planned, continued participation is most often dependent on a calculated development of the skills and knowledge needed for successful participation. For example one co-researcher told how she decided to learn how to BASE jump after watching a video presented by a motivational speaker employed by her company. She described herself as a 'corporate chick' who had never had any desire to attempt anything out of the ordinary before that occasion. She spent years learning the technical aspects of parachute jumping, moving through sky-diving to jumping from stationary balloons and finally to BASE jumping. Another participant attributed his BASE jumping expertise to a choice made while at work. He was invited on an adventure weekend with colleagues but, as he had always believed that adventure was for crazy people, he declined. However, he changed his mind when he was subsequently asked to undertake another weekend shift at work. He had not had a day off work for weeks. The outcomes of this first adventure experience activated a journey of several years attending courses and training events to build up his technical skills and environmental knowledge in order to prepare for BASE jumping. Invariably this process also involves working with an experienced mentor.

The preparation aspect of the journey is also an ongoing activity as participants continually strive to maintain fitness and update their knowledge and expertise. Most often this is context specific and involves honing required skills to perform better and also preparing for 'what if' scenarios. Big wave surfers, for example, have been known to carry heavy weights while walking on the ocean floor in order to prepare for the inevitable wipe-out. While this is usually about physical preparation, participants have also spoken about intense mental preparation to work through 'what if' scenarios and enhance skills.

Approach

Whereas the preparation phase is about developing the skills and knowledge needed for successful participation in their chosen activity, the approach stage is about how a participant approaches each event. Some events may be planned weeks or even years in advance. For example, extreme mountaineering is invariably an enormous logistical challenge. Visas and fund raising are often needed. The mountaineer may also require context specific equipment, guides and a high level of physical fitness. Even those activities that require minimal equipment, such as solo rope free climbing, might involve extensive preparation if only to work out the best route to climb a particular cliff face. Free soloists have been known to climb routes dozens of times with ropes before attempting it without ropes. Big wave surfers examine weather patterns and movements for weeks before an event.

This stage also includes the happenings immediately prior to the intended event. Equipment is readied for action. For example parachutes might need packing or surfboards waxing. This stage also includes the actions required to get ready for the event such as walking to the jump site in BASE jumping or, in kayaking, paddling to the eddy by the lip of the waterfall before the descent. This part of the approach phase is often characterised by intense emotions, a continual reassessment of, and tuning into, environmental conditions and an internal scan to assess mental and physical readiness. This phase finishes when the participant is ready for action and the decision is made to commence the activity.

Active

The active phase is when the extreme sport activity is actually undertaken. Different sports have different characteristics, for example in mountaineering this might involve dropping in and out of the approach and active phases for days where as for BASE jumping, big wave surfing or free solo climbing the active phase is usually minutes or even seconds. There are two elements to this phase: the initial commitment and the activity in flow. The *initial commitment* is best described as those moments immediately after the decision to jump or catch a particular wave has been made, when the participant is moving towards the edge of the cliff or paddling to catch the wave. As we shall show in this book this part of the active phase is often characterised by fear and mental chatter dropping away, a letting go of the need to control, a surrendering to the experience and an internal focus or listening to and trusting an inner voice. This first part of the active stage ends when the jumper is airborne or the surfer has caught the wave. The second part of the active phase, which we have called *active flow*, immediately follows on from this. The element is characterised by a momentary primordial, authentic awareness as if coming home; a release or freedom from the 'material world'; feelings that the natural world is alive, that the activity teaches that nature is greater than the human participant; complete absorption in the experience; a glimpse of the ineffable (full experience beyond the describable); an holistic sensory enhancement, effortlessness and feelings of floating, flying or weightlessness, time slowing down as participants describe being in the moment or totally present, altered perceptions of space as if entering a different world or universe, bliss, peace, calm, stillness, silence and unity, harmony or intimacy with the natural world and connecting to what is described as the 'life-force'.

Immediate post-activity

The immediate post-activity phase is where the participant emerges from the active phase but has often still not completed the broader activity. For example, the BASE jumper has finished the freefall and has released the parachute. This activity can still be problematic as the lines might cross or the parachute might spin the pilot towards the cliff. In skiing it is when the skier reaches the base of the slope, or in mountaineering when the mountaineer passes the danger zone on their way down. The body is often awash with sensations. It might last hours or days and is characterised by intense positive emotions such as elation or ecstasy and enhanced feelings of personal energy.

Post-activity

The final phase might not come into play for some time after the event but is directly attributable to the stages which preceded it. For some participants this phase might be characterised by a clarity about a participant's view on life. It is described as involving increased self-knowledge and awareness combined with humility, acute wellbeing and enhanced ecocentric attitudes, beliefs and behaviours.

How might we understand extreme sports?

There are a number of ways to understand the extreme sport experience. The dominant paradigm in this area takes a positivist approach. Researchers most often follow an experimental, theory-driven method that utilises statistics to generalise and determine cause. For example, as an outsider who is presumed to be objective a researcher could look at extreme sports and compare them to what is currently known about human behaviour. The researcher could hypothesise that as the activity involves a participant voluntarily taking part in a sport with the potential for death it must be about risk-taking. The researcher could hypothesise that for this same reason extreme sports are not common activities and therefore those who participate in extreme sports must have a personality structure that is different to the general population. From this perspective the researcher could assume that a risk-taking personality structure causes extreme sport participation. The researcher could then find a validated questionnaire that purports to assess for a risk-taking trait and compare extreme athletes with the general population.

Studying extreme sports from a mainstream theoretical and methodological standpoint limits knowledge about this phenomenon because assumptions about the findings have already been made and, as a result, studies refer to an assumed core participant group (Donnelly, 2006). Positive results might be found but a wide range of important possibilities outside of this scope might be missed. As a result findings might be meaningless and lead to inappropriate or incomplete conclusions. Policies and practices for an activity deemed to be deviant, socially unacceptable and risk-focused will differ from those for an activity that is seen to be socially beneficial and developmentally focused. Based on current understandings, extreme sports have been banned in many areas around the world (Soreide, Ellingsen & Knutson, 2007). For example, in the United States of America the National Parks Service has instigated a policy that prohibits BASE jumping (U.S. Department of the Interior, 2006). Nevertheless, participation rates in extreme sports continue to rise, and therefore we need good quality evidence in order to make effective evidence-based decisions that can best inform policy and practice, even if this evidence is only used to support business practices.

Obtaining empirical evidence of consumer perceptions toward a particular action sport, event or individual could provide sport managers and marketers

with important knowledge when planning, managing, and marketing action
sport events.

(Bennett, Henson & Zhang, 2003, p. 112)

Risk-oriented perspectives, often derived by non-participants using theory-
driven methodologies, may have made judgements that do not necessarily reflect
the lived experience of extreme sport participants (Brymer, 2005; Celsi, Rose &
Leigh, 1993; Willig, 2008). These judgements have wide-ranging ramifications.

Alternative approaches to investigating extreme sports come from an interpretive paradigm and most often involve qualitative methodologies. There are a
number of interpretive research methodologies and frameworks with slightly different focuses and intentions. A researcher interested in investigating extreme
sports through an interpretive paradigm will need to understand the particular
methodological focus in order to determine an appropriate methodology for the
specific research project. There is often confusion between different methodologies as data gathering and analysis processes seem to be very similar. Some
methodologies that could be used in studying extreme sports include ethnography, narrative and grounded theory. The aim of the following section is to
highlight each methodology and present phenomenology as being particularly
suited to the study of extreme sports. It is not the aim of this section to review or
critique the pros and cons of which methodology to utilise as in practice they are
perhaps all relevant for different purposes and each might reveal different elements that help build a more complete account of extreme sports.

Ethnography focuses on obtaining an understanding of the social world. As a
research methodology it is a systematic process that investigates cultural phenomena. From an ethnographic perspective the researcher assumes that extreme
sports participants comprise a cultural phenomenon and research is undertaken
to determine and describe the structure of the social world. An ethnographic
researcher might immerses themselves in the culture under investigation and use
observations, interviews and other qualitative methods to produce rich and
detailed interpretations at a cultural level. Ethnographic research has been presented as both a deductive and inductive methodology as ethnographers are often
informed by theory before entering a research context (Murchison, 2010).
However, for the most part ethnographers follow an inductive process where
understandings come from direct observation.

Narrative approaches to research share common ground with phenomenology
in that both recognise the primacy of lived experience and that words and language reveal valuable understandings. The main focus of a narrative approach is
the understanding that human beings give meaning to their lives through stories.
Researchers pay particular attention to the structure of the stories, the cultural
background to the stories and *by whom* and *for what purpose* the story was constructed. For some the stories told are integral to self-identity and for others
stories are powerful but superficial constructions that both reveal and conceal
identity (Smith & Spakes, 2006). As with ethnographic research, for the most
part narrative researchers employ inductive processes to understand meaning;

however, narrative researcher often also employ theoretical frameworks to inter-
pret stories (Wertz, no date). A researcher interested in extreme sports, from this
perspective, might encourage an extreme sport participant to tell their story and
then analyse this story in order to determine what the story (or narrative) reveals.
While there are a wide range of narrative research processes the main assumption is that meaning originates in stories and therefore interpreting stories is at
the core of the narrative research process.

Grounded theory is an inductive methodology that sets out to develop theory
grounded in data that explains motivations, actions and concerns about a particular group. Traditional grounded theory involves a very precise, sequential
and systematic way of gathering and analysing data to develop codes and eventually a theoretical explanation of the core concepts. However, over the years the
traditional or classic grounded theory espoused by Glaser (1978) has been influenced by other ways of knowing such as constructivism (Charmaz, 2006). A
researcher investigating extreme sports would typically be interested in explanations for participation and utilise various data sources to build theory. As is the
case with narrative and ethnography, grounded theory is no longer considered
one uniform methodology. For the most part grounded theory utilises qualitative
data but quantitative data can also be utilised. However, the aim is still to allow
theory to emerge from the data through a well-defined systematic process of data
gathering and analysis. In later stages, the researcher may spend time confirming
the theory which has emerged from their analysis.

In keeping with the aims of this book, we have drawn on phenomenology to
explicate the meaning of extreme sports participation and at the same time
modelled the application of phenomenology in a contemporary context. Phenomenology focuses on the explication of experiences and meanings as lived,
beyond cultural and psychological boundaries. Phenomenology recognises that
the 'thing' of consciousness, whether that be substantial or imagined, is united
with consciousness. That is, rather than understanding the 'outer' world and
'inner' world as separate or assuming that there is only an 'inner' world, phenomenology sees consciousness and the object of consciousness as coupled.
This process is sometimes referred to as co-constitutionality, in that the experiencing subject and the intended object of consciousness constitute each other.
In its traditional form phenomenological research is about ascertaining and
describing the core of lived experience which may well be reflected in the narratives of the experiencing participant. However, as phenomenology developed
researchers determined that it was unlikely that an essential and immutable core
could be discovered and that research would only be able to get close. By interpreting the rendered experience of others phenomenology as research can get
close to a description of experience as lived. The focus of phenomenology is
the experience, with language acting as a tool for understanding. In this way,
research becomes an understanding science as opposed to an explaining
science. Taking this stance, a researcher interested in understanding and in
explicating the extreme sport experience would find phenomenology an ideal
methodology.

A researcher interested in using phenomenology must first comprehend the principles of phenomenology in order to reorient themselves to undertake research from a phenomenological standpoint. Chapters 2, 3 and 4 outline these principles and how research reflects them. The chapters following start the process of explication so that in the final chapter, we work towards synthesising and identifying the key dimensions of the extreme sport experience situating the phenomenon in a comparative framework. We conclude by likening the extreme sport experience to that which is most closely aligned with what it is that makes us truly human – our own ancestral history.

Summary

Extreme sports, those independent leisure activities where a mismanaged accident or mistake would most likely result in death, are fast becoming activities of choice. However, there is still only a vague understanding of the human dimension of these activities. This is unfortunate as, despite their popularity, there is still a negative perception about extreme sports participation. There is a pressing need for clarity. The dominant research perspective has focused on positivist theory-driven perspectives that attempt to match extreme sports against predetermined characteristics. For the most part empirical research has conformed to predetermined societal perspectives. Other ways of knowing might reveal more nuanced perspectives of the human dimension of extreme sport participation. Phenomenology provides an ideal framework for investigating the extreme sport experience as lived. In order to undertake this effectively a researcher needs to comprehend phenomenological principles and orient themselves in a phenomenological manner. It is to this concept that we now turn.

References

Bennett, G., Henson, R. K. & Zhang, J. (2003). Generation Y's perceptions of the action sports industry segment. *Journal of Sport Management, 17*(2), 95–115.

Brymer, E. (2005). *Extreme dude: A phenomenological exploration into the extreme sport experience.* (Doctoral Dissertation), University of Wollongong: Wollongong. Available at http://ro.uow.edu.au/theses/379.

Celsi, R. L., Rose, R. L. & Leigh, T. W. (1993). An exploration of high-risk leisure consumption through skydiving. *Journal of Consumer Research, 20*, 1–23.

Charmaz, K. (2006). *Constructing grounded theory: A practical guide through qualitative analysis.* London: Sage.

Donnelly, M. (2006). Studying extreme sports: Beyond the core participants. *Journal of Sport & Social Issues, 30*, 219–224.

Glaser, B. (1978). *Theoretical sensitivity: Advances in the methodology of grounded theory.* Mill Valley, CA: Sociology Press.

Murchison, J. (2010). *Ethnography essentials: Designing, conducting, and presenting your research.* London: John Wiley and Sons.

Smith, B. A. & Spakes, A. C. (2006). Narrative inquiry in psychology: Exploring the tensions within. *Qualitative Research in Psychology, 3*(3), 169–192.

Soreide, K., Ellingsen, C. & Knutson, V. (2007). How dangerous is BASE jumping? An analysis of adverse events in 20,850 jumps from the Kjerag Massif, Norway. *Journal of Trauma-Injury Infection & Critical Care, 62*(5), 1113–1117.

U.S. Department of the Interior. (2006). *Management policies 2006: The guide to managing the national park system.* In N. P. Service (Ed.), *Use of parks.* Retrieved 7 November 2016 from www.nps.gov/policy/mp/chapter8.htm.

Wertz, F. J. (no date). Phenomenological research methods psychology: A comparison with grounded theory, discourse analysis, narrative research, and intuitive inquiry. Retrieved June 2016 from www.psyking.net/HTMLobj-3827/Wertz.Phenomenological_ Research_in_Psychology.pdf.

Willig, C. (2008). A phenomenological investigation of the experience of taking part in 'Extreme Sports'. *Journal of Health Psychology, 13*(5), 690–702.

2   Principles of phenomenology

Phenomenology provides a philosophical basis and a set of principles for understanding and describing human experience. In keeping with Husserl's dictum, *zurück zu den Sachen selbst*, or 'we must return to "the things themselves"', phenomenology is based upon a paradigm radically different to that provided by the natural sciences, That is, we seek to privilege direct encounters in a rational and reflective manner, hence the term, *phenomeno-logical* (Wertz, 2015). A phenomenologist focuses upon that which shows itself in a concrete manner, or is grasped in consciousness. This chapter outlines the main principles that frame phenomenological research and introduces some of the main phenomenological influences which underpin this text. Attempts to comprehend phenomenology are often constrained by modern empirical assumptions. One reason is that theorists working from a Cartesian paradigm fail to grasp the fundamental shift introduced by Husserl. Phenomenology called for a new understanding of reality based on the principle that consciousness is always consciousness of something. From this perspective the notion of the subject being separate from the object does not hold, particularly where the object of study is human experience.

Phenomenology was formally introduced to twentieth-century thinking through the seminal works of Edmund Husserl in the early 1900s. However, the term, 'phenomenology' had been part of philosophical language prior to the writings of Husserl and the structuring of phenomenology as a philosophy is arguably attributed to Franz Brentano, Husserl's teacher. Phenomenology is considered to be the foundation of good science, where 'science' is derived from the Latin *scientia*, meaning 'to know' or 'knowledge ascertained by observation and experiment, critically tested, [and] systematised' (*Chambers' Etymological English Dictionary*, 1965). The philosophical assumptions of phenomenology propose a return to meaning as a ground for understanding human experience. This approach was proposed to contrast with the more dominant scientific paradigm in the late 1800s, which is even more dominant today. Husserl's essential argument, as it pertains to the human sciences, is that empirical methodologies, drawing upon premises articulated by Descartes and his successors, are problematic when our quest is to understand human experience.

Husserl was of the view that the human world was not subject to the same assumptions as a natural scientific perspective and required a very different approach to the one provided by empiricism. He led a revolution through his philosophical investigations, which have considerably impacted upon our conceptions of the lived world, whether in theology, psychology, psychiatry, anthropology, law, linguistics, musicology and, more recently, neuroscience (Wertz, 2015).

In this chapter, we outline the most salient features of the philosophical basis of phenomenology. It is arguable that the assumptions which guide methodologies determine the degree to which the investigator is able to give meaning to the phenomenon and, in turn, determines the level of integrity of the findings within a particular paradigm. Within the phenomenological tradition there are those who advocate a need for a researcher to choose between, for example, the traditional phenomenology of Husserl or hermeneutic phenomenology and follow that through unwaveringly. However, phenomenology, especially as methodology, is still evolving (Laverty, 2003; Spiegelberg, 1981, 1982). Our approach to phenomenological research gives emphasis to a set of fundamental phenomenological principles that are often differently emphasised and understood by distinctive branches of phenomenology. Our intention is to provide a contemporary synthetic approach to phenomenological research and demonstrate how, and in what form, phenomenology provides a basis for understanding human experience. This is exemplified in the experience of people who engage in extreme sports.

Phenomenology as philosophy

Essentially, Husserl's aim was to turn towards the world as it is experienced in its felt immediacy (Husserl, 1977).

> Unlike the mathematics-based sciences, phenomenology would seek not to explain the world but to describe as closely as possible the way the world makes itself evident to awareness, the way things first arrive in our direct, sensorial experience.
>
> (Abram, 1996, pp. 35–36)

That is, we are encouraged to return to the taken-for-granted lived experience. The idea is that we give voice to the experience as lived rather than attempting to explain. This marks a key distinction between phenomenology and alternative theories such as Grounded Theory, Narrative and Ethnography. In each of these instances an attempt is made to explain a particular phenomenon without a commensurate change in paradigm. Grounded theory seeks to provide an underlying theory of the phenomenon, Narrative theory seeks to explain experience through a particular notion of human storying and Ethnography encourages the researcher to view participation as a cultural phenomenon.

Phenomenology developed through two main schools in Germany, known as the Göttingen School and the Munich School. Eventually, phenomenology was disseminated into France and then internationally through the works of a number of key theorists and more recently researchers. These developmental stages initiated a number of phenomenological schools of thought and philosophical thinkers which will be explored further in this text and in our exploration of lived experience of extreme sport participants.

Traditional phenomenology

Traditional phenomenology is concerned with the objects of human experiences. That is, traditional phenomenology enquires into what a given phenomenon is, as distinct from how we as humans subjectively experience or make meaning of the experience of the phenomenon. In essence, the aim of traditional phenomenology is to pave a route back 'to the things themselves'. As Husserl (1917) once observed: 'to every object there corresponds an ideally closed system of truths that are true of it' (para. 6). However, traditional concepts are often shrouded in a language that mystifies meaning. The sections which follow introduce five key principles which underpin phenomenology and its application to the study of human experience. These are: the phenomenological attitude, dualism, intentionality, *noema* and *noesis*, and Husserl's seminal concept, the lifeworld. Each of these principles inform the methodology and practice of phenomenology which are addressed in Chapters 3 and 4 respectively. Understanding these principles is essential in translating phenomenological precepts into research and practice. It is exactly this process which distinguishes phenomenology from other more thematic analytical approaches.

The phenomenological attitude

The phenomenological attitude emphasises the importance of suspending or neutralising natural intentions, defined in a phenomenological sense as the taken-for-granted assumptions which guide everyday life. When intentions are contemplated it is important not to judge until the evidence is clear. Technically, this has been described as *epoché* whereby beliefs, attitudes, valuations, judgements and natural tendencies are suspended in a phenomenological desire to consider the intended object as it appears. Phenomenological praxis attempts to be free 'from falling into an intellectualistic reflection that substitutes itself for original thought' (Balaban, 2002, p. 106). In practice this is undertaken through a process termed 'bracketing'. We shall return to this concept later. For now, it is important to appreciate that such an attitude encourages an holistic as opposed to partial understanding. Phenomenological understanding requires the appreciation of science as a whole, from the Latin, *scientia*, to make known or acquired by study, rather than a partial understanding based upon empiricism.

The phenomenological attitude considers temporality as a fundamental concept implicated in virtually every facet of conscious life. World time relates to clocks and calendar time. Internal time relates to conscious and experiential life. The third level of time, consciousness of internal time, relates to an awareness that an individual has about internal time. The phenomenological description of time therefore includes the subjective experience of internal time and the objective experience of world time. However, underlying both these versions of time is a far deeper level; an understanding of time that has been presented as the clarification of the structure of memory. Time may be understood in terms of the metaphor of frames in a movie film (Sokolowski, 2000). To remember a previous frame assumes an awareness of past. Otherwise the 'recollection' of the previous frame would be presented as present with no attachment to past. Equally, anticipation of future frames provides a similar quandary. It is these types of experience that the third level of time seeks to describe. Descriptions of this level of time or temporality rely on 'metaphor and other tropes' (Sokolowski, 2000, p. 145).

The phenomenological attitude solicits the adoption of a different point of view – one that is more radical and comprehensive than any other. Essentially, the phenomenologist must view the study in question as if observing the phenomenon for the first time, as if an onlooker or contemplator (Rinofner, 2002). This requires that we observe the world in a state of wonder, as if the familiar is suddenly unfamiliar (Merleau-Ponty, 1999). Thus, phenomenology is, in its simplest form, a method for exploring human experience and defining its nature from a perspective requiring transcendence of cultural and psychological conditioning and its ensuing understanding of self and consciousness.

Refutation of Cartesian dualism

Contemporary empiricism is based upon dualistic ideas, that is, the idea of understanding the object 'out there' from the perspective of the knowing subject. In contrast, phenomenology rejects dualism that considers mind and body as two distinct things and the idea that the world is filled with objects (objectivism) that exist independent of human experiences. The point of phenomenology is that 'there is no thing, which in any meaningful sense, exists independently of consciousness' (Crotty, 1996, p. 46). That is, from a human science perspective a phenomenon does not exist as an event in itself but is made sense of as part of human experience. Phenomenologists commonly refer to this process as 'intentionality'.

Intentionality

Phenomenology as a philosophy recognises that consciousness is consciousness of something. Consciousness does not exist as a sole or encapsulated entity: it must be directed towards a 'thing'. This premise lies at the core of phenomenological philosophy in that the concept signifies a realisation that we do not just exist inside ourselves; there is an 'outside world'. That is 'things do appear to us, things truly are disclosed, and we, on our part, do display both to ourselves and to others the way things are' (Sokolowski, 2000, p. 12). The technical term for this phenomenological doctrine is 'intentionality'.

Husserl adopted the term 'intentionality' from the work of Brentano, a descriptive psychologist. This concept differs from the empiricist's view that consciousness is empty or passive and the postmodern perspectives that emphasise that we can never know a phenomenon in and of itself. Intentionality describes a clear understanding or grasping of reality, a state whereby 'object' and 'subject' are connected, where unity exists in which the 'subject' and 'object' are co-constituted. Intentionality does not signify an intent or purpose. Crotty (1996) in his critical analysis of thirty or so studies that explicitly claimed to be examining a phenomenon using phenomenology clearly noted the misconstruction of the term intentionality.

> The everyday meaning of 'intention' seems to have taken over. In phenomenology, intentionality does not refer to conscious deliberation, or to goal-oriented behaviour, or even to the purposive activity based on habit or routine. It is an epistemological concept [...] and not a psychological one. It has to do with union of object and subject.
>
> (Crotty, 1996, p. 42)

In human terms, intentionality allows for a common world, a consciousness of something that is not purely subjective. And herein lies the ultimate goal of phenomenology: the study of the 'thing' or phenomenon.

Intending, not to be confused with intentionality, in the pure phenomenological sense of the word, differs in structure depending on the 'object' being intended. Memories, pictures, words and so forth have different intentional systems. For the researcher, one of the major concepts within intentionality is the concept of presence/absence. That is, *intending* can be of an object that is present or one that is absent. This concept is important in the sense that it allows for the possibility of the description of absent objects that may be concealed or beyond our current comprehension. Memories, for example, are the reliving of past intentionalities.

Noema *and* noesis

Inextricably linked to intentionality are the *noema* and *noesis*. To some extent the previous section has already shed light on their meaning as represented through phenomenological philosophy. The aim, here, is to explicitly determine their meaning and relationship processes. At its core, phenomenology considers that consciousness has to be consciousness of something. The *noema* is the 'what' of consciousness, that is, the 'thing' of intentionality. The *noesis* is the 'how' or process through which we define experience, the intentional acts. The importance of this consideration is that both the *noema* and *noesis* describe the 'what' and 'how' as considered through the phenomenological attitude, as distinct from the natural attitude, where the natural attitude reflects everyday life in which people, objects and even ideas are 'just there'. That is, we do not question their existence, but they are experienced as facts. From Husserl's perspective, this attitude is neither good nor bad, it simply reflects the ordinary or familiar way of being-in-the-world.

The lifeworld

During Husserl's later writings, he formulated what was perhaps his most significant achievement for the social sciences, which was his theory of the *Lebenswelt* or lifeworld (Husserl, 1970). The notion of *Lebenswelt* referred to the world as encountered and lived in everyday life, given in direct and immediate experience independent of scientific interpretations. We shall discuss this theory in some detail as it is directly relevant to our understanding of phenomena, such as the extreme sport experience.

Husserl no longer argued that the transcendental ego had any absolute status, but stated that it was 'correlative' to the world. Second, phenomenology was no longer concerned with description of a separate realm of being but rather the reflection on the description of intersubjective communal experience. A third major change in his later writing concerned his conception of phenomenology as being no longer concerned with the foundations of scientific knowledge by reflecting about scientific knowledge. Instead, Husserl distinguished between the world as known to science and the world in which we live, i.e. the *Lebenswelt*. The study of the lived world and our experience of it now became the primary task of phenomenology. Husserl drew attention to three features of the lifeworld:

1   The world of everyday experience is extended in space and time. Space and time constitute a comprehensive frame in which all the existents of our experience can be related in spatial and temporal terms with one another. Furthermore, things exhibit spatial forms as physiognomy, that is a phenomenon has particular characteristics. The physiognomic aspect does not denote a determinate figure but a generic type of spatial configuration, which allows some variation and deviation.

2   The lifeworld exhibits various regularities, as evidenced, for example, by the cycle of day and night altering with the change of the seasons. Things, according to Husserl, have their habits of behaviour. It is not from science that we learn, for instance, that stones, when lifted and released, fall to the ground, but it is a matter of everyday experience in the lifeworld. Familiarity with such regularities are of paramount importance to our existence and the practical conduct of our lives.

3   And thirdly, things in the lifeworld present themselves in certain relativity with respect to the experiencing subjects, e.g. a number of persons in a room all perceive the same objects, but each person may perceive the objects from their own point of observation. It is through intersubjective agreement, brought about in a number of ways, that we find ourselves living in one and the same life-world, with respect to the social group, however small or large.

(Gurwitsch, 1978)

The Crisis of European Sciences, to which Husserl (1970) addressed himself, was to be found in the objectivism which characterised the natural sciences. Objectivity, he argued, was not only understood by the community at large as well as by the scientific community as corresponding to reality, but was understood as being synonymous with reality – that is, it is reality. In other words, to the uncritical observer, there is no differentiation between the objective world (of atoms and particles etc.) and the lifeworld.

The implications of Husserl's position were well articulated over four decades ago by Thinnes (1977) in the following terms:

> The crisis of Western man is a direct consequence of the development of European objective science, since by implicitly assuming that scientific reality is the only source of facts, the subject loses every possibility of placing himself in everyday life. Scientific facts are theoretical constructs which cannot be grasped in immediate experience; they are ideal entities which are only available to the subject in an indirect fashion.
>
> (Thinnes, 1977, p. 123)

Husserl's argument was that science, by its very internal coherence and its formal rigour as a closed system, was seen to be engaged in a kind of ceaseless self-verifying evolution. Husserl was concerned that the 'mathematization of nature' would result in the real praxis dealing with immediate life possibilities being replaced by an ideal praxis at the level of pure thinking. The result of science (and objectivism) transcending the *Lebenswelt* in this manner would be that the *Lebenswelt* would also be concealed (Thinnes, 1977).

Consequently, the only way to address the crises and reinstate the 'reference-less subject' into the realm of immediate experience of the lifeworld was to return to the pre-scientific foundations of the objective sciences, which were to be found in the very structure of the lifeworld. This is well expressed in Husserl's slogan, *Zu den Sachen selbst*, to the '*things themselves*' which expresses his opposition to reductionism, to phenomenalism, psychological atomism and the scientism of the positivists.

Phenomenology and human experience

The development of phenomenology has produced a variety of approaches founded on the above principles but different in the practice and methodology. The following underlines those traditions that are phenomenological and that influenced our thinking and the development of the contemporary phenomenological processes to be outlined in this text.

Transcendental phenomenology

The original adoption of phenomenology is the *transcendental phenomenology* outlined by Husserl as a way of 'training the mind to perceive and intuit its own essential processes' (Laughlin, McManus & d'Aquili, 1990, p. 25). The phenomenology of Husserl is arguably the most rigorous. Essentially, Husserl's phenomenological theory is a 'method of self-discovery'. Husserl's aim was to develop a philosophy that would underlie all other philosophies (whereby the need for a multitude of systems would no longer be required), a philosophy that searched for a knowledge, understanding and explication of reality (Crotty, 1996). Transcendental phenomenology searches for objects through subjective consciousness. The ultimate aim is to return to immediate or primordial experience through intuition or insights. Transcendental phenomenology is transcendental because 'it moves beyond the everyday to the pure ego in which everything is perceived freshly, as if for the first time' (Moustakas, 1994, p. 34). Moustakas (1994) noted the inseparable nature of the process of transcendental reduction, which in a phenomenological sense signifies the journey back to intentionalities. To this aim Husserl specifically and deliberately refrained from building a philosophy that could be precisely ordered.

Existential phenomenology

Heidegger (1996), an influential German philosopher, was credited with encouraging more of an existential view of phenomenology based on a number of criticisms of Husserl's early writings and a critique of 'transcendental idealism'. Followers of the existential view of phenomenology include such eminent philosophers as Simone de Beauvoir, Jean-Paul Sartre and Maurice Merleau-Ponty. While the philosophy of Merleau-Ponty most precisely fits the term 'existential phenomenology', the roots of existential phenomenology have been traced back to the nineteenth-century philosophers, Kierkegaard and Nietzsche.

Existential phenomenologists consider phenomenology to be the philosophy of experience. For some, this is further defined by a marriage between humanistic or 'Third Force' psychology and existentialism (philosophy of being) to manifest itself as *existential-phenomenological psychology*.[1] Thus human experiences and the meaning of existence as it presents itself to awareness are honoured. Spinelli (1989) succinctly positions existential phenomenology as:

> Existential phenomenology, or existentialism – arose as a result of the refocusing on the implications of such issues for the very meaning of existence. That is, existential phenomenology set its task as exploring human potential for freedom and the limitations inherent in what it means to experience ourselves in relation to our own being-in-the-world.
>
> (Spinelli, 1989, p. xi)

Existential phenomenology recognises that the individual and the surrounding environment are inextricably intertwined. As such both the experiences of the individual and the external situation are relevant in choice making. The human being and the world thus co-constitute each other.

Essentially, the basic concepts of transcendental phenomenology are accepted by those following the existential route. However, what changes is the understanding of the essential meanings. In essence, existential phenomenology comprises four important phenomenological concepts that combine to constitute the deeper aspects of human existence. These concepts are the pre-reflective, lived structure, the lifeworld and intentionality. From an existential phenomenological perspective the pre-reflective level describes the level of awareness that is regarded as pre-language and founded upon a sense of knowing within one's own body, in essence a felt sense that is prior to cognitive awareness. The emerging sense manifests itself in consciousness as meaning. The lifeworld describes the world in which we live and subjectively experience. It is the world of immediacy of our experiences, immediately as we live it.

> The life-world is the world that we count on without necessarily paying it much attention, the world of the clouds overhead and the ground underfoot, of getting out of bed and preparing food and turning on the tap for water. Easily overlooked, this primordial world is always already there when we begin to philosophize. It is not a private but a collective dimension – the common field of our lives and other lives with which ours are entwined – and yet it is profoundly ambiguous and indeterminate, since our experience of this world is always relative to our situation within it.
>
> (Abram, 1996, p. 40)

Lived structure from an existential phenomenological perspective defines the purpose of an empirical phenomenology, in that phenomenology attempts to reduce meaningful experience that presents itself in awareness in order to describe the underlying factors (lived structure).

Intentionality, for existential phenomenologists, extends the original Husserlian meaning and relates to the understanding that every human experience is world-directed. That is, being human means that we are necessarily being-in-the-world. Intentionality is thus at the core of phenomenological understanding where 'objects' are manifestations in the real-world and not just within our own minds. In fact the very notion of a distinction between our mind and the object of our mind is antithetical to the foundational principles of phenomenology. Human experience is unique in that humans are the only beings with the ability to be aware of their existence. Though this point may be contentious, this awareness corresponds to an inseparable link between existence and the world, an intersubjective awareness.

A unique aspect of the existential phenomenological perspective is the assertion that human experience is necessarily entwined with embodiment. That is, being an experiencing human being is being as a human body (Macann, 1993). Essentially, the personal body allows for the realisation of experiences and therefore the experiences of others. On the surface the importance of the body in experience would seem to be sensible, after all we are all manifest in physicality, if our heart stops moving so do we. However, whilst many experiences may be physical, it may not be true to say that all experiences are physical.

There are, however, potential pitfalls for those rigidly following existential phenomenology. First, the subjective experiences and meanings as lived at this moment potentially ignore sociocultural systems. That is, the focus tends to be on the individual's relationship to the object, which, in turn, limits the sharable aspect of the experience (Spinelli, 1989). Spinelli uses the example of a snow-flake. Whilst all snowflakes are different they all concede to a set of six basic rules. It is these rules that define the snowflake as a snowflake.

Concepts such as class, poverty and capitalism may be ignored or taken as non-existent. Equally, processes such as evolution and adaptation might be dismissed (Harris, 1979). However, ideas around culture and society are at once liberating and limiting. Boundaries are set and barriers created that can often come 'between us and our immediate experience of objects' (Crotty, 1996, p. 5). The ultimate task of the phenomenological investigator is to be open to exploring the nature of the experience whilst suspending our own and the co-researchers' meaning systems. That is, in phenomenological studies, the convention to avoid 'objectifying' terms such as 'subject' and refer instead to 'participant' or, in our case, to 'co-researcher', to emphasise that the participant in the research is contributing to our knowledge or understanding.

An effective understanding and introspection process, as required to understand a phenomenon, such as extreme sports, would need to accept a range of ways of being-in-the-world. These may include transpersonal or transcendental experiences. Pure phenomenology assumes that such experiences cannot be reduced to subjective experiences. For example, in phenomenology as a philosophy, intuition is simply the presence of an object. If we use the example of *thinking about* the potential of a baseball game as opposed to watching the game, Sokolowski (2000) posits:

> Our watching of the game is our *intuition* of the game. This is all that intuition is in the phenomenological vocabulary. Intuition is not something mystical or magical; it is simply having a thing present to us as opposed to having it intended in its absence.
>
> (Sokolowski, 2000, p. 34)

The traditional phenomenological understanding of a phenomenon may also prove limited in understanding the total picture. Aspects of the experience linked to the phenomenon in question may be outside the awareness of the individual or our understanding of the human world. For example, data gathering may depend on the verbal ability of co-researchers (participants) or the phenomena may be difficult to describe verbally.

> True enough, the 'things themselves' prove elusive. In describing what comes into view within immediate experience, we draw on language and therefore on culture. These are tools we have to employ. For that reason, we end not with a presuppositionless description of a phenomena, but with re-interpretation.
>
> (Crotty, 1996, p. 3)

Despite the assertion that phenomenology requires that the researcher describe the phenomenon as lived, language and culture may present barriers to our understanding of the experience itself.

Hermeneutic phenomenology

As with all phenomenology, hermeneutic phenomenology is about getting back to the things themselves but acknowledges the role of interpretation in this process. That is, language is regarded as intrinsic to our understanding of human experience. However, that does not mean that as phenomenologists we use language as an excuse to limit our exploration of human experience and get back to the things themselves, as we are human beings first and only second born into cultures and languages which may colour experience. Essentially, hermeneutic phenomenology comprises the study of experience together with meanings associated with the experience: it is about openness to meaning and to possible experiences. As with other phenomenological traditions the hermeneutic interpretations of phenomenology by scholars such as Ricoeur (e.g. 1966), Gadamer (e.g. 1977) and van Manen (1990, 1997) have their own peculiarities and implications for methodological practices drawing upon a phenomenological paradigm.

For Ricoeur, a twentieth-century French philosopher, hermeneutic phenomenology developed out of dissatisfaction with the structuralist position so popular in his day (Laughlin, 2001; Sweeney, 2002). Ricoeur determined that texts and the experiences of those influenced by or living the texts are required to truly comprehend the phenomenon under investigation. That is, a dialogue between text and experience was required. However, the essential focus is on the primacy of interpretation. Ricoeur's hermeneutic phenomenology speaks of the 'creative power of language' (Jervolino, 2002, p. 394) and often took as its starting point the interpretation of symbols and myths. These are most clearly explored in his volume on metaphor (Ricoeur, 1986). Central to the phenomenological exploration is the notion of text and, in particular, the fixing of discourse by writing. Still, language is seen as the 'primary condition of all human experience' (Jervolino, 2002, p. 396) and discourse the process of bringing experience to language. However, understanding another's discourse is considered an imperfect translation.

Language makes us human and perhaps also limits our capacity to communicate. Language is our way of making sense of the world but also suggests a lack of neutrality, a dilution of 'reality', a value-laden system of communication. Also, as we have noted earlier, it is possible that some experiences are not language based and that language (at least English language) is not required to comprehend meaning. As recognised by many of the traditional wisdoms, some experiences are physical metaphors in themselves. It is arguable that some knowledge does not require language.

Gadamer, a leading continental philosopher who contributed to the development of hermeneutic phenomenology, argued that any attempt to comprehend reality is already filtered by one's past education and experience. As such, the act of knowing or interpreting can interfere with our ability to comprehend the 'thing' of experience. Nevertheless, Gadamer in his attempts to extend human understanding to all forms of human experience, remained somewhat vague in defining his concepts. For example, critics question the applicability of his processes for validating and distinguishing false from true interpretations (Moran, 2000). Others focus on the potential for dialogue to enforce a power-based knowledge. Gadamer's philosophy influenced our thinking about phenomenology not so much as a way forward but as a warning of potential pitfalls.

From Ricoeur we accept the reality of otherness and the imperfection of understanding implicit within his 'paradigm of translation' (Jervolino, 2002, p. 399). Hermeneutic phenomenology is essentially the construction of an interpreted understanding of an aspect of the human lifeworld. A complete and final description of a phenomenological object is impossible, as any object is more complex than 'any explication of meaning can reveal' (van Manen, 1990, p. 18).

> When speech, language and thought patterns generated from experiences in the world are used, they always involve an interpretive process: but the aim here is to try to disclose the most naïve and basic interpretation that is already there but as yet is unelaborated in the life world experience, a phenomenological hermeneutic.
>
> (Willis, 2001, p. 7)

Essentially, the hermeneutic phenomenologist becomes an interpreter of interpreters. The process of interpretation is explicitly creative and accepting of the implication that analysis of data sources may result in many interpretations (Klein & Westcott, 1990). However, the intention is always to remain true to the principles of phenomenology and move towards an explication of experience as lived.

The hermeneutic phenomenologist openly makes use of various forms of text to understand the phenomenon. The work of poets, authors, artists and cinematographers may be explored in the desire to fully explicate understandings of our 'immediate common experience in order to conduct a structural analysis of what is common, most familiar, most-evident to us' (Willis, 2001, p. 19). However, the aim of hermeneutic phenomenology is still to seek and explicate universal meanings.

The relationship between text and experience as outlined by van Manen's hermeneutic phenomenology is in the writing process (van Manen, 2002). The researcher is focused on the object of study with the explicit aim of showing, describing and interpreting the true nature of the phenomenon. Thus phenomenology is indelibly linked to language. However, as has already been noted, some experiences, as will be evident in our descriptions of extreme sport participation, may lie outside the scope of language.

So, as with the transcendental and existential phenomenologies, the definition of hermeneutic phenomenology is seen to be dependent on the whims of the phenomenological explorer. However, on closer inspection the scientific nature of hermeneutic phenomenology differs only in its realisation and focus on interpretation. For transcendental and existential phenomenology the aim is to describe the essence of an experience whether as a direct description of an object or the expression of a lived experience. For the hermeneutic phenomenologist the description contains a strong element of interpretation. Thus phenomenology becomes hermeneutic in the original sense of the word where it assigns the act of interpretation. The texts used in this interpretation process include historical as well as interview data. The aim remains to get *back to the things themselves*, though the realisation is that interpretation is required. In this instance interpretation is considered in terms of pointing out the meaning of something as well as pointing to something that is potentially concealed.

Transpersonal phenomenology

A relatively new addition to the phenomenological tradition is transpersonal phenomenology or transpersonal-phenomenological psychology. The approach may be applied to the understanding of a range of experiences from the transpersonal, transcendent, sacred or spiritual experience which has often existed outside the mainstream areas of the social sciences and is more commonly understood in terms of pre-reflective sensibilities.

The phenomenological approaches described thus far are appropriate for exploration of those experiences that can be articulated in everyday language and are more commonly recognised by communities of people. In the case of transpersonal phenomenology, phenomenology has been effectively used in transpersonal studies (or transpersonal psychology – the Fourth Force) that aim to describe those experiences that are beyond common, but are still shared by the few. The central point here is that some experiences are of an exceptional nature. Transpersonal viewpoints recognise the relevance and legitimate experiences of those who have had extraordinary experiences. While human beings experience the world through reflective and pre-reflective awareness, the transpersonal realm is posited as existing 'prior to' the reflective/pre-reflective realm (Valle & Mohs, 1998). These experiences might include out of body experiences, visions, near death experiences, mystical experiences, meditative experiences, ecstatic experiences, personal transformations, unitive experiences and even those relating to peak experiences, bliss, awe and wonder (Anderson, 1998; Laughlin, 1988; West, 1998). These may include experiences characterised by stillness and peace, love and contentment for all, an absence of a sense of 'I', a sense of pure being without the need for space, time standing still, bursts of insight, surrender of the need for control and extraordinary transformations. Proponents of such a viewpoint have included psychologists and theorists such as William James (1971), Carl Jung (1964), Viktor Frankl (1966, 1984), Ludwig Binswanger (Sindoni, 2002), Rollo May (1983) and more recently John Rowan (2001) and Ken Wilber (1993, 2001).

Transpersonal phenomenology recognises that some experiences are outside the traditional understanding of intentionality: that is, some experiences are without an object and therefore by default without a subject (Barnes, 2003). In other words transpersonal phenomenology argues that previous understandings about consciousness were more about mind than consciousness (Valle & Mohs,

1998). As such, transpersonal experience is an experience that is prior to the pre-reflective/reflective realm (Anderson, Braud & Valle, 1996). In their words:

> It is, therefore, mind, not consciousness per se, that is characterized by intentionality, and it is our recognition of the transintentional nature of Being that calls us to investigate those experiences which clearly reflect or present these transpersonal dimensions in the explicit context of phenomenological research methods.
>
> (Anderson et al., 1996, p. 27)

Transpersonal phenomenology recognises that consciousness is no longer consciousness of something, it is just consciousness. In one instance, it has been described as referring to 'beyond being' and 'nothingness'.

Transpersonal phenomenology recognises and accepts that some experiences may transcend traditional descriptions conceived in terms of intentionality as articulated by Husserl. Thus, transpersonal phenomenology positions itself as a phenomenology that attempts to honour the totality of human experience, often transcending more concrete aspects of human experience. Transpersonal phenomenology is concerned with describing those spiritual, infinite, unitive, transformational experiences outside the everyday experiences of self, of others and the world around us.

Summary

This chapter provides an overview of the basic tenets of phenomenology, as well as the branches of the discipline since its early introduction by Husserl in the late 1800s. For phenomenology to be phenomenology it must have an essential commonality or core, it must be founded on a particular paradigm, with its own assumptions and implications. Phenomenology is an attempt to 'get back to the things themselves'. It is far more than a mere representation of our subjective worlds, it considers a 'real lived world' with equally 'real lived experiences' as the foundation of our knowing. In this sense, it strives to arrive at 'truth'. This is the essence of phenomenology.

The study of human experience requires us to remain open to accept both personal and transpersonal experience. Even those experiences where subject and object are merged into one existence or non-existence and which, contentiously, cannot be conceived in terms of intentionality in the strict sense, are nevertheless human experiences. Like the guide for the intrepid mountaineer, the chapters following provide a map which stakes out the key features of the territory.

Note

1 It is recognised that arguments exist that question the relationship between European Existential Psychology and American Humanistic Psychology.

References

Abram, D. (1996). *The spell of the sensuous: Perception and language in a more than human world.* New York: Vintage books.

Anderson, R. (1998). Introduction. In W. Braud & R. Anderson (Eds), *Transpersonal research methods for the social sciences: Honoring human experience* (pp. xix–xxiv). Thousand Oaks, CA: Sage.

Anderson, R., Braud, W. & Valle, R. (1996, April 11–14). *Disciplined inquiry for transpersonal studies: Old and new approaches to research.* Paper presented at the 76th Annual Convention of the Western Psychological Association, San Jose, CA.

Balaban, O. (2002). Epoche: meaning, object, and existence in Husserl's phenomenology. In A. Tymieniecka (Ed.), *Phenomenology world-wide: foundations – expanding dynamics – life-engagements: A guide for research and study* (pp. 103–113). Dordrecht, the Netherlands: Kluwer Academic Publishers.

Barnes, J. (2003). Phenomenological intentionality meets an ego-less state. *Indo-Pacific Journal of Phenomenology*, *3*(1), 1–17.

Crotty, M. (1996). *Phenomenology and nursing research.* South Melbourne, Victoria: Churchill Livingstone

Frankl, V. E. (1966). *The doctor and the soul.* (R. Winston & C. Winston, Trans.). New York: Alfred A. Knopf.

Frankl, V. E. (1984). *Man's search for meaning.* New York: Simon & Schuster.

Gadamer, H. (1977). *Philosophical hermeneutics.* (D. E. Linge, Trans.). Los Angeles, CA: University of California Press.

Gurwitsch, A. (1978). *Human encounters in the socialworld.* (F. Kersetn, Trans.). Pittsburgh, PA: Duquesne.

Harris, M. (1979). *Cultural materialism: The struggle for a science of culture.* New York: Random House.

Heidegger, M. (1996). *Being and time: A translation of Sein and Zeit.* (J. Stambaugh, Trans.). Albany, NY: State University of New York.

Husserl, E. (1917). *Pure phenomenology, its method and its field of investigation: Inaugural lecture at Freiburg im Breisgau.* Retrieved 24 September 2002 from www3.baylor.edu~scott_moore/essays/Husserl.html.

Husserl, E. (1970). *The crisis of European sciences and transcendental phenomenology.* Evanston, IL: Northwestern University Press.

Husserl, E. (1977). *Cartesian meditations: An introduction to phenomenology.* (D. Cairns, Trans.). The Hague: Martinus Nujhoff.

James, W. (1971). *The varieties of religious experiences: A study in human nature* (5th ed.). London: Collins.

Jervolino, D. (2002). Paul Ricoeur and hermeneutic phenomenology. In A. Tymieniecka (Ed.), *Phenomenology world-wide: foundations – expanding dynamics – life-engagements: A guide for research and study* (pp. 392–402). Dordrecht, the Netherlands: Kluwer Academic Publishers.

Jung, C. (Ed.). (1964). *Man and his symbols.* London: Aldus Books.

Klein, T. & Westcott, M. R. (1990). The changing character of phenomenological psychology. *Canadian Psychology*, *35*(2), 133–158.

Laughlin, C. D. (1988). Transpersonal anthropology: Some methodological issues. *The Western Canadian Anthropologist*, *5*(December), 29–60.

Laughlin, C. D. (2001). Phenomenological anthropology. Retrieved 6 August 2001 from www.carleton.ca/~claughli/phenanth.htm.

Laughlin, C. D., McManus, J. & d'Aquili, E. G. (1990). *Brain, symbol and experience: Towards a neurophenomenology of human consciousness*. Boston, MA: New Science Library, Shambala.

Laverty, S. M. (2003). Hermeneutic phenomenology and phenomenology: A comparison of historical and methodological consideration. *International Journal of Qualitative Methods*, *2*(3), Article 3.

Macann, C. (1993). *Four phenomenological philosophers*. London: Routledge.

May, R. (1983). *The discovery of being: Writings in existential psychology*. New York: W. W. Norton & Company.

Merleau-Ponty, M. (1999). *Phenomenology of perception*. (C. Smith, Trans.). London: Routledge & Keegan Paul.

Moran, D. (2000). *Introduction to phenomenology*. London: Routledge.

Moustakas, C. E. (1994). *Phenomenological research methods*. Thousand Oaks, CA: Sage.

Ricoeur, P. (1966). *Freedom and nature: The voluntary and the involuntary*. (E. V. Kohak, Trans.). Evanston, IL: Northwestern University Press.

Ricoeur, P. (1986). *The rule of metaphor*. London: Routledge & Keegan Paul.

Rinofner, S. (2002). Fathoming the abyss of time: Temporality and intentionality in Husserl's phenomenology. In A. Tymieniecka (Ed.), *Phenomenology world-wide: foundations – expanding dynamics – life-engagements: A guide for research and study* (pp. 134–145). Dordrecht, the Netherlands: Kluwer Academic Publishers.

Rowan, J. (2001). The phenomenology of the centaur. *Transpersonal Psychology Review*, *5*(2), 29–41.

Sindoni, P. R. (2002). Ludwig Binswanger, the inspiring force. In A. Tymieniecka (Ed.), *Phenomenology world-wide: foundations – expanding dynamics – life-engagements: A guide for research and study* (pp. 657–663). Dordrecht, the Netherlands: Kluwer Academic Publishers.

Sokolowski, R. (2000). *Introduction to phenomenology*. Cambridge: Cambridge University Press.

Spiegelberg, H. (1981). *The context of the phenomenological movement*. The Hague, Netherlands: Martinus Nijhoff Publishers.

Spiegelberg, H. (1982). *The phenomenological movement* (3rd ed., with Karl Schuman (Ed.)). The Hague, Netherlands: Martinus Nijhoff Publishers.

Spinelli, E. (1989). *The interpreted world: An introduction to phenomenological psychology*. London: Sage.

Sweeney, R. (2002). Paul Ricoeur, on language, ethics and philosophical anthropology. In A. Tymieniecka (Ed.), *Phenomenology world-wide: foundations – expanding dynamics – life-engagements: A guide for research and study* (pp. 641–645). Dordrecht, the Netherlands: Kluwer Academic Publishers.

Thinnes, G. (1977). *Phenomenology and the science of behaviour*. London: George Allen and Unwin.

Valle, R. & Mohs, M. (1998). Transpersonal awareness in phenomenological inquiry: Philosophy, reflections and recent research. In W. Braud & R. Anderson (Eds), *Transpersonal research methods for the social sciences: Honouring human experience* (pp. 95–113). Thousand Oaks, CA: Sage.

van Manen, M. (1990). *Researching lived experience: Human science for an action sensitive pedagogy*. New York: State University of New York Press.

van Manen, M. (1997). *Researching lived experience: Human science for an action sensitive pedagogy* (2nd ed.). London, ON: The Althouse Press.

van Manen, M. (2002). *Writing in the dark: Phenomenological studies in interpretive inquiry*. London, ON: The Althouse Press.

Wertz, F. J. (2015). Phenomenology methods, historical development, and applications in psychology. In J. Martin, J. Sugarman & K. L. Slaney (Eds), *The Wiley handbook of theoretical and philosophical psychology: Methods, approaches, and new directions for social sciences* (pp. 85–102). New York: Wiley-Blackwell.

West, T. (1998). On the encounter with a divine presence during near-death experience: A phenomenological enquiry. In R. Valle (Ed.), *Phenomenological inquiry in psychology: Existential and transpersonal dimensions* (pp. 387–406). New York: Plenum Press.

Wilber, K. (1993). *The spectrum of consciousness* (20th anniversary edition). Wheaton, IL: Quest Books.

Wilber, K. (2001). *A theory of everything: An integral vision for business, politics, science, and spirituality*. Boston, MA: Gateway.

Willis, P. (2001). The 'Things Themselves' in phenomenology. *Indo-Pacific Journal of Phenomenology*, *1*(1), 1–16.

3 Translating principles into practice

Researching the constituents of human experience poses significant challenges. We have already alluded to the limitations of a natural scientific approach in the previous chapter, in which we outlined some of the basic tenets of phenomenological philosophy and how these assumptions relate to researching human experience. We asserted that while phenomenology has various branches depending on theoretical perspectives, the fundamental principles of phenomenology are adhered to consistently. We argued that phenomenology is the most appropriate perspective from which to gain an understanding of the essence of human experience. This chapter provides an introduction to the ways in which various theorists have translated phenomenological assumptions into the research process. The purpose is to lay the groundwork for our own methodology in the chapter following.

Husserl provided a philosophical framework as opposed to a method for undertaking research. The translation of the philosophical assumptions into practice is potentially problematic. For example, in a review of many published papers that claimed to be phenomenological Crotty (1996b) claimed that while many studies were seemingly consistent with the premises of a phenomenological paradigm they were simultaneously missing the whole point. The main confusions were linked to the comprehension of the phenomenological ideas of 'experience', 'phenomenon', and 'bracketing', as well as an understanding of the processes required to accumulate and analyse data in a phenomenological manner. Crotty argued for a return to the origins of phenomenology as opposed to what he saw as a North American hybrid approach to phenomenology. He begins his argument with a plea that phenomenologists return to the origins of the movement, and argues that the phenomenological process is 'an attempt to regain a childlike openness in our encounter with the world' (Crotty, 1996a, p. 158). Giorgi's (2010) critique of some methodological approaches reiterated this point and the need to be guided by philosophical principles.

A number of key theorists have provided a basis for human science, and in turn, a basis for phenomenology. Each of these approaches privilege understanding as opposed to seeking explanations as a foundation for their endeavours. These include the ancient Greeks, modern philosophers including Brentano and Dilthey, the psychoanalysts from Freud onwards, and psychologists including

William James and contemporary qualitative researchers (Wertz, 2015). This chapter only considers those models which are drawn from phenomenological principles and are posited by contemporary researchers as suitable for the study of human experience. Chapter 4 will translate the processes in the current chapter into a practical research methodology that may be applied to a range of human experiences. Our intention is to provide a contemporary synthetic approach and demonstrate how, and in what form, phenomenology provides a basis for understanding human experience as represented in the experience of people who engage in extreme sport.

As previously presented, some writers on phenomenology have argued that a researcher interested in phenomenology as a methodology should choose to follow a particular branch or phenomenological method. Indeed, we would concur that a researcher claiming to follow the phenomenology of Husserl or the methodology of Giorgi (1997, 2009) is advised to follow these processes unambiguously. However, phenomenological methodology is still evolving and there is a need to consider the research context while still staying true to the principles of phenomenology. The interpretation and application of these principles are not always clear. The supposedly monolithic phenomenological movement displays commonalities and differences in the processes for *getting back to the things themselves*. Many of the so-called common factors in phenomenological processes turn out to be only common to some. Claiming that one is 'doing' phenomenology does not necessarily mean that phenomenology has been 'done' (Crotty, 1996b). In this explication, we have attempted to be faithful to and learn from some of the founding figures of the phenomenological movement. We thus provide a basis for researchers to utilise the method outlined in their own search for understanding and explicating human experience. We do not claim that the ideas are original, but on the contrary, we trust that they are in harmony with the assumptions of the leading writers in the field. These writings are not always consistent, and we will reflect some of the diversity of ideas in the sections following.

To reiterate, our approach is guided by a set of fundamental phenomenological principles and influenced by four branches of phenomenology: transcendental phenomenology, existential phenomenology, hermeneutic phenomenology and transpersonal phenomenology. While there are a number of theorists who have presented methodological notions of how to carry out phenomenology we will focus on those that exemplify these four branches of phenomenology.

Transcendental phenomenology

Exponents of a broad transcendental phenomenology include Amedeo Giorgi (2009) and Clark Moustakas (1994). Though a close inspection of both methodologies reveals distinct differences between their approaches, the ideas behind the methodologies developed are intended to reflect the phenomenology of Husserl. Researches from this tradition tend to focus on phenomenological research as a series of precise, usually linear, process steps. For example, Giorgi

(2009), arguably the gold standard for those wishing to follow Husserlian phenomenology, presents five distinct steps in the phenomenological process. The researcher first assumes the phenomenological attitude before getting a sense of the whole, allocating meaning units, transforming meaning units into lived-meanings and developing a synthesis of the lived experience. Moustakas (1994) delineates a broader perspective on the phenomenological method which begins before the topic is even chosen. He distinguishes between the preparation stage, the data collection stage and the data analysis stage. A researcher conducting research into human experience has a responsibility to ensure the study meets appropriate standards of rigour and quality. The topic should be grounded in what Moustakas termed autobiographical values and meaning. He encourages the researcher to develop a set of questions to guide the research process before conducting an intensive interview. The researcher should then conduct a comprehensive review of all related literature and set criteria to locate co-researchers. Finally, the researcher is encouraged to develop textural and structural descriptions through organisation and analysis of the data. Moustakas thus distanced himself from Husserl who deliberately refrained from developing a structured system.

In the preparation stage emphasis is placed upon the importance of formulating the question. The question should have personal and social meaning and be precisely worded with every word defined, clarified and explained. As an illustration Moustakas presented a study explicating time to show how the original researcher was totally absorbed in his own relationship with time. Only after this relationship was fully explored did the researcher formulate a question. Moustakas then showed how each key word was described and defined by the researcher.

The preparation stage involves the selection of what are termed 'co-researchers' as opposed to research subjects. Essentially co-researchers need to have experienced the phenomenon, be available and agree to the instructions and agreements as related to the ethical considerations guiding the research. However, in Moustakas' example there are considerations regarding pre-interview interviews and the co-researchers' commitment to open-ended investigation of the phenomenon through interviews.

Before gathering data, Moustakas emphasises the importance of a complete review of literature. Four kinds of literature review are identified: integrative, theoretical, thematic and methodological. An integrative literature review draws conclusions, outlines methods, evaluates data, arrives at interpretations and presents findings from studies that are relevant to the topic. The methodological review focuses on research methods used. Theoretical literature reviews focus on theories related to the study. A thematic review organises and presents core themes. Reviews should include technical and non-technical literature.

Once the preparation is complete the researcher is ready for data collection. At this stage the transcendental phenomenologist is encouraged to conduct interviews that are informal and open-ended. The researcher's aim is to create an appropriate, comfortable atmosphere that allows for a full description of the phenomenon in question. Before starting the interview the researcher needs to ensure that they have assumed the phenomenological attitude, bracketed effectively and continue to do so throughout the interview process. For the transcendental phenomenologist bracketing, or *epoché*, describes the act of suspending any and all presuppositions or pretentions to scientific truth, natural truth or individual biases about the natural world to instead focus on analysis and explication of lived experience.

The data analysis stages for Giorgi and Moustakas are different. Giorgi speaks about the development of meaning units. Moustakas recommends a process that moves through a complete transcript to horizontalisation, then thematisation, then rechecking against the original transcripts. In this step the phenomenologist is encouraged to refrain from creating a hierarchy from the items described. Each item is to be viewed, initially, as having equal value or significance. Individual textural descriptions are then completed with verbatim examples. A structural description is constructed and textural and structural descriptions are used to describe meanings and essences. Finally, the individual analyses are integrated to form a universal description and these descriptions are compared and contrasted to the literature previously identified.

In summary, transcendental phenomenology is considered a pure and distinct form of phenomenology with a specific role for investigating consciousness. The method described has a role for intuition akin to sophisticated yogic meditation to gain and articulate an understanding of the phenomenon:

> Another major distinction is the emphasis on intuition, imagination, and universal structures in obtaining a picture of the dynamics that underlay the experience, account for, and provide an understanding of how it is that particular perceptions, feelings, thoughts, and sensual awareness are evoked in consciousness with reference to a specific experience such as jealousy, anger, or joy.
>
> (Moustakas, 1994, p. 22)

This view has been transformed into a precise linear construction of processes and steps designed to explore human phenomena. Some of the recommendations such as precisely formulating the question and ensuring that co-researchers have experienced the experience are fundamental. However, precise systems do not guarantee quality. For example, when we turn to our own study on extreme sports, which are not everyday experiences, it is feasible that the uniqueness of the experience dictates a different approach.

Existential phenomenology

Phenomenological research methodologies that arguably fit within the broad existential approach to human science include those developed by the contemporary existential psychotherapist, Ernesto Spinelli (1989) and an Australian nurse researcher and theorist, Michael Crotty (1996a, 1996b). Spinelli provides a clear account of a phenomenological method. The central criteria being that any exploration must be guided by the absence of any imposition of beliefs, biases, theories, hypothesis and explanations. Thus, an initial state of explorer naïvety or un-knowing supports a process of phenomenological reduction. The word 'reduction' is not be confused with the meaning espoused by the natural sciences but is the gradual discovering of what constitutes the phenomenon in question.

Three basic steps are posited: the first step requires the researcher to bracket all previous understandings. For Spinelli this concept does not entail a bracketing that equates to that proposed by transcendental phenomenology. What is required is an attempt to bracket biases 'as far as was possible' and to develop 'more of an open mind' (Spinelli, 1989, p. 17). The aim is to develop conclusions from the actual experience, rather than prior assumptions. In this way the researcher not only deliberately avoids a narrow, pre-determined focus but also avoids the common bias of finding only what was expected.

Essentially, Spinelli (1989) recognised the impossibility of transcendental bias in favour of an attempt to be open to the phenomenon and approaching the phenomenon with an attitude of naïvety. Even if bracketing to this extent is not likely or feasible the act of recognising biases and presuppositions weakens their influence on our capacity to apprehend meaning. The researcher is thus encouraged to cultivate an attitude of doubt and openness.

The second step is the rule of description. That is, describe as opposed to explain. The intention is to differentiate between any attempt to immediately explain or question the findings. Thus the need for a hypothesis or theory to frame the findings is not only negated but contra-indicated. The point is that experiences should be described on their own merits and not as a function of some theory or hypothesis. Similar to the transcendental notions, the third and final step involves horizontalisation or equalisation. Each item is to be viewed as, initially, having equal value or significance. The ideas presented by Spinelli thus provide scaffolding for the complexities of engaging in phenomenological research.

Crotty (1996a) links his methodology to the European traditions of phenomenology in a number of ways. First he notes that bracketing and opening ourselves to immediate experience are prerequisite but different phenomena. Bracketing involves the disciplined and persistent setting aside of all previous knowledge, perceptions and understandings. Opening up to immediate experience of the phenomenon entails surrender. That is, in opposition to general perceptions about science, the phenomenologist does not desire or attempt to control or manipulate matters. In this instance the researcher is encouraged to be open to the experience, listen, meditate and let the experience speak for itself. A passive, contemplative attitude is required.

As we have already argued, language may create a barrier to complete understanding. Crotty considered that descriptions are inevitably limited by and embedded in the thought patterns and language of our cultures (Crotty, 1996b). Potentially, the best that can be achieved is a minimisation of such limitations by 'using' language in describing the phenomenon. This of course presents complications, as descriptions might become confusing or over-complicated, as words acquire new meanings or understandings. In effect, language can only allude to the essence of the phenomenon, it cannot truly illuminate. Phenomenology necessarily becomes an hermeneutic science. The task of the phenomenologist adopting an existential perspective is to unmask the experience by working through all those layers that hide the essential nature of the phenomenon.

Whilst accepting the inevitable limitations presented by language, the phenomenologist still has the task of determining the essence of the experience, as far as possible. The challenge is to determine whether the characteristics described are wholly and truly the essence of the phenomenon being explored. For example, could the description depict some other experience? Or does the description distinguish itself from all other experiences? Or can the experience exist without the elements described? The final telling point is when the description fits. Thus, what was previously implicit has become explicit as a direct result of deliberate and methodical explorations.

The phenomenological process is thus defined in a format that can be followed and that can be adhered to by the inexperienced researcher and yet remain close to the original tenets of the philosophy underpinning the method. Yet there are still questions that spring to mind. Does this process signify a solo exploration? What about using other people's material? Would not poetry or film contribute to the exploration process? A phenomenologist can work closely with co-researchers and therefore become a principal researcher in a shared endeavour. However, for a phenomenologist to work with an 'other', the other in question must also become a phenomenologist. Each person collaborating in the exploration of the phenomenon in question must be prepared to explore the nature of his or her own experience, perhaps with guidance or coaching, but still as a phenomenologist. That is, co-researchers are not only chosen for the fact that they have experienced the phenomenon, or that they are able to talk about and articulate the phenomenon but also that they are able to undertake (albeit guided) phenomenological reduction and exploration. This in itself raises further questions about the explication of experiences that are outside of the principal researcher's experience and outside the explicit interest of the co-researchers' ability to apply a phenomenological method.

There is an alternative extension of the phenomenological method that can be explored. A process that allows for a deeper level of understanding, within the exploration of lived experience. We propose that the answers can be found by exploring hermeneutic phenomenology.

Hermeneutic phenomenology

Leading proponents of the application of hermeneutic phenomenology are Max van Manen (2000) who has written extensively on methodology in education and the human sciences, and Susann Laverty (2003). For van Manen, hermeneutic phenomenology is more than just a response to the realisation that language limits our ability to reveal the phenomena. Hermeneutic phenomenology is a marriage between hermeneutics, phenomenology and semiotics. Where phenomenology defines a person's orientation to lived experience, semiotics defines the linguistic approach to research and hermeneutics describes how a researcher 'interprets the "texts" of life' (van Manen, 1990, p. 4). Research in the human sciences is a balance between accepting the need for an element of structure without alienating the spirit of humanity. Essentially hermeneutic phenomenology claims to have no method *per se* and researchers are advised to be vigilant against 'the seductive illusion of technique' (van Manen, 1990, p. 3). Despite these warnings hermeneutic phenomenology does provide guidelines. Perhaps the most important guideline is the indelible link between writing and research.

As indicated in the previous chapter the essential nature of hermeneutic phenomenology is that the reporting of experiences necessarily involves the process of interpretation. An attempt to balance an awareness that whilst life is complex and complete descriptions of experience unattainable, the explication of some aspect of life remains significant. Essentially, the phenomenological reduction as originally described is deemed impossible. As Heidegger (1996) so eloquently pointed out, it is perhaps impossible to separate oneself from one's past experiences and understandings. Yet the attempt to get as close as possible to *the things themselves* is worthwhile. We are not suggesting that the researcher avoid rigour or be side-tracked; rather, extra rigour is required as the researcher remains focused upon the phenomenon in question.

We now turn to the hermeneutic phenomenological research method. Six dynamically interconnected activities are posited by van Manen (1990). His intention is not to provide a detailed step-by-step procedure but simply a guide. The aim is to make clearer the hermeneutic understanding of the research process, which in itself helps to develop a dynamic emergent textual understanding. In the end, while being grounded in the phenomenological principles, the actual method used may be particular to a specific research topic or context. The first of the six activities involves the researcher being committed to and interested in a specific phenomenon or 'turning to the nature of lived experience' (van Manen, 1990, p. 31). Here the researcher sets out to explore and eventually describe some element of human experience. The realisation being that the experience can never be explored whilst being lived, it necessarily has to involve a degree of reflection to be realised. As such any verbalisation is always a reflection or interpretation of a past event. The overall aim is to textually model the essence of a lived experience. We start with an experience itself and end with a text that animates the very nature of the experience. As such any lived experience can be questioned, explored and explicated. The challenge for researchers is to orient towards an experience in such a way that the essential nature and meanings are recalled as potential explications of the experience. Thus the researcher should identify an experience that is of intense interest.

As with most other phenomenological disciplines the identification process is followed by a formal development of a phenomenological question. Invariably the question does not stand alone; an interest or sense of curiosity will often be part of the researcher's greater experience. The question must then clearly define the topic being explored. A unique component of the hermeneutic approach is the requirement for the researcher to live the question as if becoming the question. It is perhaps most appropriate to pose the question in its broadest sense, to ask 'what is' or 'what is it like', as in 'what is it like to experience a jump from a building 1,000 metres off the ground, and only have a parachute which you trust will protect your life?'. Of course to ask a question assumes the exploration of an answer. In hermeneutic phenomenology this is best defined as a journey towards describing the 'what-ness' of the experience (van Manen, 1990, p. 46). Equally, an hermeneutic phenomenological researcher must pay attention to prior knowledge. Significantly, any attempt to ignore or bury prior knowledge would inevitably result in that knowledge creeping into a researcher's reflection processes. It is thus better to acknowledge and come to terms with prior assumptions, beliefs and understandings and make them explicit. This might even be part of the written documentation associated with the research. In this way a researcher is able to ensure, as best as is humanly possible, that the mystery – that is, the phenomenon – is explored in its own terms.

This process of translating experience into text inevitably involves the challenge of metaphor. To render the meaning of the metaphor explicit requires that we move beyond explicit language to describe the nature of the experience and achieve sufficient closeness to reveal 'the thing itself'. Thus we explore the meaning of a phenomenon through language, just as the experience displays itself through emotions or behaviours. This is not a postmodern attempt to focus on the story but an explication of the experience through stories (Churchill, 2002). The objective is to uncover what is lived and pre-language, and bring it more fully into textual being.

The use of additional material

Hermeneutic phenomenology is similar to other versions of phenomenology in investigating the lived experience as opposed to a theoretical presentation of the experience. For hermeneutic phenomenology this entails a broad search for material that might help with revealing the nature of the experience. However, as all material is potentially an interpretation of lived experience the phenomenologist needs to be attuned to how this reveals the essence of the phenomenon. Arguably, the first place to look for understanding is the researcher's personal descriptions of the experience. This of course assumes that one has experienced the phenomenon under question. Whilst the original text would not be phenomenological, ensuing thoughts and reflections might begin the phenomenological process. The presupposition is that personal experiences may reveal something about the experiences of others and of course *vice versa*.

It is often important to trace the words that describe the phenomenon back to their original meaning to understand what the words themselves have to say about the phenomenon. Similarly, it is often useful to consider terms or phrases that relate to the phenomenon or mystery being questioned. However, some of the major sources of information are those texts that a researcher acquires from others. The voices and experiences of others should be honoured and appreci-ated. Sometimes a researcher might ask for the experiences to be in written form, and sometimes interviews will be audio or video recorded. In the case of the interview the researcher would either be gathering information or discussing the meaning of the phenomenon with the interviewee focusing on the phenomeno-logical question at hand.

The interview process, which is invariably central to phenomenological research, may depend on relationships and the abilities of the co-researcher. Van Manen (1990) makes some suggestions on format. For example, the primary researcher might begin by asking a co-researcher to focus on an experience and describe what it was like. The essence being to ensure the process remains focused on revealing something about the nature of the phenomenon in question. The practice of hermeneutic phenomenology encourages the use of close obser-vation, literature, biography, diaries, journals and art. Van Manen (2007) describes the process as stemming from the 'pathic power' of phenomenological reflection in which pathic knowing inheres in the senses in our encounter with the other. We are thus encouraged to enter the lifeworld of the co-researcher.

Essentially the researcher rigorously gathers relevant anecdotes. This could include poetry and other human expression that might help with the exploration (Laverty, 2003). The important point here is that the story or poem should be significant to our explication of the phenomenon. Biographies often provide rich experiential descriptions that can be used for phenomenological exploration. Diaries and journals, either concurrent or historical, may also provide rich insights. Art, cinematography, music, sculpture and painting might all provide valuable insights; however, the researcher may have the task of interpreting a different type of language – a tactile or visual language. The focus, though, is on the meaning that language helps to uncover not the language itself.

The third activity involves hermeneutic phenomenological reflection. This involves continually moving between parts of the experience to the whole experience to obtain greater depth. The researcher uses the interpretation process to search for a deeper unity of meaning and continually tests interpretations against new textual chunks. This cyclical process is undertaken with creativity and acceptance of the certainty of presuppositions. The focus is to arrive at a determination and explication of the phenomenon in question. The researcher conducts thematic analysis or the formulation of a thematic sense or meaning. The aim is to organise and order the research as distinct from following strict rules. Themes might be developed from specific texts before being considered as a part of the whole. In his more recent writings, van Manen also refers to mantic meaning, which refers to our understanding of the imagery revealed to the reader through his or her own reverberation with the material.

Themes have various purposes and structures. Themes are a focus of meaning; they are simplifications, descriptions of aspects of the phenomenon. Themes are a point along the journey to a full explication, a way of giving shape to the text. Essentially, themes and our pathic understanding and explication of themes develop as a way of organising the text resulting in discovery and insights about an aspect of a phenomenon. Themes can be isolated by considering the whole text and formulating a phrase that expresses the essence of the text.

Thematic analysis is often part of the overall process of explication. The hermeneutic (or meaning making) interview is a continual conversation, reflection and theme interpretation. The analysis – or, the term we prefer, explication – involves collaborative discussions with co-researchers holding a phenomenological interest. When developing the thematic structure or meaning units van Manen (1990) recommends using the fundamentals of lived body (corporeality), lived space (spatiality), lived time (temporality) and lived other (relationality or communality) to reflect the foundational structures of lived experience. These four fundamentals, sometimes referred to as 'existentials', are considered universal lifeworld themes that permeate human lifeworld independent of cultural, historical or social context. The process of thematic development does not necessarily result in an explication of the unique description of the phenomenon. It is therefore important to distinguish between the essential elements and incidental elements. For this the phenomenologist uses free imagination; that is, themes are imaginatively changed or deleted to test their relevance. For instance, experience derived from meditation, dreams, imagery and bodily and emotional cues may form part of the theme development.

A unique contribution by van Manen to an hermeneutic phenomenological approach is expressed in his fourth activity; writing. While he emphasises that in practice research and writing cannot be separated the aim is to create a phenomenological text.

> Writing is not just externalizing internal knowledge, rather it is the very act of making contact with the things of our world. In this sense to do research is to write, and the insights achieved depend on the right words and phrases, on styles and traditions, on metaphor and figures of speech, on argument and poetic image. Even then writing can mean both insight and illusion. And these are values that cannot be decided, fixed or settled, since the one always implies, hints at, or complicates the other.
>
> (van Manen, 2002a, p. 237)

Writing, in the phenomenological sense, is considered as two distinct levels, the practical and the reflective. The practical relates to the 'mundane issues of methods, techniques, form, and style'. The reflective level entails such issues as metaphysics, truth, limits of language, interpretation and the phenomenological meaning (van Manen, 2002b, p. i). The essence being that writing is a process that engulfs the phenomenological exploration from its inception.

Writing is not just about giving expression to the words of the co-researcher but also about listening to both the words and the meanings associated with silences. Like words, silence can be deeply meaningful, whether serving the function of expressing what may be difficult to express, or indicating that which is too difficult to express. Silences are thus listened to, and form part of the process of meaning making. In this sense, they add to the quality of the text. Silence might also be an expression of tacit knowing whereby we know more than we are able to put into words, where words become ineffective. It is feasible that what is beyond the linguistic skills of one person can be put into words by another. For example, a person may have experienced a phenomenon but they may not have the desire or linguistic capacity to enter into an exploration or description. Silence can also be ontological in the sense that moments of silence might signify profound insights or the realisation that we are in the presence of potential truth.

Writing provides distance between action and reflection. Writing up represents a powerful process that is vastly different from the traditional writing up of research reports. The act, or perhaps it should be the art, of writing is paramount. Writing formalises thought, allows for a deeper reflection as if we are engaged in making public an understanding of our own depth. Writing simultaneously distances and unites the writer with the lifeworld. At its core, the process of writing and rewriting is the most important skill possessed by the phenomenological researcher adopting an hermeneutic stance.

The fifth activity in van Manen's approach is to maintain a strong and 'oriented' relation. In this sense the term 'oriented' means that there is no attempt to separate life from theory. In contrast to other social sciences, such as ethnography, phenomenological writing exhibits a commitment and involvement in the lifeworld being studied. Abstraction is avoided in an attempt to remain connected to the phenomenon. The notion of strength implies the continued and exclusive focus on the phenomenon. The ensuing texts need to be deep and rich.

Finally, in the sixth activity both the parts and the whole need to be balanced. The researcher needs to consider their ethical responsibilities towards themselves and others who may be involved. For some phenomena transformations may take place or a new learning that has arisen as a result of conversations may result in anger or anxiety. The researcher may require considerable creativity in developing the information-gathering processes. Less common experiences may be difficult to comprehend by those who have not lived the experience. In this case constraints with general validation and information gathering are obvious restrictions. The writer might organise writing to mirror the structure of the phenomenon or as subdivided texts that relate to the themes. The text might relay the journey taken or be expressed in a more analytical format. The text may build up to reveal the phenomenon or start with the phenomenon and then fill in essential descriptions. Equally, a text might start with the concepts of lived time/space/body/other and create a dialogue from this starting point. A researcher could also use a combination or invent something new.

Transpersonal phenomenology

Transpersonal phenomenologists are most often interested in exceptional, sacred or spiritual experience. Those human experiences which are invariably outside the realm of traditional discourses of study are therefore difficult to put into words. While this area of research is less well known, insights from proponents such as Valle and Mohs (Valle 1998; Valle and Mohs 1998, 2007) allow us to broaden the scope of phenomenological enquiry. Valle is a contemporary theorist and practitioner who writes about consciousness and Mohs comes from a nursing background, and has contributed to our understandings of Eastern and Western spiritual philosophies. Their work provides essential guidance when studying potentially extraordinary experiences. At its core, transpersonal phenomenology accepts non-duality as an experiential reality. Researchers are encouraged to pay more attention to symbolic or archetypal information or become more familiar with bodily, feeling or insightful language. The researcher needs to demonstrate a level of listening that honours different ways of knowing; a listening that involves emotional awareness and awareness of self. A more radical approach was proposed by Braud (1998) who expands this concept even further by recommending that researchers merge with the object of study.

> Such a step involves paying full attention to *what is known directly to the eye of the spirit;* this type of knowing seems to require a change or transformation in the investigator's *being.* It requires that the investigator *become* what is being studied and to know it as *subject* rather than as object.
>
> (Braud, 1998, p. 51)

This process is referred to as *dadirri* in Aboriginal culture and denotes a deep spiritual skill, based on mutual respect.

Summary

In this chapter we have investigated a number of phenomenological theorists who have contributed to the translation of phenomenology as a philosophical approach to phenomenological practice. We have focused on four branches of phenomenology outlined in Chapter 2 and shown how the approaches adopted by significant theorists broadly adhere to the principles outlined as essential for undertaking a phenomenological study, while still being attuned to the essential nature of each theoretical perspective.

Essentially, phenomenological approaches to studying human experience would seem to be just as diverse as the fields of thought that support them. The process which we will outline is adapted from the works reviewed and explored as there are some commonalities. However, ultimately it would seem that the essence of the process needs to be faithful to the question being asked and to the phenomenon being explicated. Our purpose in reviewing each of the above theorists is to demonstrate the approaches outlined. Our prime purpose is to persuade the student of phenomenology to appreciate that there is no single perfect methodology and that each study needs to develop a methodological approach appropriate to the aims of the study while still adhering to phenomenological principles. Contemporary approaches also emphasise the need for rigour in research studies allowing for replication. What seems to distinguish the different approaches is the underlying belief about how this can be best done. Being true to phenomenology and to the experience in question requires an open-ended approach. That is, an approach that necessitates an attentive, aesthetically awake and receptive awareness of the lived experience of the other. Some common values to achieve this objective include humility, awe, wonder, appreciation, respect and delight. The chapter following will describe the operationalisation of the principles outlined in Chapter 2 and the practice guidelines articulated above with a particular emphasis on the extreme sport experience.

References

Braud, W. (1998). Integral inquiry: Complementary ways of knowing, being and expression. In W. Braud & R. Anderson (Eds), *Transpersonal research methods for the social sciences: Honoring human experience* (pp. 35–68). Thousand Oaks, CA: Sage.

Churchill, S. D. (2002). Stories of experience and the experience of stories: Narrative psychology, phenomenology, and the postmodern challenge. *Constructivism in the Human Sciences, 7*(1&2), 81–94.

Crotty, M. (1996a). Doing phenomenology. In M. Parer & Z. Unger (Eds), *Proceedings of qualitative research methods workshop* (pp. 6–12). Melbourne, Australia: Office of Continuing Education, Monash University Clayton Campus.

Crotty, M. (1996b). *Phenomenology and nursing research.* Melbourne: Churchill Livingstone.

Giorgi, A. (1997). The theory, practice, and evaluation of the phenomenological method as a qualitative research procedure. *Journal of Phenomenological Psychology, 28*(2), 235–260.

Giorgi, A. (2009). *The descriptive phenomenological method in psychology: A modified Husserlian approach.* Pittsburgh, PA: Duquesne University Press.

Giorgi, A. (2010). Phenomenology and the practice of science. *Existential Analysis, 21*(1), 3–22.

Heidegger, M. (1996). *Being and time: A translation of Sein and Zeit.* (J. Stambaugh, Trans.). Albany, NY: State University of New York.

Laverty, S. M. (2003). Hermeneutic phenomenology and phenomenology: A comparison of historical and methodological consideration. *International Journal of Qualitative Methods, 2*(3), Article 3.

Moustakas, C. E. (1994). *Phenomenological research methods.* Thousand Oaks, CA: Sage.

Spinelli, E. (1989). *The interpreted world: An introduction to phenomenological psychology.* London: Sage.

Valle, R. (1998). Transpersonal awareness: Implications for phenomenological research. In R. Valle (Ed.), *Phenomenological inquiry: Existential and transpersonal dimensions* (pp. 273–279). New York: Plenum Press.

Valle, R. & Mohs, M. (1998). Transpersonal awareness in phenomenological inquiry: Philosophy, reflections and recent research. In W. Braud & R. Anderson (Eds), *Transpersonal research methods for the social sciences: Honouring human experience* (pp. 95–113). Thousand Oaks, CA: Sage.

Valle, R. & Mohs, M. (2007). Transpersonal awareness in phenomenological inquiry: Philosophy, reflections, and recent research. *Alternative Journal of Nursing, 10*, 1–16.

van Manen, M. (1990). *Researching lived experience: Human science for an action sensitive pedagogy.* New York: State University of New York Press.

van Manen, M. (2000). www.phenomenologyonline.com.

van Manen, M. (2002a). Writing in the dark. In M. van Manen (Ed.), *Writing in the dark: Phenomenological studies in interpretive inquiry* (pp. 237–253). London, ON: The Althouse Press.

van Manen, M. (2002b). *Writing in the dark: Phenomenological studies in interpretive inquiry*. London, ON: The Althouse Press.

van Manen, M. (2007). Phenomenology of practice. *Phenomenology & Practice, 1*(1), 11–30.

Wertz, F. J. (2015). Phenomenology methods, historical development, and applications in psychology. In J. Martin, J. Sugarman & K. L. Slaney (Eds), *The Wiley handbook of theoretical and philosophical psychology: Methods, approaches, and new directions for social sciences* (pp. 85–102). New York: Wiley-Blackwell.

4 Phenomenology and the extreme sport experience

An hermeneutic phenomenological methodology

In the previous chapters we presented some fundamental principles of phenomenology and outlined four branches of phenomenological practice. This chapter outlines a set of context specific procedures which have salience to phenomenological research and, in particular, researching the extreme sport experience. At one level, phenomenological research seems to be a perfectly simple process. However, the practice of phenomenology is challenging for researchers, embedded within a traditional natural scientific or empirical-based paradigm with its emphasis upon causality, measurement and notions of verification. Furthermore, the natural scientific paradigm assumes a distinction between subject and object. This attitude is the taken for granted 'background' of all research. In this chapter, we detail a specific methodological process for undertaking a form of phenomenological research in which the 'taken for granted' assumptions of object and subject are questioned, and we also give credence to the role of interpretation in our descriptions. The chapters following demonstrate the application of this approach, drawing upon phenomenological principles to explicate and gain a phenomenological understanding of the extreme sport experience. We draw upon the work of a number of phenomenologists, with an emphasis upon the work of hermeneutic phenomenology. We also extend the field of research phenomena by recognising the potential for transpersonal or extraordinary experiences.

Selecting a research topic

Most phenomenological research commences with a search for a suitable topic for exploration. Essentially seven interacting pragmatic concerns need to be realised. A project should be manageable in the time allowed and the horizons of the topic should be clearly specified. Ideally, the aims should be capable of being expressed in a single sentence. The topic should be simple, focused and concrete in its exploration of a specific relationship. Such relationships are, by definition, human experiences informed by the concept of consciousness being 'intentional'. Furthermore, the researcher should be practically able to inquire into the topic. The topic will hopefully be inspiring to the researcher and trigger intellectual passion. Finally the topic should focus on an object of interest that is still unknown or builds upon what is known. Beyond this, the phenomenological researcher has a responsibility to ensure rigour, careful data collection and disciplined analysis. Each of these principles informs the approach outlined in this book.

The ultimate goal of phenomenological research is to work towards defining the core of the experience. That is, to put into language the invariant features of the phenomenon. The formal researcher needs to be disciplined as she or he is explicit and careful about observations, decisions, judgements and processes. The researcher recognises that research is always value laden and depends on personal and cultural views on soundness, trustworthiness and worth. Equally, characteristics such as our respective backgrounds, training, worldviews and skills potentially influence all stages of the research process, from defining questions to communicating the findings. In the current research endeavour, we recognise that those who participate in extreme sports, whom we term co-researchers, are the experts in their fields of endeavour. We thus need to focus on the relatively simple objective of explicating the experience of extreme sports participants.

Selecting a research topic

For this project the phenomenon to be considered is *the extreme sport experience*. In the first instance the topic was the focus. The desire was to understand how and why some people choose to engage in extreme sports. The study evolved into a phenomenological study as a result of a growing dissatisfaction with traditional ways of knowing and an appreciation for the power of a phenomenological approach to explicate the lifeworld of extreme sports people.

Preparation

Good research is organic in nature as it evolves in both the intent and method. The preparation stage involves considerable time and effort. Often the phenomenon is difficult to define or writings claiming to uncover insights into the experience textualise widely different concepts. Researchers need to define exactly what will be included and not included. Additionally, drawing upon the phenomenological concept of intentionality, the phenomenological researcher is interested in human experience. That is, if the researcher were interested in headaches the researcher would not regard the headache as independent from the person suffering from the headache but as a deeply personal experience. This highlights a key distinction between phenomenology and a natural scientific approach in which the object of study is most often regarded as independent of the subject. In keeping with the assumptions of human science, the preparatory process requires moving away from metaphors of human behaviour as 'reductionistic' or 'causal' and towards an understanding and explication of lived experience with all its variations.

The role of assumptions needs to be kept in mind. For example, the researcher may need to consider the potential role of gender and any bias which may reflect their own gender-based assumptions. To the degree to which we engage in what we term reflexive process, we reflect upon our own mental processes, theoretical and experiential presuppositions and make our assumptions explicit. While this process starts in the preparatory stage in practice it is a continual process over the course of each stage of the research. The researcher is advised to start keeping a journal from the very beginning.

Reflection

In the current research, Brymer kept a diary of his experiences, assumptions and reflections during the research process. In practice this process is organic, recursive and part of the research process. Reflection is sometimes deliberate and intended but at other times can emerge when least expected – while playing in the surf or on your walk.

Focusing on the question

Any research initiative which seeks to gain a rigorous understanding of lived experience requires that we focus on formulating the research question. The question may not be static, but it provides the structure or scaffolding of the research enterprise. Focusing on the question requires some degree of circumscribing the field of interest and definition of the object of study. However, from a phenomenological perspective, the process is more complex as we need to reflect upon our own natural scientific assumptions, often borne out of an unconscious bias towards an explanatory or empirical scientific world view, in which both causality and dualism are the bedrocks of scientific thought.

Let's illustrate this point with an example. If we were to frame a question in relation to extreme sport, such as: what is the role of risk-taking in extreme sport? From a phenomenological perspective, this question is saturated with assumptions, most importantly, that extreme sports may be understood by drawing upon a predefined concept, known as risk-taking. No doubt, a scale of risk-taking with excellent psychometric properties could also be identified. In contrast, a phenomenological researcher is more interested in a rigorous description of the phenomenon, as it emerges in the lifeworld of the research participants. Such a methodology allows us to ask many inductive questions which lie beyond the dominant natural scientific paradigm. There are a range of qualitative methodologies which could be brought to bear upon the above question. For instance, a grounded theory approach might also be interested in the constructs which define the extreme sport experience, but from this perspective the grounded theory researcher is more interested in developing a theoretical model of motivation for engaging in extreme sports. Similarly, a more traditional thematic analytic methodology might be employed to study the themes which characterise participant experience in extreme sport. In this instance the researcher might ask a seemingly similar question but the notion of intentionality would not apply and the question might focus upon the subjective experience of participants rather than focus upon the lived experience.

In the process of focusing the research question in our study of the experience of extreme sport, we commenced by asking ourselves, 'what exactly is an extreme sport?'. Defining the topic and intent of the study was the only way of ensuring that we were studying the appropriate participants who engage in the experience which in turn would, of course, influence each aspect of the research journey. While we all have assumptions that we know what an extreme sport is, it soon emerged that there are a variety of views on the matter and that some decisions in relation to the definition of the topic was imperative. If the boundaries were not defined appropriately the study would collapse before it even began! Thus the search for definitions included formal and informal methods but drew upon a broad perspective of human science, which privileges questions regarding meaning, values and experience as opposed to methods concerned with prediction and control. Second, the task involves reviewing previous studies pertaining to the phenomenon being explored, thus providing a basis for building upon prior understandings or knowledge.

Defining the boundaries

Reading the literature it soon became clear that the phrase 'Extreme Sport' encompasses a variety of activities that are traditionally associated with 'adrenaline junkies' or 'risk-taking'. Skateboarding, street luge, snow sports, mountain sports, moto-cross and surfing have been presented as examples of such sports. Many writers were using the same descriptor for different activities and different levels of the same activity. Furthermore, even within the descriptor certain predetermined assumptions were being proffered; namely the relationship to risk. In the literature, activities such as BASE jumping, bungee jumping and whitewater rafting were often grouped together as if they represented comparable activities. In a similar way activities such as whitewater kayaking was assumed to be one activity. However, whitewater kayaking can take place in an environment where the most likely outcome of a mismanaged mistake is getting wet, or at the other extreme when kayaking over waterfalls the likelihood of mismanaged mistake is death. Equally, a tourist can undertake a whitewater rafting trip or a bungee jump with little knowledge of the activity or the environment. However, a BASE jumper requires an in-depth knowledge of the environment and activity.

Extreme sports were defined as those *independent leisure activities where a mismanaged mistake or accident would most likely result in death.*

Defining the boundaries

The researcher needs to explore the work of writers and researchers who have extended ideas on the phenomenon, building upon previous research. The most common way of defining boundaries is to define inclusion and exclusion criteria. In the early stages it is important to not rule anything out, regardless of presuppositions in relation to the topic. The definitions may start broad but eventually need to precisely encompass the experience being addressed. Phenomenological studies routinely require participants to articulate their experience to some degree. However, the researcher also has responsibilities to facilitate the exploration of the topic. For example, what are the experiences of those who jump off cliffs armed with only a parachute; who surf waves as big as a house (or bigger); who ski sheer cliffs; who would willingly kayak over waterfalls for the experience itself?

Narrowing the focus, broadening horizons

In the process of focusing on and defining the research question, and furnished with a new understanding of a method of delineation, a proposed study may well take on a revised direction. Previous understandings may be categorised as relevant or not relevant as we are more open to the phenomenon and an emerging understanding of it. In the development of a phenomenological study, the researcher is required to continually revisit the topic under study. Unlike traditional approaches where the question may remain static the phenomenological researcher may well revisit the topic and engage in a process which we term 'narrowing the focus'. We also refer to 'broadening horizons', a phenomenological term meaning background with potential for emergence. This requires us to be perceptive to subtleties of the phenomenon which may not be obvious at this stage of the developing study. It is thus incumbent on the researcher to maintain a focus on the phenomenon in question in order to ensure that appropriate experiences are included and inappropriate ones excluded. Narrowing the focus and broadening the horizon is essentially a process of being attuned to the subtleties of the phenomenon, and being aware of these subtleties in defining the research journey. For example, in this study the experience of mountaineering provided one such challenge. At its best, high altitude mountaineering is most definitely an extreme sport. However, tourists with enough money have also been dragged to the roof of the world. Thus we needed to be narrow in our acceptance of mountaineering accounts. The inevitable downside of such decisions is the potential that certain rich accounts might have been missed. However, this was deemed preferable to the contamination that would have occurred if such decisions had not been made.

The process of narrowing the focus and broadening the horizon also helps determine the boundaries of the experience being investigated. While for some experiences the boundary is quite clear, for others such as the extreme sport experience the boundary might be more fuzzy. As part of this process it is important to determine 'the difference that makes the difference' for those engaged in the phenomenon being investigated. For example, in the extreme sport context the inclusion criterion was that participants needed to partake in adventure activities, for leisure, where a mismanaged mistake or accident would

Narrowing and broadening

For example, in the current exemplar, we were able to narrow our focus onto specific types of activity which resulted in a broadening of potential leisure pursuits. We differentiated between BASE jumping, where participants jump off cliffs, buildings and bridges with only one parachute and no mechanical aids to remind them to pull the release cord and skydiving where two parachutes and mechanical aids are used and there is space all around. In climbing, the definition of extreme sport provided a clear line between those who climb at a high level with ropes and those who climb without the additional safety of ropes. However, for some activities, such as skiing, we relied on the knowledge of those participating to indicate if they would categorise their sport as extreme. At the same time other sports such as cave-diving, proximity flying, solo unsupported expeditions in extreme environments and certain mountaineering activities were added to the list.

most likely result in death. Thus, to fully explore the extreme sport experience it is important to comprehend the almost-extreme sport experience. On occasion we have made that point explicit when exploring thematic material in the ensuing chapters.

Lastly, there is an important assumption guiding the interest of the phenomenological researcher, that is, to think of the 'subject' of the research as a 'participant' and 'co-researcher' who has expert knowledge of the phenomenon, and the imperative to return to the experience itself. In our example, the question guiding the investigation was 'what is your experience of the sport in which you engage?'. This is a distinctive question, and quite different to such questions as: how do extreme sport participants perceive their involvement in extreme sport activities? That is, phenomenological enquiry, supported by the principle of rejecting dualism, works towards obviating subject–object distinctions which are characteristic of the natural sciences. The approach, drawing upon intentionality, privileges a perspective in which consciousness is always consciousness of the object, in other words, the 'subject' and 'object' are co-constituted in the act of human experience.

Gathering data

Gathering data lies at the foundation of the phenomenological task. The term 'data' is unfortunate, as it has connotations of something separate from the self. We are interested in human accounts of phenomena, taking into account the fact that experience-near phenomena are co-constituted. That is, the *human world* in which we live does not, in a phenomenological sense, exist completely independent of self. The world as object would not cease to exist if we cease to exist, but the necessary understanding of phenomena is dependent upon our lived sense of the phenomena. Similarly, data (or human accounts) may include a range of sources, such as digital movies, poems, biographies and autobiographies and, most importantly, focused conversations.

Co-researchers are chosen for their ability to assist the investigation in terms of having sufficient lived experience and an ability and desire to unravel and give voice to the mysteries that make up or constitute the experience. Co-researchers are not chosen for their knowledge of the phenomenological framework and no attempt is made to change co-researchers into phenomenological researchers. Potential co-researchers are approached for their expertise. Co-researchers are contacted prior to a focused interview in order to explore their willingness to engage in the exploration of the experience. That is, to ensure they have the required skills and are comfortable articulating their experiences in depth. While different sources vary in their estimation of the number of co-researchers needed for a research project, in our experience the final number will be dependent on co-researcher's skills, interviewer skills and the phenomenon being investigated. However, we concur with Giorgi that studies should have a minimum number of three experts in the phenomenon. The interviewer or principal researcher requires the skills to draw out aspects of the experience which the co-researcher may not even realise are part of their experience.

Co-researchers

Co-researchers who have contributed to understandings for this book include twenty-two participants from BASE jumping, proximity flying, rope free solo climbing, big wave surfing, extreme mountaineering, extreme skiing and waterfall kayaking.

The interview

The most important quality to bring to the phenomenological interview is a deep sense of curiosity where the 'taken for granted' is regarded as unfamiliar. That is, the exploration of human action and experience constitutes an 'intriguing quest into the unknown' (Gergen, 1990, p. 29). The stance being advocated applies not only to the experience being investigated and the recording of information and recollections but also the interview flow. These guidelines provide an appropriate context in which to effectively and respectfully explore participants' experience.

Fundamentally, discussions on the experience of co-researchers take the form of focused exploratory interviews. Central to any such exchange is the necessity that the interviewee experiences the encounter as safe. The psychotherapy literature is useful here, in advocating the requirements for such an interview; that is, clarity round the purpose of the interview, understanding the process to be followed, and third, the difficult to define, but intrinsic importance of the rapport established between the parties. The role of the interviewer is to rebalance the inherent power assumptions often associated with interviewer–interviewee relationships. That is, the interviewer enters into a collaborative relationship with the interviewee who is acknowledged as an expert in the area being explored.

We can all reflect upon our own experiences of feeling safe in interview situations and the attributes which contribute to feeling safe, or the absence of such feelings. However, the focus of the phenomenological research interview is always on the experience in question rather than getting to know the person as a therapeutic client.

In practice, as the co-researcher is not expected to be familiar with phenomenology, the interview may involve the researcher providing the co-researcher with explanations and motivations for the research project and the research approach. The interviewer may initially need to direct the process through probing questions but very quickly engages in a more exploratory collaboration underpinned by a sense of curiosity. The interview process follows what has been termed 'a highly unstructured, open-ended format' in which we, as researchers, seek to gain some degree of empathic attunement to the experience of the other and, at the same time, to provide the conditions so that the interviewee is facilitated to articulate in-depth responses. To do this effectively the interviewer cultivates an attitude of being present for the co-researcher and demonstrates this through body language, attention and genuinely prioritising the interviewee's narrative.

The researcher's goal is to keep the interview focused on the question underpinning the research and develop depth in the co-researchers' responses. Wertz (2015) has described the process as a 'wedding of rationality and observation' in its adoption of a process which is characterised as being methodical, systematic, critical, self-correcting and progressive. To develop appropriate depth the interviewer's role is to aid in the process of verbalising, and bringing to awareness, what may previously have been an act. The process of explication is guided by encouraging the co-researcher into a state of re-living and giving expression to the experience, developing action-based knowledge into representational knowledge and supporting the process of verbal clarification. This process might best be described as a process of revelation, from the Latin *revelare* which means to 'lay bare', as the researcher seeks to uncover the invariant structure of the phenomenon.

In practice, the interview process begins with rapport building prior to recording the interview. Participants are given time to confirm their understandings of the purpose of the study and express comfort with the process. Whilst there is some evolution in the specific method, the focused element of the interview process invariably begins with a request from the researcher for a brief history into each co-researcher's journey to initiating their chosen activity. The next stage of the interview process explores the structure of the experience itself by evoking images, sensations, sounds and the like. The interview is characterised by a degree of intimacy which might differ depending on the experience being explored but which is nevertheless essential. In contrast to traditional interviews where the interviewer always leads the interview, over time the phenomenological interview may well be led by the interviewee. The participant is encouraged to talk in the first person and describe their own lived experience. The interviewer observes and listens carefully in order to notice verbal and non-verbal responses that invite further clarification and his or her own responses to the unfolding of the interview. Depth is gained by keeping in mind the phenomenological principle of intentionality. In practice the interviewer asks for examples, uses reflections, summaries, articulates observations and even uses probe questions and a knowledge of their own responses to the interview in an effort to organise and understand an interviewee's experience.

We strongly advocate a process of active listening where we attend to gestural and affective elements of the interview, including our responses to the material being shared. There is an argument that videotaping interviews has advantages in this regard. The whole process is underlined by five qualities: respect for the participants involved; developing a climate of trust as far as this is possible in the time allocated to the process; an acceptance of participants' realities; a fullness of attention to minimise distortion or filtering, denial and projection of both the interviewer and interviewee; and finally the attitude of the researcher needs to be characterised by reflectivity and integrity. These qualities are well summarised by texts on cultural competence and their privileging: humility; curiosity; self-awareness; willingness and open-heartedness.

As interviewers we need to continually reflect upon our preconceptions, and making these explicit in the spirit of Husserl's notion of 'bracketing' while recognising the hermeneutic phenomenological perspective on how this is done. Bracketing is best captured by the idea of mindful awareness as we adopt an 'emic' perspective. It may seem simple to describe but more difficult to put into practice. For the beginning researcher, one approach to approximate the values being described is to gain an understanding of 'presence'. This often takes a great deal of preparation and the beginning interviewer might well be advised to prepare for interviews. For example, engaging in exercises such as spending a few minutes alone prior to an interview session doing mindfulness activities with a view to developing awareness of one's own preconceptions, and consciously 'putting these aside' in the process of engaging in the interview.

In our experience, a major challenge is the conflict between allowing the co-researcher to maintain a fluid description whilst at the same time attempting to take note of gestures, phrases or words that need revisiting. For some this might mean a second interview in order to clarify certain terms and phrases otherwise

---

Place of interview

In our research, interviews have most often been conducted in places chosen by the co-researcher, which may have been their home, or another place where they felt most comfortable. This meant that interviewees were more likely to feel safe, and happy to engage in a reflective process which underpins the most successful interviews.

missed. Thus the process involves a simultaneous broad and narrow focus on the meaning of the experience, sometimes exploring the experience as a whole and at other times exploring the meaning of specific words or phrases, but always with the intention of making sense of the experience as experienced. That is, we search for understandings and meanings over the course of the human encounter, referred to as 'the interview'; continually clarifying and expanding upon co-researcher meanings and nuances of meaning.

Exploring the phenomenon

As we have made clear, the aim of phenomenological research is to go beyond the 'insignificant surface' to reach a 'profound depth' in a move to articulate characteristics of the phenomenon. This requires a transition from the exploration of the phenomenon on an individual basis to an understanding of the phenomenon across individuals, often referred to as moving from an ideographic to a nomothetic approach. In practice this requires working with a number of co-researchers. While some approaches advocate specific numbers – for example Grounded Theory refers to saturation – the important idea in hermeneutic phenomenology is to gain sufficient data to arrive at the essential structure or range of themes across a group of participants. The gathering of sufficient data is a recursive process and in practice interviews may still be taking place while the researcher is explicating other texts. The processes required to achieve this objective involves the following:

Exploring interviews

The interview should be recorded and transcribed. However, immediately following the interview and before transcription, whilst maintaining as open a state as possible, it is important to listen to the interview in order to grasp a sense of the whole. This reflective space allows us to relive the interview process and to recall the importance of gestures and silences. In our experience, we will often listen to each recording a number of times before and after the transcription to gain a sense of the whole. The next process is to read and re-read each individual interview transcript still with the aim of gaining a sense of the whole lived experience. Only once this has been done is each transcript explicated as a separate entity to identify themes, though all transcripts are revisited as themes become more explicit.

The stage following may use one of a variety of computer assisted qualitative data analysis software (CAQDAS) programs. All CAQDAS programs assist with the systematic retrieval of data, they are tools, and cannot substitute for the intellectual work of the researcher in explicating meaning. There are computer programs which claim to analyse data, but they rely on algorithms and do not meet the requirements of phenomenological research.

There is no single method for interpreting text, and even phenomenological studies will vary from study to study in their emphasis. In some sense, each study will have specific requirements, which will require the method of explication to be consistent with the aims and method of the study. Nevertheless, the process of interpretation involves more than just reading or exploring the raw text as if separated from the experience itself, and the process should align with the principles of phenomenology. Hermeneutical research is inevitably both rational and unconscious and therefore creative and rigorous. The same report or action can be interpreted in a number of ways depending on the interpreters (both primary researcher and co-researcher) and the information or context that surrounds the text. Text is considered within its 'emergent context' or as part of a flowing interdependent process. Thus interpretation involves more than just developing two dimensional themes from written texts. Yet, arguably, consistency and transparency rely on the methodical management of the research process. Through interpreting the readings of others and our own trial and error we accept the inevitability that our explication involves some degree of interpretation.

Both formal and non-formal understandings of potential themes are continually questioned, challenged and assessed for relevancy as we move through transcripts and other material. This is an iterative process. The researcher might question interpretations such as: 'what are the emergent themes as presented?' 'am I interpreting this text from a position of interference from theory or personal bias?', 'what am I missing?'. Often this results in initial thematic understandings being rejected, changed or filed as variations.

Towards the phenomenological description

Phenomenological descriptions are not about reproducing matters of fact, chronological events, inner feelings, theoretical explanations, socio-cultural narrative or psychological explanations. The researcher needs to look beyond the manifest descriptions and identify themes and invariant meanings. Yet this process is the most challenging aspect of explication. How, exactly, does one know that the description one ends up with is indeed phenomenological? The answer lies in the degree to which one's description is faithful to the phenomenon. Our argument is that the specific technique required to achieve this goal cannot be predetermined, but the principles of such research can be articulated.

The primary activity involves understanding the nature of the phenomenological theme. Themes in a phenomenological sense are concerned with exploring meaning structures as opposed to repetitive concepts. Thus the process involves gaining familiarity with the phenomenon in question. The outcome, though potentially considered in terms of the phenomenological traditions of structural, textural and creative descriptions, should nevertheless not restrict the phenomenological researcher from producing descriptions consistent with phenomenological or theoretical assumptions.

There are a number of systems for achieving the same ends. Some phenomenological methodologists advocate the fine coding of data. *Codes* are based upon identifying meaning units. *Codes* can then be constellated to form *themes*.

Themes can then be further constellated to form *general themes* and these themes are then articulated to form your *phenomenological description*. In keeping with our own principle advocating that each researcher and context has some unique demands the methodology needs to be consistent with the theoretical underpinnings of phenomenology and will often emerge from the researcher's experience of the phenomenon being investigated.

In our experience, it is not unusual to commence identifying themes, and then recommence a project and start again as we gain greater familiarity with the text. That is, the initial reading and re-reading enables us to gain an understanding of each co-researcher's experience beyond that gained from the interview process. In approaching the data after an initial attempt to identify themes, we may well begin to differentiate between those elements that might be related to the experience (e.g. some motivations for beginning to participate in extreme sport) but were not core elements of the experience. To this end, we follow the process of free imaginative variation. That is, we explore themes by imaginatively changing or deleting themes to test for validity.

In practice, both verbal and non-verbal aspects of the interviews are attended to. Thus, we highlight all phrases that are potentially of interest and note any relevant non-verbal considerations and may make notes of such considerations. Metaphors become particularly important, as they often harbour particular meanings which are less accessible to simple descriptions. Our notes are reconsidered in terms of potential underlying thematic phrases or meaning units.

Free imaginative variation

An example derived from our research involved ideas around fear. It was not uncommon for participants to refer to *fear* in relation to the activities they engaged in, but, more importantly, fear started to assume particular meanings in the transcripts and had more to do with challenging instinctual responses. The more we reviewed the material, the more we were able to envisage the theme of fear as being quite different to the more commonly assumed meanings of the term which have to do with recoil, avoidance and retreat.

Identifying emergent themes

Part of the process is to consider *emerging themes* to determine any potential connections. There are a number of ways to identify emerging themes. Initially, we may extract all relevant phrases and keywords and consider them in terms of emerging themes. This may also be done by coding data and constellating the codes. The process of Mind Mapping might be productive in this process as meanings are never linear. In this way certain initial thematic ideas are grouped and further defined.

Identifying general themes

Second order themes are considered against the original transcripts to ensure accuracy of explications. The process is repeated again and again, testing the assumptions, until explications gain some solidity and form. It is essential to keep notes and speculative ideas as we work with the material. All data sources (transcript or other account) are considered on their own merit before we work on synthesising material and formulate *general themes*. This synthesis provides the basis of the phenomenological description.

Other first-hand accounts

As with the interview transcripts relevant first-hand accounts are read or watched (sighted in the case of visual material) in order to gain an understanding of the phenomenon as a whole. Each account is considered on its own merit and notes eventually taken to document interpretations of meanings. In the instance of the example being presented in this text, not all the material was designed specifically for a phenomenological research study of meanings. Often material from such sources is considered in the light of interpretations prepared from co-researcher interviews. We have found it useful to also share our findings with co-researchers, and gain their feedback on our explication. A common response has been a level of excitement, to see their experience captured and articulated in ways which went beyond their own descriptions.

Writing

Essentially, phenomenological practice involves writing. That is, writing and giving expression to phenomena also doubles as a revisit and deeper analysis of the experience itself. Furthermore, as we write, further examples and accounts may well present themselves, which of course require further analysis on their own merit. Writing in phenomenology is not the same as traditional approaches, as the unit of meaning cannot be simple descriptions of the other, descriptions are always intentional, in the sense that consciousness intends the object of consciousness. The initial sojourn into the realms of writing might take the traditional route of exploring the literature as a separate entity followed by detailing the research process. In our experience, this process is not always conducive to the phenomenological attitude.

We may begin the research process with a desire to explore the structure of the experience but may not be fully aware of the nuances of the experience. That is, we may wish to develop an understanding of what the experience is but had not recognised phenomenology as the most appropriate approach, let alone what branch of phenomenology best lends itself to addressing the research question. The point being an initial review of the literature needs to be undertaken, yet we also need to avoid setting up a range of presuppositions, which would detract from approaching the phenomenon from a naïve stance.

We propose a threefold organising principle: the first is to discuss the relevant elements of phenomenology including the theory and practice that may frame the study, the second is to identify and articulate typical or recurring understandings that are assumed to be part of the experience but perhaps are not, and the third, to focus upon the experience itself. The conclusion, more accurately described as a synthesis, is a rigorous process in which all elements are brought together as a phenomenological description.

Holding the focus

For many hours of most days we have had the experience of being absorbed by the process of explicating the essence of the phenomena we are exploring. Formally, a researcher may start by following a set of documented pathways, however, much of the thematic understandings are evoked in those quiet times, possibly whilst walking on the beach or in a semi-dream state before and after deep sleep. Both authors have lost count of the times that dreams have awakened us with ideas or when we may have been prevented from falling asleep as concepts gestated in our minds. Researchers engaging in phenomenology need to accept that the process can be all-encompassing. Intuition cannot be ruled out as part of a process of gestation. In our experience, it is only in living and breathing the experience over time that we become sufficiently engrossed in the desire to reach beyond the naïve and explore the essence. This becomes part of the creative process which is most difficult to describe.

The scholar engaging in phenomenological research needs to make space in which he or she feels able to reflect upon both the interview data and their own experience of the interview with a view to making sense of the experience. Phenomenology is founded upon the principle of co-constitutionality, that is, the researcher has an active role in the process of explication and making sense of the phenomenon. Phenomenology is an inductive process where the phenomenon needs to be granted the opportunity to 'speak to' the researcher. Nevertheless consideration also needs to be given to issues around reliability and the obligations to engage in the research process which allows some degree or replication.

Writing up the research

In engaging with the research project, we move away from a focus on writing up a research report, towards the idea of authoring a text. Drawing upon a phenomenological stance, we need to step out of the bustle of everyday life and slow down as part of the process to explore the phenomenon and engage in reflexive practice and find just the right word, expression or phrase. Text is relational in that it reflects our relation with the phenomenon and the phenomenon might even dictate the structure of the written document. The quality of the text can indicate the degree to which the researcher has demonstrated rigour and fidelity in relation to the phenomenon. Van Manen (1997, 2002) expresses this well by identifying five features which are most likely to be observed in the mantic (how the text speaks) aspect of a phenomenological text: lived throughness, evocation, intensity, tone and epiphany. Thus the resulting phenomenological text, if successful, is concretely part of the lifeworld, is vivid and evocative, and develops intensity and thickness in the descriptions and discussions. The researcher as author allows the text to give voice to the phenomenon in a way which resonates with the reader and thus enables the reader to gain his or her own sense of the phenomenon.

Phenomenological investigators, whether in psychology, education, sport or adventure create textual descriptions which are also about the desire to gain connection or phenomenological intimacy with the experience being explored. Those studies that explore the familiar may well evoke nostalgia and recognition of the inherent qualities of the experience in the reader while others that explore experiences outside of the everyday, such as the sacred, may evoke wonder as the reader is introduced to new understandings outside of normal awareness. In the final analysis our intention is to evoke or bring to mind the essence of the phenomenon being investigated whilst at the same time arriving at a final description untainted by attributes determined from immediate experience. At this stage it might also be appropriate to reflect on other phenomenological or philosophical writings that might help explicate the phenomenon under investigation.

Summary

Phenomenological exploration in practice privileges the research question and an approach or particular stance, over prescribed techniques or methodologies. Following technique too rigidly may even blind the researcher to the essence of the phenomenon in question. We have outlined a series of activities: focusing on the question; gathering information; exploring the phenomenon; focusing on writing; holding the focus; and writing up the research. Each of these activities assist in developing a methodology to help the researcher undertake a phenomenological study based upon phenomenological principles. Still, in the end the reader must judge. Words cannot be the experience, they can only replace the things that they name. Words point to an experience but by pointing one can hopefully gain a sense of the phenomenon which is the 'thing' of the study. Some events might actually challenge the phenomenological description.

References

Gergen, K. J. (1990). If persons are texts. In S. B. Messer, L. A. Sass & R. L. Wolfolk (Eds), *Hermeneutics and psychological theory: Interpretive perspectives on personality, psychotherapy, and psychopathology* (pp. 28–51). New Brunswick, NJ: Rutgers University Press.

van Manen, M. (1997). *Researching lived experience: Human science for an action sensitive pedagogy* (2nd ed.). London, ON: The Althouse Press.

van Manen, M. (2002). *Writing in the dark: Phenomenological studies in interpretive inquiry*. London, ON: The Althouse Press.

Wertz, F. J. (2015). Phenomenology methods, historical development, and applications in psychology. In J. Martin, J. Sugarman & K. L. Slaney (Eds), *The Wiley handbook of theoretical and philosophical psychology: Methods, approaches, and new directions for social sciences* (pp. 85–102). New York: Wiley-Blackwell.

5 The risk hypothesis

Extreme sports such as BASE jumping, waterfall kayaking and big wave surfing have been characterised as independent leisure activities where the most likely outcome of a mismanaged accident or mistake is death. There continues to be a widely held and theory-driven presupposition that extreme sports are synonymous with risk and participation merely a function of an inbuilt drive for risk-taking or adrenaline seeking. This assumption stems from a model of behaviour which assumes that aspects of human motivation are determined by innate characteristics. While risk-taking behaviour in general is complex and multi-dimensional, with roots in physiological, psychological, social and environmental notions, in extreme sports these are most often described as deficient characteristics which differentiate extreme sport participants from 'normal' populations and explain why certain people participate in activities where death is a foreseeable outcome. On closer analysis, however, these approaches are limited. From a phenomenological perspective it is important to gain an understanding from those who have lived experience of extreme sports. In this chapter we explore risk and risk-taking in extreme sports in order to explicate the relationship between risk and the extreme sport participation more closely.

Risk is a culturally constructed phenomenon stemming from modern society's deep-seated aversion to and obsessive desire to be 'liberated' from uncertainty. Risk was initially a construct used to understand outcome probability and magnitude in gambling (Creyer, Ross & Evers, 2003; Davidson, 2008). As modern society has become fixated with safety, risk has gradually become a negative descriptor synonymous with the unacceptable face of danger and society's primary preoccupation with 'rendering it measurable and controllable' (Davidson, 2008, p. 6). Society has become so preoccupied with risk reduction and safety-seeking that activities not immediately accepted by the majority are labelled problematic, abnormal, and, in some instances, deemed illegal!

In sport, risk is most often about the probability of physical danger. In extreme sport this has come to mean very high uncertainty, a very high probability that something will go wrong and a very high chance of death as the outcome. Typically, participation has been considered as negative, deviant and even pathological. Motives for participation in extreme sports are most often attributed to a need for the so-called adrenaline rush or because participants are crazy 'Extreme Dudes' taking unnecessary and socially unacceptable risks. Participants are often portrayed as selfish teenage boys 'fascinated with the individuality, risk and danger of the sports' (Bennett, Henson & Zhang, 2003, p. 98). Media and advertising representations have mirrored these presuppositions. The assumption is that risk acts as a motivator for participants with little skill but a desperate desire to connect with the image of glamour associated with adrenaline and danger. Why else would someone willingly undertake a leisure activity where death is a potential outcome?

Extreme sports and risk-taking

Theoretical perspectives that focus on linking extreme sports to risk-taking have focused on psychological and psycho-social explanations. The main psychosocial theory that has been put forward to explain participation is Edgeworks (Laurendeau, 2008). The key psychological theories include type 'T' (Self, Henry, Findley & Reilly, 2007), and sensation seeking (Breivik, 1996; Goma, 1991; Robinson, 1985; Rossi & Cereatti, 1993; Schrader & Wann, 1999; Shoham, Rose & Kahle, 2000; Slanger & Rudestam, 1997; Straub, 1982; Zarevski, Marusic, Zolotic, Bunjevac & Vukosav, 1998). Recent work in genetics and the link to sensation seeking has added to the explanations for why extreme sport participants do what they do. These perspectives all suggest that participation in extreme sports is beyond the control of the participants. Instead participants are assumed to somehow be propelled towards extreme sports by their particular psychological make-up.

Edgeworks and extreme sports

One model that attempts to account for voluntary risk-taking within a sociological framework is termed Edgeworks (Lois, 2001; Lyng, 2004). The notion of Edgeworks refers to an individual's desire to explore the edge or limits of her/his own control in specific risk contexts. The theory suggest that all 'risk-takers' share the same characteristics and as such participating in extreme sports is motivated by the same underlying factors as found in stock-traders, vandals and those involved in unprotected sex and sadomasochism (Lyng, 2004). Some individuals, described as edgeworkers, feel heightened control over their own lives and experience intense positive feelings immediately after events where psychological and physical limits are pushed. Thus, some people might be more effective in situations requiring higher risk. Proponents of Edgeworks suggest that participants move through four stages. The first is the preparation stage where individuals might be a little nervous and anxious. The second is the performing stage which is characterised by thoughtless action. The third is the aftermath stage where participants feel omnipotent, and the last stage is where participants defuse feelings in order to prepare for the next event.

One study that explicitly considered Edgeworks in the extreme sport of BASE jumping found support for this notion in that BASE jumpers were deemed to pass through the four stages as mentioned above. However, the study also found that participants often reported motivations that include fun, being alive, and deep personal transformations and positive aspects of their chosen activity (Allman, Mittlestaedt, Martin & Goldenberg, 2009). Similar findings have been previously reported where participants relate that they do not push the boundary of their control and in fact prefer to stay well within their comfort zones (Celsi, Rose & Leigh, 1993). If the limits of control were being over-extended then the preference was to leave participation for another day. That is, participants play safe rather than take risks.

The type 'T' explanations

Those exploring type 'T' in the extreme sports context explain participation as a positive means to live out a deviant personality trait (Self et al., 2007). The theory differentiates between 'type-T' (arousal seeking) and 'type-t' (arousal reducing/avoiding). These types fall at the opposite ends of a continuum with conflicting motivational preferences. Big T's are described as preferring uncertainty, unpredictability, high risk, novelty, copious variety, complexity, ambiguity, low structure, high intensity and high conflict. Small t's prefer certainty, predictability, low risk, familiarity, little variety, simplicity, clarity, high structure, low intensity and low conflict. The 'type-T' personality is considered to be biologically based and relatively stable throughout life. Extreme sports participation is considered to be a deviant need for uncertainty, novelty, ambiguity, variety and unpredictability (Self et al., 2007). The study undertaken by Self and others focused on theorising extreme sports as activities undertaken by type T participants from a market perspective. They concluded that some extreme sports participants might fit the type T personality structure. However, they also recognised that if the type T was relevant it may only be for those few pioneers.

The sensation-seeking perspective

Sensation seeking is probably the most well-known construct for explaining extreme sport motivations. Sensation-seeking theory suggests that there is an inherent need in some individuals to continually search for risky, complex or novel experiences. The sensation-seeking hypothesis in its usual form draws upon trait theory, suggesting that individuals are born with a desire for seeking out sensation and that in order to maintain an optimal level of stimulation, the sensation-seeker requires an arousal level that is higher than that required by the non sensation-seeker. From this perspective, extreme sports participants are categorised as having similar personality structures to those participating in other unhealthy activities such as excessive drug taking. With increasing interest in genetics, studies exploring the genome have unearthed a gene associated with inherited biological traits that correlate with sensation seeking. The DRD4 (or sometimes D4DR) gene was discovered in experiments conducted in Israel and was subsequently linked to alcoholism and drug abuse. The long allele of this gene has been associated with such so-called risk-seeking behaviours. No studies have successfully made the connection between genetics and extreme sports, yet some theorists have made the considerable leap of suggesting that there is an association between extreme sports and the DRD4 long allele (Baker, 2004; Dennison, 1995; Zuckerman, 2000).

Attempts to relate sensation seeking to extreme sports have often not been supported by research. In part this is because the definitions used for many studies are unclear. This lack of clarity and consistency confuses the issue rather than provides a definitive answer to the question: why do people engage in extreme sports? One study that effectively considered the extreme sport issue was conducted by Slanger and Rudestam (1997). These investigators defined the characteristics of an extreme sport and tested and compared participant characteristics against other sport types. A multi-faceted quantitative and qualitative study was undertaken to explain extreme and high physical risk-taking behaviour. Participants from rock climbing, skiing, piloting a small plane and whitewater kayaking were divided into an extreme group and a high-risk group. Consistent with the definition presented in the first chapter, Slanger and Rudestam defined extreme sports as activities where the likely consequence of an error was death. A group from bowling, gyms and other sports competitors were matched for age and acted as the control group. Standard questionnaires on sensation seeking, death anxiety, repression-sensitisation, generalised self-efficacy and physical self-efficacy were administered. A structured interview that probed views on perceptions of motivation, risk, pain, disinhibition, death, mastery, control and self-efficacy was also conducted. While many of the findings of their study will be discussed elsewhere in this book, it is important to note here that no significant difference between the extreme, high or low risk groups was found in relation to sensation seeking. Simply put, the data does not support the sensation-seeking hypothesis.

Studies focusing on sensation seeking as an explanation for extreme sport participation question the validity of relating sensation seeking to the extreme sport experience and thus challenges the validity of the assumed relationship between risk and the extreme sport experience. This is a view supported by several contemporary investigators who consider that sensation seeking is not sufficient to explain the motivations of extreme sports enthusiasts (Brymer & Schweitzer, 2013a, 2013b; Houge Mackenzie, Hodge & Boyes, 2011; Kerr & Houge Mackenzie, 2012; Monasterio, 2007). The most likely explanation is that participation in extreme sports has little to do with sensation seeking and that to place extreme sports on one end of a risk continuum is misleading.

These findings are also supported by modern studies attempting to define some extreme sports in terms of personality types more generally. For example, studies investigating multiple personality characteristics in mountaineers and BASE jumpers found that while on average extreme sports participants exhibited some differences in novelty-seeking, self-directedness and harm-avoidance when compared to normative groups and those classed as low-risk sports participants, the large variation across all measures was not indicative of a defined personality profile (Monasterio, Alamri & Mei-Dan, 2014; Monasterio, Mulder, Frampton & Mei-Dan, 2014). That is, they did not find a personality type that defined an extreme sport participant. This suggests that there are multiple motivators for participating in extreme sports.

In summary, the dominant sociological and psychological perspectives on extreme sports offer an argument that personality traits, socialisation processes and previous experiences work to compel a participant to put their life at risk through extreme sports. From these theoretical, risk-taking perspectives extreme sport participation is (1) an innate need or drive for thrills and uncertainty; (2) pathological and unhealthy; and (3) a focus in undertaking an activity which is tantamount to searching out death. Whilst for some, the initial motive to participate might be about the risk, thrills, glamour and the excitement of these activities, there is evidence refuting these claims and, furthermore, demonstrating that motives change with continued participation.

Despite the fact that the risk focus has dominated research on extreme sports over the last few decades it is interesting to note that this was not universally accepted. For example, over four decades ago a study found that extreme sport participants displayed low levels of anxiety, a strong sense of reality and emotional control (Ogilvie, 1974). Participants exhibited self-responsibility and were deemed to be resourceful, energetic and adaptable. Men and women shared characteristics that included above average intelligence, above average desire for success and recognition, above average independence, self-assertiveness and forthrightness. In another study mountaineers were found to be low in neuroticism and high in extraversion (Goma, 1991). Extreme individuals have been described as being more relaxed and less governed by super-ego than the average population (Breivik, 1996). Perhaps not the typical characteristics of someone who would want to take irresponsible risks due to a pathological problem.

A focus on the genetic predisposition for risk-taking or the risk-taking personality would also be hard pushed to explain why a person chooses skiing or BASE jumping above surfing or mountaineering, an active choice often made many years in advance of participation. If risk-taking was the aim it is also questionable that participants would take years preparing and ensuring safety before undertaking their chosen activity. Let alone six years to plan one BASE jump (Swann & Singleman, 2007) or fourteen years to plan one expedition (Muir, 2003). Explanations that focus on risk might be too simplistic and based on naïve non-participants' viewpoints as opposed to the experience itself. The tendency to focus on theories that search for labels involving 'risk' and/or 'thrills' is entirely missing the point. Extreme sports are not necessarily synonymous with risk and participation may not be about risk-taking.

Studies have also indicated that extreme sport participants are not inclined to search for uncertainty or uncontrollability. For example, the study by Celsi et al. (1993) referred to numerous examples of well-respected extreme sport participants who considered that they participated well within their personal capabilities. The preference was to leave participation for another day if they felt that the limits of their control were being extended. Athletes expend considerable time and effort to develop high level skills and a deep understanding of their particular activity and also engage in extensive planning. They deliberately become very familiar with all the variables including the environment, their equipment and their current capabilities and values.

Any assumption that participants might take risks through overconfidence or overestimation of their abilities is also erroneous (Brymer & Oades, 2009; Celsi et al., 1993; Pain & Pain, 2005). Celsi and others assert:

> It is one thing to risk overconfidence while making a $2 lottery bet, where little is risked on the outcome, and quite another to trust your life to a potentially fatal and frightening behaviour without carefully weighing the outcomes.
>
> (Celsi et al., 1993, p. 17)

Extreme sport participants are most often careful, well trained, well prepared, self-aware and prefer to remain in control. For example, a research study undertaken with extreme climbers determine that 'individuals do not want to put their lives in danger by going beyond personal capabilities' (Pain & Pain, 2005, p. S34). Despite the commonly held perspective participants are not out to intentionally risk their life and are instead highly disciplined athletes who have engaged in extensive training and preparation. They are well aware of their strengths and limitations in the face of danger.

Evidence that extreme sports may not be about risk has also come from a statistical comparison between the death rates of motorcyclists, BASE jumpers and climbers (Storry, 2003). The study found that in the UK the death rate for climbers was 1:4000 which compares favourably against motorcycle riding where the death rate is 1:500. Another study investigating death rates in BASE jumpers undertook an analysis of 20,850 BASE jumps in Norway over eleven years and found that the death rate was 1:2,317 jumps and whilst the injury rate was higher they were in the main linked to sprains and bruises (Soreide, Ellingsen & Knutson, 2007). Furthermore, adventure sports in general are less likely to cause injury than more traditional sports. Controlling for time engaged in sport activity, a rugby player is 50 times more likely to be injured than a rock climber or skydiver and running or jogging is reportedly ten times more likely to result in injury (Buist et al., 2010; Flores, Haileyesus & Greenspan, 2008; Gabbett, 2000; Llewellyn, Sanchez, Asghar & Jones, 2008; Neuhof, Hennig, Schöffl & Schöffl, 2011). Further, evidence suggests that extreme sports trigger positive psychological health and deep personal changes in constructs such as courage and humility (Brymer & Oades, 2009; Willig, 2008). The stereotype of extreme athletes as risk-taking adrenaline junkies may be too simplistic a perspective that reflects a naïve non-participant's anxieties as opposed to the lived experiences of participants, especially those of the most accomplished veterans.

A participant perspective

A phenomenological perspective focuses specifically on the experiences of participants in an activity, often drawing upon the indigenous terms that arise from that experience and shape the way that it is experienced and articulated. From this perspective it is important to investigate the extreme sport experience through those that have had the experience. In this section we explore the meaning of risk through the words of practicing extreme sport athletes. Michael Bane (1996), a windsurfer reflecting on his own extreme sport experience, was succinct and to the point:

> Much of the early research on risk concentrates on a phrase I am coming to hate, thrill seeking. I am not sure what this means, and it doesn't seem to me that the researchers are that far ahead.
>
> (Bane, 1996, p. 24)

Bane's perception is not unique. Extreme sports participants regularly point to experiences other than risk when trying to define their extreme sport involvement. Rarely if at all is risk mentioned as a motivator or an important aspect of the experience. In fact most often other more positive aspects are presented as reasons and descriptors. For example, mountain climbers have been quoted as considering that they climbed as a quest to find and test the self, an exploration into self-fulfilment. This is perhaps best highlighted in the words of John Harlin:

> I have used climbing as a medium for introspection into my own mind and have tried to understand my own reactions to stimuli, particularly between emotion and muscle coordination. Before training, the coordination of mind and body is not stable when one is on a two-thousand-foot ice wall with a tenuous belay. After training the personal understanding of oneself that occurs in the intricate alpine experience can be developed and used outside of this experience. In other words, it can be borrowed and projected. This ultimately leads to a physical and emotional control of one's self. I believe that this control is an important prerequisite to creativity.
>
> (Harlin cited in Houston, 1968, p. 58)

Lynn Hill a climber who had proved herself top of her field on numerous occasions, often to a level where death would be the most likely outcome of a mismanaged error or accident reportedly stated that she did not like the 'extreme' label because of the presupposition about its perceived relationship to danger and risk.

> Extreme to me means doing something that is dangerous and risky. And that was never my motivation as a climber. The reason I climb is more about learning about myself as well as the sense of partnership with my climbing partners within the natural environment. It has nothing to do with how dangerous it is.
>
> (Olsen, 2001, p. 59)

These perspectives are not just from those who have reflected on their experiences as part of their writing. Those interviewed for the current study explain that the activity is not undertaken for the risks.

> Some of the biggest risks I face are on the roads because really you know the most dangerous thing I encounter are people. I don't feel like I'm putting my life in any greater danger going on an adventure whether it's climbing Mt. Everest or walking across the desert. But I do when I get out on the road. So we face risks in our lives every day and I don't really draw a big distinction. I do feel safer when I'm in the natural world. I do feel safer when I'm on the Arctic Ocean or in the Himalaya than I do out in the home environment when I'm driving around.
>
> (Co-researcher, mid 40s)

In this quote the participant explains that he does not undertake mountaineering for the risks. He considers that activities that society takes for granted such as driving are far more dangerous. In the interview he continued to explain that he is taking greater risks when walking city streets at night than he does when undertaking an expedition. From his perspective non-participants' focus on risk is misguided:

> Most people label people like myself as thrill seekers or risk-takers. The person who is labelling me is way off course.
>
> (Co-researcher, mid 40s)

A BASE jumper and co-researcher in this study was also quite clear that he was not comfortable about being labelled an extreme athlete and that many socially acceptable activities are far more risky than BASE jumping:

> I hate the word extreme too, because it's overused, it's got a connotation of recklessness, lack of control. It's got a connotation of unnecessary risk-taking and although in my life I have taken unnecessary risks like we all do; you know, we all jay walk or we all drive ten k's over the limit or we drive when tired or do something like that or travel to some third world country where there's an uprising. But no, I certainly don't want to be put in that category.
>
> (Co-researcher, late 30s)

In fact the BASE jumper explained that if he felt there was a chance that he might die from a particular BASE jump he would walk away from the site and return when conditions were favourable. In the interview he explained that risk is not the focus and in fact he clarifies the opposite is closer to the truth. Extreme sports are undertaken because the participant enjoys life.

> I don't and most people who do these activities don't [do it for the risks]; they do it because they enjoy living.
>
> (Co-researcher, late 30s)

For the participant the essence of the extreme sport experience is about learning everything about the constraints of the activity in order to be confident about participating.

> Learn everything possible about the sport; learn about weather conditions, learn about wind, learn about what wind does in and around buildings and structures and cliffs, etc. so you know what you can do and what you can't do.
>
> (Co-researcher, late 30s)

As a comparison this participants points to potential alternatives that might be socially acceptable but are also perhaps the biggest risk of all:

> Try my hardest to manage all risks and reduce the chance of making a mistake. I certainly don't want to sit at home and watch television and grow fatter than I am, doing nothing.
>
> (Co-researcher, late 30s)

Another BASE jumper was also clear about the void between the typical perspective on risk and risk-taking and his own understanding of his chosen leisure pursuit:

> They all think we're being irresponsible towards our children putting our life at risk. Yet you know the irony of that is that well there are many ironies here … there are sort of philosophical and intellectual ironies … you know that life is a 100 per cent fatal condition … everyone is going to die … you have to die … and one of the problems of this society is that we don't pay enough attention to that fact …
>
> (Co-researcher, mid 40s)

Later in the interview he explained that as death was a certainty the real risk was ignoring this fact and as a result missing out on opportunities because of fear. The participant went on to explain that he would not undertake BASE jumping if he thought that he was putting his life at risk. However, to reach this point takes a considerable amount of training and discipline. He explained that when he was first interested in BASE jumping he obtained formal qualifications in parachute physics in order to become fully aware of the constraints involved. He considered that success was dependent on knowledge:

> Good intellectual grasp of all of the technology they're using and the environment they're going into and the situation that they're putting themselves in and their own physical and mental limitations and that's how you get to be a successful adventurer, otherwise you get to be hurt or dead and that's not where the satisfaction is, being hurt or dead.
>
> (Co-researcher, mid 40s)

A BASE jumper in her 30s supported this point by pointing out that undertaking an extreme sport takes great discipline and that those who do not have such discipline would not last in the sport:

> You know people tend to get weeded out of the sport by the rigours, by the discipline of what you have to do. Because if you're not disciplined about it every time … it's not a sport where you know 90 per cent of the time I will pack it right … it's a sport where you have to pack it right 100 per cent of the time, where you have to launch right 100 per cent of the time, where you have to be able to control malfunctions a 100 per cent of the time … because you know 99.5 per cent of the time still gets you hurt or dead.
>
> (Co-researcher, late 30s)

A BASE jumper in his 70s spoke about risk with a particular focus on the assumed relationship to the adrenaline rush. He explained that in his early career he had what he called an adrenaline rush which almost resulted in his death:

> I've had situations where I've had tunnel vision and it cuts your brain off as well, where you can't control it. I nearly died actually in California on one of my early jumps where I got tunnel vision. I became obsessed with one thing and obliterating everything else … and I was screaming towards the ground. I forgot all my training, I was obsessed with getting these twists out.

He continued:

> When I started getting this ground rush, I cut away, I went back into free fall at four hundred feet, you know, which is a suicidal thing to do, suicidal, because I had problems with control, I forgot all my training, because of the adrenaline, probably. And they reckon I hit the deck at the point where the parachutes blossom, you know. They reckon I hit the ground at fifty mile an hour and what saved my life was a million to one chance. There are these flood canals, they're about twenty feet deep; I hit right on the edge of that.
>
> (Co-researcher, early 70s)

He went on to explain that the usual experience involved mental clarity and feelings of being relaxed. At the same time the idea of risk and addiction to adrenaline is seen as undermining the very essence of what it means to be an extreme sport person. Adrenaline is linked with a loss of control, increased danger and almost inevitable demise.

However, these perspectives cannot be explained by considering that extreme sports participants are somehow denying or unaware of the potential downside of their chosen activity. Extreme sport participants know that the slightest mistake could mean death. There is no illusion as to the seriousness of the potential consequences.

> If we got something wrong, then death would have been imminent.
>
> (Co-researcher, mid 40s)

Extreme sport participants invariably report that they know that there is no second chance when things go wrong. In order to minimise this potential, extensive training and safety processes are undertaken by extreme sport athletes:

> So for example, the big thing in BASE is safety, so you've got a potential problem analysis you go through; you know – these things might kill me, this is what I'll do to prevent that from happening.
>
> (Co-researcher, mid 30s)

If risk is a function of consequence and likelihood and risk-taking in extreme sports is about an unhealthy and pathological desire for danger, uncontrollability and uncertainty, then extreme sports are not risky let alone about risk. The negative consequence of a mismanaged accident or error may be devastating but the likelihood is low. By following the phenomenological imperative and listening to the voice of extreme sports athletes as they describe their lived experience we learn that extreme sports participants are quite clear that they do not search for risk and that many socially acceptable activities are inherently more dangerous. But then accepting this proposal could lead to the argument that living is the riskiest activity of all. After all the consequences of living is death and death is most definitely a certainty. Perhaps too much energy is spent trying to pathologies those that are not like us?

> I sometimes think psychologists see too much pathology out there … To the contrary, these are people who are pushing the envelope and that's their life. They would not want the life of someone who never pushes the envelope. To them, that is an unlived life.
>
> (Farley cited in Terwilliger, 1998, p. 4E)

The focus on certain activities being risk oriented may reflect a modern morbid aversion to risk or obsessive desire for safety-seeking. One only has to consider the evolution of humanity to appreciate that this construct called risk has always been a part of life, it is only relatively recently that the lack of certainty and the need to control our surroundings has been boxed as a construct and labelled, let alone labelled as something deviant. It may be that the essence of extreme sport participation is a function of other factors and that a participant accepts that certain risks, whether death or injury, are involved, just as a potential lover accepts the risk of rejection.

Summary

Extreme sports participation is not about the search for risk or the need to take risks. In order to experience the wonder of love one has to accept the potential for not being loved in return and, one would expect, the feelings of rejection or personal annihilation that might accompany such an acceptance. Equally to experience hope indicates that one has risked disappointment. Yet disappointment or rejection are not the aim. Similarly, risk-taking is not the experience. After all, just because an extreme sport participant does not back away from the risks involved in their chosen activity it does not mean that they are chasing the risks. In the same way that a person does not chase disappointment or rejection when searching for the wonders of hope or love. It is love and hope that are the experiences. Perhaps, then, the experience lies elsewhere. That is, rather than these activities being about the threat of losing something of value they are more about the opportunity to gain something of value. Later in the book we will show that the extreme sport experience is so powerful for extreme sport adherents that it is worth managing the potential risks along the way.

Is it not comforting to think that we are not like extreme sports people, and do not have the same personality structure which results in such activities? We can live in harmony with our lives and happily consider the other as deviant. And certainly, if it is not about risk-taking *per se*, but risk is an element of the journey, it still may be that the outcome searched for is not socially acceptable, for it may be about a deep-seated desire for death? Perhaps that is the outcome of value? It is to this question that we will now turn.

Acknowledgement

Parts of this chapter were published in an article in *Annals of Leisure Research* in 2010, available online: *www.tandfonline.com/doi/* 10.1080/11745398.2010. 9686845.

References

Allman, T. L., Mittlestaedt, R. D., Martin, B. & Goldenberg, B. (2009). Exploring the motivations of BASE jumpers: Extreme sport enthusiasts. *Journal of Sport and Tourism*, *14*(4), 229–247.

Baker, C. (2004). *Behavioral genetics: An introduction to how genes and environments interact through development to shape differences in mood, personality and intelligence*. Washington, DC: AAAS Publications Ltd.

Bane, M. (1996). *Over the edge: A regular guy's odyssey in extreme sports*. New York: Macmillan.

Bennett, G., Henson, R. K. & Zhang, J. (2003). Generation Y's perceptions of the action sports industry segment. *Journal of Sport Management*, *17*(2), 95–115.

Breivik, G. (1996). Personality, sensation seeking and risk taking among Everest climbers. *International Journal of Sport Psychology*, *27*, 308–320.

Brymer, E. & Oades, L. (2009). Extreme sports: A positive transformation in courage and humility. *Journal of Humanistic Psychology*, *49*(1), 114–126.

Brymer, E. & Schweitzer, R. (2013a). Extreme sports are good for your health: A phenomenological understanding of fear and anxiety in extreme sport. *Journal of Health Psychology*, *18*(4), 477–487. doi:10.1177/1359105312446770.

Brymer, E. & Schweitzer, R. (2013b). The search for freedom in extreme sports: A phenomenological exploration. *Psychology of Sport and Exercise, 14*(6), 865–873. doi: DOI 10.1016/j.psychsport.2013.07.004.

Buist, I., Bredeweg, S., Bessem, B., van Mechelen, W., Lemminkl, K. & Diercks, R. (2010). Incidence and risk factors of running-related injuries during preparation for a 4-mile recreational running event. *British Journal of Sport Medicine, 44*, 598–604.

Celsi, R. L., Rose, R. L. & Leigh, T. W. (1993). An exploration of high-risk leisure consumption through skydiving. *Journal of Consumer Research, 20*, 1–23.

Creyer, E., Ross, W. & Evers, D. (2003). Risky recreation: An exploration of factors influencing the likelihood of participation and the effects of experience. *Leisure Studies, 22*, 239–253.

Davidson, L. (2008). Tragedy in the adventure playground: Media representations of mountaineering accidents in New Zealand. *Leisure Studies, 27*(1), 3–19.

Dennison, R. (Writer). (1995). *Risk: Yelling in the face of life* (Director: R Dennison).

Flores, A., Haileyesus, T. & Greenspan, A. (2008). National estimates of outdoor recreational injuries treated in emergency departments, United States, 2004–2005. *Wilderness Environmental Medicine, 19*(2), 91–98.

Gabbett, T. (2000). Incidence, site, and nature of injuries in amateur rugby league over three consecutive seasons. *British Journal of Sport Medicine, 34*, 98–103.

Goma, M. (1991). Personality profiles of subjects engaged in high physical risk sports. *Personality and Individual Differences, 12*(10), 1087–1093.

Houge Mackenzie, S., Hodge, K. & Boyes, M. (2011). Expanding the flow model in adventure activities: A reversal theory perspective. *Journal of Leisure Research, 43*(4), 519–544.

Houston, C. S. (1968). The last blue mountain. In S. Z. Klausner (Ed.), *Why man takes chances* (pp. 48–58). New York: Doubleday.

Kerr, J. H. & Houge Mackenzie, S. (2012). Multiple motives for participating in adventure sports. *Psychology of Sport and Exercise, 13*(5), 649–657.

Laurendeau, J. (2008). 'Gendered Risk Regimes': A theoretical consideration of edgework and gender. *Sociology of Sport Journal, 25*(3), 293–309.

Llewellyn, D., Sanchez, X., Asghar, A. & Jones, G. (2008). Self-efficacy, risk taking and performance in rock climbing. *Personality and Individual Differences, 45*, 75–81.

Lois, J. (2001). Peaks and valleys: The gendered emotional culture of edgework. *Gender and Society, 15*(3), 381–406.

Lyng, S. (2004). *Edgework: The sociology of risk-taking*. New York: Routledge.

Monasterio, E. (2007). The risks of adventure sports/people. *The Alpinist, 19 November*. Retrieved 1 November 2016 from www.alpinist.com/doc/web07f/rb-erik-monasterio-mountaineering-medicine.

Monasterio, E., Alamri, Y. & Mei-Dan, O. (2014). Personality characteristics in a population of mountain climbers. *Wilderness Environmental Medicine, 25*(2), 214–219.

Monasterio, E., Mulder, R., Frampton, C. & Mei-Dan, O. (2014). Personality characteristics of BASE jumpers. *Journal of Applied Sport Psychology, 24*(4), 391–400.

Muir, J. (2003). *Alone across Australia*. Camberwell, Victoria: Penguin Books Australia.

Neuhof, A., Hennig, F., Schöffl, I. & Schöffl, V. (2011). Injury risk evaluation in sport climbing. *International Journal of Sports Medicine, 32*(10), 794–800.

Ogilvie, B. C. (1974). The sweet psychic jolt of danger. *Psychology Today, 8*(5), 88–94.

Olsen, M. (2001). *Women who risk: profiles of women in extreme sports*. New York: Hatherleigh Press.

Pain, M. T. G. & Pain, M. A. (2005). Essay: Risk taking in sport. *The Lancet, 366*(1), S33–S34.

Robinson, D. W. (1985). Stress seeking: Selected behavioural characteristics of elite rock climbers. *Journal of Sport Psychology, 7*, 400–404.

Rossi, B. & Cereatti, L. (1993). The sensation seeking in mountain athletes as assessed by Zuckerman's sensation seeking scale. *International Journal of Sport Psychology, 24*, 417–431.

Schrader, M. P. & Wann, D. L. (1999). High-risk recreation: The relationship between participant characteristics and degree of involvement. *Journal of Sport Behaviour, 22*(3), 426–431.

Self, D. R., Henry, E. D., Findley, C. S. & Reilly, E. (2007). Thrill seeking: The type T personality and extreme sports. *International Journal of Sport Management and Marketing, 2*(1–2), 175–190.

Shoham, A., Rose, G. M. & Kahle, L. R. (2000). Practitioners of risky sports: A quantitative examination. *Journal of Business Research, 47*(3), 237–251.

Slanger, E. & Rudestam, K. E. (1997). Motivation and disinhibition in high risk sports: Sensation seeking and self-efficacy. *Journal of Research in Personality, 31*, 355–374.

Soreide, K., Ellingsen, C. & Knutson, V. (2007). How dangerous is BASE jumping? An analysis of adverse events in 20,850 jumps from the Kjerag Massif, Norway. *Journal of Trauma-Injury Infection & Critical Care, 62*(5), 1113–1117.

Storry, T. (2003). The games outdoor adventurers play. In B. Humberstone, H. Brown & K. Richards (Eds), *Whose journeys? The outdoors and adventure as social and cultural phenomena* (pp. 201–228). Penrith: The Institute for Outdoor Learning.

Straub, W. F. (1982). Sensation seeking among high and low-risk male athletes. *Journal of Sport Psychology, 4*(3), 246–253.

Swann, H. & Singleman, G. (2007). Baseclimb 3 – The full story. Retrieved 30 July 2008 from www.baseclimb.com/About_BASEClimb3.htm.

Terwilliger, C. (1998, 28 March). Type 'T' personality. *The Denver Post*, pp. 1E, 4–5E.

Willig, C. (2008). A phenomenological investigation of the experience of taking part in 'Extreme Sports'. *Journal of Health Psychology, 13*(5), 690–702.

Zarevski, P., Marusic, I., Zolotic, S., Bunjevac, T. & Vukosav, Z. (1998). Contribution of Arnett's inventory of sensation seeking and Zuckerman's sensation seeking scale to the differentiation of athletes engaged in high and low risk sports. *Personality and Individual Differences, 25*, 763–768.

Zuckerman, M. (2000). Are you a risk taker. *Psychology Today, Nov/Dec*, 130. Retrieved 3 November 2016 from www.psychologytoday.com/articles/200011/are-you-risk-taker.

6   The death-wish hypothesis

Extreme sport participation is commonly assumed to be tightly paired with death. After all, the potential of a mismanaged accident or mistake is death – not injury or embarrassment, not even financial ruin, but death. Further, it is often assumed this relationship must be an unhealthy one, a secret, or perhaps not-so-secret, desire for death or an unconscious wish for self-annihilation without having to reveal one's intentions. Or to put this differently, an activity designed with the sole purpose of killing oneself without admitting the intent, perhaps akin to a clandestine suicide. Some may conjecture that extreme sport participation is nothing more than a death wish. Certainly, this perception has been voiced and research has been carried out which attempts to confirm this view.

A number of theories have been offered to explain the unhealthy link between extreme sports participation and death. One suggests that participants focus on attempting to cheat death in a desire to alleviate anxiety about the potential of their own death. Another theory is that participants are living out delusions of immortality. Whichever understanding is voiced, the relationship is negative. Otherwise, why would a participant go to such lengths to disguise their intent by hiding it under the banner of sport?

Undoubtedly, people do die as a result of undertaking extreme sports. Deaths and 'near misses' are often conveyed in the media. Even during the course of writing this chapter, such incidents have been reported. A recently released movie, *Sherpa*, highlights the dangers and deaths associated with mountaineering and Mount Everest. The potential for some so-called extreme sports to result in death has been documented by Palmer (2000). The issue for Palmer is the marketing and commodification of extreme sports as tourist activities. She used as examples the deaths on Everest and the Interlaken raft disaster to question the wisdom of tourists who willingly trust their lives to people they have never met for the sake of rafting a river or ascending a mountain. The focus in her writing is on the questionable motives of the operators whom she considers to be openly marketing disasters waiting to happen. She argues that to trust your life to a tourist operator is tantamount to a death wish. Still, people also die whilst crossing the road, but does this mean that anyone who crosses a road has a death wish or any other deliberate and unhealthy relationship with death?

A significant factor distinguishing extreme sports is that a mismanaged accident or error would most likely result in death, and this discourse is about those activities that involve participants who willingly develop skills in activities where death is a potential outcome. Given that 'normal' people do everything possible to avoid such situations, it may well appear reasonable to conclude that participants must be acting out of a death wish. Perhaps, though, the focus is not death in itself but some other outcome, just as the focus for crossing the road is not death (even though death is a possibility) but some other outcome.

The aim of this chapter is to examine the assumptions that participation in extreme sport is about a desire for death, a desire to cheat death or even an experiential narrative on immortality. We have seen in the previous chapter how extreme sport participants do not focus on risk and in fact consider the thought of taking unnecessary risks an alien concept. Here, we will provide evidence demonstrating that the perception of extreme sport participation is about an unhealthy connection to death is a long way from the reality of the extreme sport experience.

The death wish: an introduction

In Western society, death has acquired negative connotations to such an extent that we often avoid serious contemplation of its existence, yet death is perhaps our only certainty, even more so than taxes. Arguably, in the twenty-first century, we engage in the denial of death on many levels; that is, between the inevitability of death and death as an abnormal, taboo concept. Death has become something to be feared. As an extension to this fear, certain activities have been negatively labelled.

The motivations are many and varied. The relationship between life and death has been a central theme in Heidegger's phenomenology and his notions of being-towards-death and an authentic existence, and in the existential philosophers with their writings on authenticity (Gosetti-Ferencei, 2014). In applying these ideas to extreme sport, Alvarez suggested that some people may desire death in order to 'escape confusion, to clear their heads' (Alvarez, 1972, p. 130) and that in order to 'to break through the patterns of obsession and necessity which they have unwittingly imposed on their lives' they engage in activities which seem to invite death (Alvarez, 1972, p. 131).

> Consider a climber poised on minute holds on a steep cliff. The smallness of the holds, the steepness of the angle, all add to his pleasure, provided he is in complete control. He is a man playing chess with his body; he can read the sequence of moves far enough in advance so that his physical economy – the ratio between the effort he uses and his reserves of strength – is never totally disrupted. The more improbable the situation and the greater the demands made on him, the more sweetly the blood flows later in release from all that tension. The possibility of danger serves merely to sharpen his awareness and control. He argues that there may be people who kill

themselves through their involvement in extreme sport in an effort 'to achieve a calm and control they never find in life'.

(Alvarez, 1972, p. 130)

In reflecting upon the potential for a fatal accident, Alvarez suggests that the accident might result not from a conscious desire or 'impulse of despair', but from something less direct. That is, a climber, for instance, may want to die but in such a way that s/he does not have to accept responsibility for her/his actions.

Again, this explanation may reflect the actions of some but does it indicate that the extreme sport experience is all about a desire for death? Surely, spending years of hard work and training to become a BASE jumper, for example, would suggest that this is not the case (Allman, Mittlestaedt, Martin & Goldenberg, 2009). Nevertheless, many psychoanalysts have argued, death can be sought in subtle ways. It is not necessary to consciously desire death. Still, something is missing from this simplistic viewpoint: surely there would be easier ways of searching out death? Yet, at one time the explanation that participation was about an unconscious death wish was frequently cited and extreme sports were considered a way to attain respite from an unconscious, ever-present desire for death.

In spite of the evidence, the notion of 'the death wish' persists. Bane (1996) tells of an encounter with a friend and psychologist at a party in which both friend and psychologist assume, despite his denial, that Bane must have a deep-seated death wish. In Bane's words:

'I am not saying I don't want the rush', I reply, 'but I am saying the rush is only a tiny part of what's there, the experience'.

Heads nod knowingly.

'I want you to meet a woman I'm dating', a close friend of mine says one night, 'she's a shrink, and she's fascinated by people with death wishes'.

'I do not', I say emphatically, 'have a death wish'.

'Have some more pizza' he says.

Later I am at a party at a friend's advertising agency. I am cornered by a young woman in a basic black dress, long blonde hair hanging down her back. She steers me out of the flowing herd, into an eddy, sits me down on a desk chair, and pulls up a bench across from me. She leans forward on her elbows, and I notice her eyes are a muddy blue. *I am*, I think, *trapped in a Calvin Klein commercial*.

'Tell me what it's like', she says, stopping just short of licking her red lips, 'when you think you are going to die'.

I can't help myself. I break out laughing.

'I wouldn't know', I say.

She is clearly offended.

'Wouldn't know or won't say?'

I take her hands in mine. They are slightly sweaty.

'I am not crazy', I say. 'And I intend to live for ever'.

I stand up. She jots her number on a piece of paper.

'Call me when you're ready to talk', she says, tossing her hair. On the way out of the office, I toss the paper in the garbage.

(Bane, 1996, p. 66)

These might be the writings of someone with an undisclosed desire to die but perhaps once again we need to think of our motivation to pathologise behaviour rather than celebrate the diversity of experience, which constitutes human activity and skilled sportsmanship.

The death instinct

Psychoanalysis is founded upon Freud's discovery of the unconscious. In his writing on what he termed drive theory Freud posited the existence of two complementary forces, Eros and Thanatos, or 'life instinct' and 'death instinct', as fundamental drives. The psychoanalytic theoretical framework thus explains extreme sport participation as indicative of an unconscious search for death, more commonly described as a 'death wish'. The extension of the death wish (Thanatos) is that any activity that knowingly involves the potential for death is evidence of suicidal tendencies or expressive of a death wish – in technical terms, a function of the Thanatos factor. Consequently, participation in activities that 'played with' death is seen as evidence for pathological and unconscious impulses associated with self-destructive needs or wishes.

One study exemplifying this approach investigated deep sea scuba diving (Hunt, 1996). Death in deep scuba diving can result from numerous events including decompression sickness, embolism and oxygen toxicity. Hunt quoted a technical diver expressing a desire to play a game with death as a justification for participating at a level where death is a possible outcome. Interestingly, however, the diver that Hunt quoted also emphasised that the ultimate aim was to complete the dive successfully and that if prior preparations indicated a potential for death, then the dive would not be undertaken.

Hunt applied psychoanalytic theory to exploring risk, pain and injury in the case of the male scuba diver. The analysis of the deep diver's unconscious life supposedly explained his desire to dive and the serious injury he could sustain while diving. Hunt understood the diver's intentions as sometimes courting disaster and perhaps a function of a 'desire to master conflicts rooted in early experiences with absent or abusive fathers' (Hunt, 1996, p. 619). She also considered that the same individual was highly intelligent and curious and had developed considerable technical and physical skills over an extended period of time. She does, however, concede that the results of her study are speculative.

Perhaps there are easier and quicker ways to kill oneself? As Ogilvie (1974) concluded, explanations like Hunt's are true some of the time but not sufficient to accurately represent the extreme sport experience. If death was the ultimate aim, whether consciously or sub-consciously, participants would not, as noted in the previous chapter, spend so much energy on ensuring their safety. Still, to the outsider the death wish explanation is naïvely attractive, easy to understand and comfortable. However, it may be that a deeper understanding would refute this claim – a view shared by Tutko, a researcher specialising in extreme sport athletes, who wrote over three decades ago 'when I first started out in this field, my original prejudice was the prevalent theory at the time – the death wish idea' (Tutko cited in Groves, 1987, p. 190). Needless to say, his opinion changed as his experience grew. For Zuckerman 'the "death wish" is a myth' made up by those 'who can't understand the rewards' (Zuckerman cited in Koerner, 1997, p. 3).

Death anxiety

Death anxiety is related to an awareness of the fundamental concept of death and non-existence. Essentially, it is hypothesised that human development has been facilitated by our intelligence and, in particular, our ability to think in abstract terms. With this enhanced ability comes an enhanced self-consciousness and awareness. This awareness leads to the burden of being able to contemplate our own death (Becker, 1962). This view is consistent with the hypothesis that extreme sport represents a desire to achieve control over our own mortality or, in other terms, 'to cheat death' (Schrader & Wann, 1999, p. 427).

Drug taking and unsafe sex have been interpreted as behaviours that set out to cheat death. The hypothesis is that there is a logical extension from these activities to recreational pursuits, often labelled 'high-risk' recreation. One study that investigated this phenomenon using the fifteen-item Death Anxiety Scale developed by Templar (1970) as part of a broad analysis of participants who undertake 'high-risk' recreational activities concluded that death anxiety did not contribute to the prediction of involvement in high-risk recreation (Schrader & Wann, 1999). However, rather than accepting this finding the authors suggested that the reason for the lack of significance was twofold. First, as the age of the typical participant was about twenty-two years old, they were most likely in denial. Second because the state in which the test was carried out (Kentucky, USA) was highly religious, individuals had increased hope for immortality and therefore less anxiety about death. Both explanations may have a degree of relevance but perhaps engaging in extreme sport activities is not about death anxiety and therefore measuring death anxiety is a fruitless activity. Furthermore, as the activities tested were not explicitly defined as extreme sports, any explanation is problematic. It is also important to recognise that athletes in general have demonstrated lower than normal death anxiety (Kumar, Pathak & Thakur, 1985). This represents a typical example where theory is used to determine the outcome as opposed to staying with the experience of the participant.

The Templar Death Anxiety Scale was also used in the multi-test research project introduced in Chapter 5 with activities classified as extreme, high-risk and lower risk participants (Slanger & Rudestam, 1997). In this study participants included athletes from rock climbing, kayaking, skiing and small plane piloting. Each activity was separated into extreme participation and high-risk participation. In this instance, as is the case in this book, the extreme group were defined as those that participated to a level where a mismanaged error would most likely result in death. The study found no difference in the extreme, high-risk and lower-risk groups for death anxiety, suggesting that there is little basis for assuming a relationship between death anxiety and extreme sports, or for assuming that extreme sport participation could be a type of counter-phobic behaviour. Relating extreme sport participation to a desire for death, or an attempt to cheat death is simply not supported by the research to date.

Nevertheless, there is undoubtedly some relationship between the extreme sport experience and death. This relationship was noted by Todhunter (2000) whilst processing the exploits of numerous athletes involved at the extreme end of their sport. Most notably, when he was taken climbing by an expert climber Todhunter reflected on the influence of his own psychological perceptions and attitudes on his ability to climb. In the attempt to undertake a significantly difficult climb whilst maintaining 'a rapid, thoughtless pace' the climb seemed easier, the culmination of which was a feeling of unique elation. Todhunter reflected that:

> In nearly twenty years of intermittent climbing, I have never felt such intense satisfaction in the mountains. For a few minutes, there on the ridge, I accept that it might be worth dying for.
>
> (Todhunter, 2000, p. 16)

Here, it could be argued, is an example of an experience that is so intense that even if death was the result it would have been worthwhile. Yet, as we have argued, dying is not an intentional part of the extreme sport experience. Death is not sought, nor is participation part of a death-related anxiety or about a perception of immortality, but engagement in such experience, at least in the example cited, involves an acceptance that the experience would be worth dying for.

Death and the symbolic relationship

Another approach used to explain extreme sport and potential confrontation with death proposes that participants make a symbolic deal with death, using nature as the playing field and their body as currency. Proponents of this approach suggest that extreme sports are just a medium for some Western athletes to test their capacity to resist suffering. The proposition is that, almost as a response to a crisis in Western society, individuals involved in extreme sports are engaged in a contest which provides an ideal outlet for testing courage and resources. This contest is not against other athletes but is lived out as a 'hand-to-hand fight with nature'. Individuals only superficially or metaphorically consider that their activity might result in death. The extreme sport participant becomes the master of their activity by attempting to participate on a par with death in order to 'steal some of its power' (Le Breton, 2000, p. 7).

The 'symbolic deal with death' hypothesis is not without its limitations. Le Breton's thesis is limited in that he equates endurance activities with extreme sports and considers that participants are often 'people with no particular ability' (Le Breton, 2000, p. 1). However, his contention that participation in the realm of death could actually be exceptionally positive is fascinating. He also argues that participation might be a way of experiencing what has, until now, only been accepted as part of the ascetic or spiritual domain or, at the very least, a pathway to living life to its fullest. Experiences considered exceptional in everyday life might be a common occurrence for the extreme sport participant.

We argue that participants do not have a death wish or any other unhealthy connection to death. Researchers who have attempted to get to know extreme sports on a more intimate level share this perspective. For example, Ogilvie argued that the idea that extreme sports athletes were somehow pathological was just a myth that endures irrespective of the evidence. As emphasised by a participant in Ogilvie's (1974) extreme sport study some four decades ago:

> I didn't get all this grey hair for nothing in 47 years, without being careful. It's easy to die young if you want to. I have no ambitions to die young at all.
>
> (Ken Miles cited in Ogilvie, 1974, p. 94)

A point echoed in many other studies that represent the words of athletes as opposed to being blinkered by logical-empiricist assumptions.

Farley recorded the following impressions almost thirty years ago after meeting numerous extreme sports participants at a film conference:

> What I learned from talking to these people was that they wanted to live. They have a 'life-wish'. Because they have an exciting life they don't want to end it.
>
> (Farley cited in Groves, 1987, p. 190)

In our experience, the sentiments expressed are the same today as they were thirty or forty years ago. Participants have a strong sense of reality and a willingness to take responsibility for their own actions. Participants themselves may be the best judges of the extreme sport experience. It might be that the observations made by Farley point to a deeper appreciation of the relationship between death and the extreme sport experience. Extreme sport activities support a process where death is understood and accepted in a unique way or even that participants of extreme sports experience certain realisations about death that make possible a more powerful experience of life.

Participation in 'extreme' activities is about engaging with life. Like the assumptions about risk, the assumption that extreme sport participation is unhealthily connected to death has completely missed the point; instead, participants describe a very healthy connection to live life to its fullest, to celebrate life, a 'life-wish'.

We don't have a death wish, we have a life wish! A wish to live life to the fullest and if by chance we do die skydiving, then at least we died doing what we loved.

(A participant who had engaged in 1,000 jumps cited in Celsi, Rose & Leigh, 1993, p. 19)

Participation is thus not about cheating death – instead, the reality of death is invariably accepted as part of life. The inevitability of death was acknowledged by Celsi et al. (1993) in their study of skydiving participants. Whilst skydiving might be outside the set of criteria for extreme sport as currently defined (since a skydiver has technological support and extra parachutes) death does occur and is a real possibility. Celsi et al. found that while participants did not hope for death they accepted that death was part of skydiving.

Participants are very much aware that death is a real possibility; they do not have any illusion about immortality. For example, even in the study by Le Breton (2000) an explorer succinctly expressed his awareness of the potential of his imminent death before attempting to fly a microlight across the Atlantic.

Two weeks before lift-off I was living as though I was expecting to die the next day. I was sure I would never come back from the crossing. When I hit the accelerator for lift-off I said farewell to life. It's an absolutely terrifying feeling that never leaves you.

(Guy Delage cited in Le Breton, 2000, p. 4)

Yet the explorer continued, despite these feelings. In the study outlined in this book participants expressed similar notions about the relationship between participation and death. In particular, participants focused on a desire to remove the element of chance, as far as this is possible, as chance might bring them too close to the potential of death. A typical representation of this point was that participants worked very hard to minimise the influence of chance, as chance was unacceptable:

I reckon you have to stop a little bit before that, because, you know, at that '*Russian Roulette*' point you're already very close to death and that's just not a place you want to be. I don't and most people who do these activities, don't; they do it because they enjoy living.

(Co-researcher, mid 30s)

So what have we learnt so far?

The contention that death is consciously or unconsciously sought, or that death is in some way cheated through extreme sports, is a misunderstanding of the extreme sport experience. Equally, participants do not consider themselves immortal and, as Todhunter (2000) wrote, extreme sport participation does have a close and powerful relationship to death.

So the question has to be: if participants express a desire to live and note that the experience is about living life to its fullest, how is this related to participation in an activity that could result in death? There is a paradox: expose oneself to the potential of death in order to live a full life. Philosophy has something to say about this issue in that philosophy as a discipline allows for the exploration of death. After all, human life is limited; our destiny is to die.

The meaning of death in the context of living life to its fullest has seldom been addressed in contemporary philosophical thought. In philosophical terms, death has been discussed in terms of its place in society, the afterlife, its function in religion and bioethics to name but a few. However, these analyses do not foster a resolution to the aforementioned paradox. Unlike risk, there are philosophical and theoretical writings on the relationship between death and living life to its fullest. The following paragraphs consider philosophies and philosophers that in some way aim to shed light on this paradox. The intention is not to seek a theoretical explanation but to find other portrayals of the phenomenon.

Reflections on death

The existential phenomenologists have had a long interest in meaning and in death in human existence (Koestenbaum, 1978). Death has been approached from the viewpoint of symbolism and reality, its relationship to human behaviours and emotions, its relationship to time and our reactions to our impending death. In exploring the extreme sport experience, the essence of the existential position is that death is inescapable and by accepting the inevitability of one's own death, one can live fully. By accepting death, one discovers a new urgency in life and focus is switched to the essentials of life. Thus, all threats to existence are removed and death loses its intimidating power. One learns to live with meaning and vitality. This perspective is, of course, not unique to an existential perspective, but has long been espoused in works stemming from the wisdom traditions, such the Tibetan Book of the Dead.

Heidegger's (1996) phenomenological exploration of being and time includes extensive writings on death which led to his deliberations on being-towards-death. Death is seen as the point at which life comes to an end. Heidegger recognises that death is generally experienced as belonging to others and not to ourselves. Heidegger questions this state of being and realised that 'no one can take the other's dying away from him' (Heidegger, 1996, p. 223). Essentially, death, in Heidegger's view, is a personal matter. Death belongs to each *Dasein* (Being). Or in other terms 'death is always essentially my own' (Heidegger, 1996, p. 223). Thus, death is each person's own solitary journey which cannot be experienced through others.

Heidegger further decreed that every Being is old enough to die as soon as s/he is born. However, as death is the end of every human life we cannot directly experience our own death. Thus, in no small way every *Dasein* lives journeying towards its own death. How we live in recognition of this realisation, of this inevitability, is what makes the difference. In the words of Heidegger:

Death is the possibility of the absolute impossibility of Da-sein. Thus *death* reveals itself as the *ownmost nonrelational possibility not to be bypassed.* As such it is an *eminent* imminence. Its existential possibility is grounded in the fact that the Da-sein is essentially disclosed to itself, in the way of being-ahead-of-itself. This structural factor of care has its most primordial concretion in being-towards-death. Being-towards-the-end becomes phenomenally clearer as being toward the eminent possibility of Da-sein which we have characterised.

(Heidegger, 1996, p. 232)

In Heidegger's view, death can be categorised in three ways. First, it is 'my' unavoidable end to life. Second, death should be viewed as the possibility of 'me' no longer existing (ownmost possibility) and third, no one can die for 'me' (non-relational). Thus, death can only be confronted '*ahead of the event* in an attitude Heidegger calls being-towards-death' (Macann, 1993, p. 97). Yet we observe that we often do not consider our own deaths and act as if we have an eternity to undertake what we desire. In fact, as Heidegger pointed out, 'even "thinking about death" is regarded publicly as cowardly fear, a sign of insecurity on the part of the *Da-sein* and a dark flight from the world' (Heidegger, 1996, p. 235).

Death, according to Heidegger, should be thought about, should be faced as an imminent inevitability as death sits squarely as a matter of life. That is, rather than evade or attempt to veil this reality Heidegger encourages us to acknowledge and accept death and somehow 'make it our own'. Being intimate with the certainty of our own death enables a freedom from those dark clutches that create anxious concerns. Facing death is individualising; that is, it requires facing ourselves as we really are. In Heidegger's view, the ideal aim would be to live life with the realisation that death is a distinct and imminent possibility. This assertion eloquently articulated by Heidegger should not be mistaken as a call for an obsessive focus on death. Instead framing death in such a way opens up the potential 'to find rich significance in living' (Higgins, 1998, p. 48), providing encouragement to live life to its fullest, 'a tool for seizing the day, every day' (Higgins, 1998, p. 49).

Accordingly, people take hold of their own life by focusing on its end in such a way that they are individualised. Accepting the inevitability and truth of our own death and its ever-present potential changes the way life is lived and supports a process whereby each person moves towards living life authentically. Arguably this acceptance is rare and difficult; fear holds us back and life is described as being lived inauthentically (Soll, 1996). An inauthentic life in this context means that we conform to the pressures of social norms and their tranquillising rewards. Such a life is in flight from death; a person may verbally affirm mortality but does not truly believe it. In living one's life authentically, it is necessary to accept our destiny, which involves the acceptance of the reality of our own death. It is through this process that we achieve a sense of autonomy and focus (Young, 1996). Authenticity, then, could be seen as deriving from the true and genuine experience of the realness of death, an acceptance of one's own mortality, essential for living a full human life. The response to the potentiality of death is that consciousness tends to withdraw to the deeper or core elements of being. Similar experiences are recounted through the world's mythological history. For the mystic, the shaman and, perhaps, the extreme sport participant, the effect of such an experience is that 'life is then richer, stronger, and more joyous' (Campbell, 1973, p. 230).

Other perspectives on the death–life relationship come from a range of wisdom traditions, the most well-known of which is arguably Buddhism. A central tenet of Buddhist philosophy is the impermanence of life. According to Buddhism, all life, including human life, suffers from birth and death. Death therefore is an integral part of life and, by extension, life is an integral part of death. Buddhist philosophy succinctly reminds us that whilst we may not know when, where or how we will die, death is ever-present (Humphreys, 1993). Contemplating this inevitability in such a way that one becomes experientially aware of the ever-present potential of our own death each day liberates us from deception and laziness in living our lives (Gyatso, 2001).

> Since I shall soon have to depart from this world, there is no sense in my becoming attached to the things of life. Instead I will take to heart the real essence of my human life.
>
> (Gyatso, 2001, p. 43)

One Buddhist text, *The Tibetan Book of the Dead*, explores death as a continual process, not just an end to life (Fremantle & Trungpa, 1975). For Wicks (1996) the texts are a reminder to live life.

> Our habitual patterns of expectation and reaction to circumstances often produce a deathlike stagnation and unanimated redundancy within our experience. As a release from this benighted condition, there remains the permanent possibility of experiencing a liberating transformation of character and a 'rebirth' of personality.
>
> (Wicks, 1996, p. 71)

Death is thus seen as a continual cycle of personality transformations. Accepting death also means that we should learn how to live well (Rinpoche, 2002). Contemplating our own death introduces us to the essence of our own mind. If the reality of death is ignored then life will remain unfulfilled. In other terms, only by recognising how fragile life is, can we come to know how precious life is (Rinpoche, 2002).

Zen Buddhist philosophy also indicates that death, or at least the facing of death, provides a direct path to understanding the true nature of self. Parkes (1996) draws on Ancient Zen philosophy to make this point:

> If you are not a hero who has truly seen into his own nature, don't think that [non-ego] is something that can be known so easily … you must be prepared

to let go your hold when hanging from a sheer precipice, to die and return again to life ... Supposing a man should find himself in some desolate area where no one has ever walked before. Below him are the perpendicular walls of a bottomless chasm. His feet rest precariously on a patch of slippery moss, and there is no spot of earth on which he can steady himself. He can neither advance nor retreat; he faces only death.

(Ekaku cited in Parkes, 1996, p. 92)

Thus one is brought back to life with new vigour. Essentially, death should be learned in an experiential way as opposed to an objective or abstract way. That is, to understand death (and therefore experience life to the fullest) one should enter into 'its way of being' (Parkes, 1996, p. 93). Parkes again calls on the words of a Zen master, Suzuki Shosan:

This is what Shosan means by exhorting his readers to 'learn death': we can learn from death by entering into its way of being, its falling away at every moment, and thereby come to 'live having let go of life'.

(Parkes, 1996, p. 93)

Of course we can never truly experience our own death – we can only hope to get as close as possible to the experience. It has been observed that 'only the man who gives up his life shall learn to live' (Humphreys, 1993, p. 72). Hindu philosophy takes this further, showing that not only is entering the truth of death essential to living a full life but, also, to ignore this experiential reality is to live life as a living death (Chaudhuri, 1990).

The Taoist philosophies place human beings solidly as part of nature (Malpas & Solomon, 1998). Death is neither revered nor cherished, neither celebrated nor feared. Death is just that – death. According to Ames, the Taoist view on death is one of tolerance for its place in human existence. Without death, life would be 'static, transparent, predictable and tedious' (Ames, 1996, p. 60). Thus, death is seen as a positive presence that enables life to be lived more fully 'making it more intense and poignant' (Ames, 1996, p. 60).

We have argued that philosophy, both Western and Eastern, presents a view in which it is argued that an experiential appreciation of death is essential in terms of our appreciation of life. As well as the philosophical perspectives already discussed, Eastern philosophers who follow Taoist views and Western philosophers such as Montaigne and Nietzsche have considered death as an existential conception. Whilst it must be accepted that viewpoints are often culturally and historically embedded, there would seem to be a striking similarity in what such apparently disparate philosophies have to say about death. Often, writings and recommendations posit a view that becoming somehow unfastened from life seems to reverse the process and enables a re-entering into life with a heightened vitality.

Nietzsche philosophised that living towards death infuses life with the desire to live every moment to its fullest. In his classic work *Zarathustra's Discourses*

Nietzsche (1995) even recommended that 'one should learn to die' (Nietzsche, 1995, p. 77). For Nietzsche as well as the contemporary existential psychotherapists, life is best understood from a perspective that is distant or departed from itself. Thus, any process that enables a viewpoint outside of one's life also provides a more complete picture of one's life and makes possible a return to a fuller life and freedom from superficiality.

A number of psychiatrists and psychotherapists have looked closely at the role of death in living. For example, Kubler-Ross (1975) considered that only by accepting death as part of life can we hope to fully appreciate what it means to live with meaning. Confronting death brings freedom from the future, freedom from the illusion of personality and vanity and a glimpse of eternity. Life, even the worst bits, become live entertainment. Death provides a route to clarity, a pathway to a different view on life:

> The presence of death is an eraser that clears off much that is filling the blackboard. When life gets too cluttered and confused, when you have somehow strayed from the path, consult with death. Thoughts of death clarify and clear the blackboard of unimportant material.
>
> (Horwitz, 1996, p. 13)

These philosophical perspectives on death, ever present in the experiences of the extreme sports person, present a view insisting that to live is also to die; one cannot exist without the other. The challenge is to learn how to live whilst one moves towards death, for death is a certainty. This challenge would seem to be best performed when death is genuinely accepted as an ever-present possibility in one's own human existence. Accepting this reality requires that each of us face up to our own limited existence; only then is life truly, authentically lived. This acceptance does not imply that death is the point of existence or that death is in any way celebrated as an end in itself – merely that accepting death as real removes its power and opens up possibilities that are precious and infinitely exciting.

The extreme sport experience can be seen as one route towards experiencing one's own death as a real and imminent potential and thereby affirming life. Arguably, extreme sports bring us experientially (or as near as is possible) face to face with our own death in a real and genuine way. The relationship to death exemplified in the decisions to participate in extreme sport, whether consciously or unconsciously, leads to an ability to live life to the fullest extent. After all, when sitting in the eddy preparing to shoot a waterfall, or standing on the cliff readying oneself to jump, one is accepting that death is a real possibility. In the words of one extreme participant:

> For me, my sports are a direct tap into what I call the 'life force'. I don't want to die, and I especially don't want to die a slow death of desperation, without adventure. We'll all be a 911 call sooner or later, but I'd prefer mine to happen in the midst of an open-eyed life experience.
>
> (In Gadd & Rubenstein, 2003, p. 25)

William James, one of the most eminent psychologists in the history of the discipline, noted 'it is only by risking our persons from one hour to another that we live at all' (James cited in Koerner, 1997, p. 2) – a realisation also accepted by those studying near-death experiences and mythology (Campbell, 1973, 1993). That is, accepting and experiencing the reality of our own death may well be the door to something more, something special, that might even lead to an enhanced consciousness within a life lived well.

Summary

Although this might be scant comfort to those of us who lie awake concerned for our loved ones, extreme sport participation is not about the death wish or a desire to cheat death. We have argued that the experience of bringing death to our waking consciousness may well have positive outcomes for living in the present. That is, by approaching death, one comes to accept death, which in turn enables life to be lived more fully. This may well be what happens when one participates in an extreme sport. This idea is consistent with the narratives of extreme sport participants which is characterised by a life wish, referred to by Freud as Eros, and a desire to live life to its fullest.

Yet this aspect of the extreme sport experience cannot be the whole experience but an element that might contribute to a more complete understanding of people who engage in activities in which danger is fundamental. Equally, if it was as easy and straightforward as discussed above, would we not all be lining up to partake of our chosen activity? Our relationship to death is complex and represents just one element in understanding the motivations for participation in this human endeavour. For the closer we get to the potential annihilation of our person, the more we seem to want to turn back. Something within us warns us of our impending doom. Yet if we would just move past that warning, as extreme sports participants seem to do, a special experience might await. Still, we are compelled to restrain our enthusiasm. For a fuller exploration into this phenomenon we must turn to fear.

References

Allman, T. L., Mittlestaedt, R. D., Martin, B. & Goldenberg, B. (2009). Exploring the motivations of BASE jumpers: Extreme sport enthusiasts. *Journal of Sport and Tourism*, *14*(4), 229–247.

Alvarez, A. (1972). *The savage god: A study of suicide*. New York: Random House.

Ames, R. T. (1996). Death as transformation in classical daoism. In J. Malpass & R. C. Solomon (Eds), *Death and philosophy* (pp. 57–71). London: Routledge.

Bane, M. (1996). *Over the edge: A regular guy's odyssey in extreme sports*. New York: Macmillan.

Becker, E. (1962). *The birth and death of meaning*. New York: Free Press.

Campbell, J. (1973). *Myths to live by*. London: Souvenir Press.

Campbell, J. (1993). *The hero with a thousand faces*. London: Fontana Press.

Celsi, R. L., Rose, R. L. & Leigh, T. W. (1993). An exploration of high-risk leisure consumption through skydiving. *Journal of Consumer Research*, *20*, 1–23.

Chaudhuri, H. (1990). *The essence of spiritual philosophy*. New Delhi: Indus.

Fremantle, F. & Trungpa, C. (1975). *The Tibetan book of the dead: Great liberation through hearing in the bardo*. (F. Freemantle & C. Trungpa, Trans.). Boston, MA: Shambhala.

Gadd, W. & Rubenstein, B. (2003, 1 September). Why I go extreme. *New York Times*, pp. 24–25.

Gosetti-Ferencei, G. (2014). Death and authenticity: Reflections on Heidegger, Rilke, Blanchot. *Existenz*, *9*(1), 53–62.

Groves, D. (1987). Why do some athletes choose high-risk sports? *The Physician and Sports Medicine*, *15*(2), 186–193.

Gyatso, G. K. (2001). *Transform your life: A blissful journey*. Ulverston: Tharpa.

Heidegger, M. (1996). *Being and time: A translation of Sein and Zeit*. (J. Stambaugh, Trans.). Albany, NY: State University of New York.

Higgins, K. (1998). Death and the skeleton. In J. Malpas & R. C. Solomon (Eds), *Death and philosophy* (pp. 83–97). London: Routledge.

Horwitz, T. (1996). My death. In J. Malpas & R. C. Solomon (Eds), *Death and philosophy* (pp. 5–16). London: Routledge.

Humphreys, C. (1993). *The Buddhist way of life*. New Delhi: Indus.

Hunt, J. C. (1996). Diving the wreck: Risk and injury in sport scuba diving. *Psychoanalytic Quarterly*, *LXV*, 591–622.

Koerner, B. I. (1997). Extreeeme: The peril the thrill. The sheer rebellion of it all. High-risk sport adds spice to the humdrum of American lives. *U.S. News Online* 30 June. Retrieved 10 July 2004 from www.uwnews.com/usnews/issue/970630/30extr.htm.

Koestenbaum, P. (1978). *The vitality of death: Essays in existential psychology and philosophy*. Westport, CT: Greenwood Press.

Kubler-Ross, E. (1975). *Death: The final stage of growth*. Englewood Cliffs, NJ: Prentice-Hall.

Kumar, A., Pathak, N. & Thakur, G. P. (1985). Death anxiety and locus of control in individual, team and non-athletes. *International Journal of Sport Psychology*, *16*, 28–288.

Le Breton, D. (2000). Playing symbolically with death in extreme sports. *Body and Society*, *6*(1), 1–11.

Macann, C. (1993). *Four phenomenological philosophers*. London: Routledge.

Malpas, J. & Solomon, R. C. (1998). Death and philosophy. In J. Malpas & R. C. Solomon (Eds), *Death and philosophy* (pp. 1–4). London: Routledge.

Nietzsche, F. (1995). *Zarathustra's discourses*. (R. J. Hollingdale, Trans.). London: Penguin Books.

Ogilvie, B. C. (1974). The sweet psychic jolt of danger. *Psychology Today*, *8*(5), 88–94.

Palmer, C. (2000, September 11). Extreme sports a risky business for tourists. *Media Release*. Retrieved 2 November 2016 from www.adelaide.edu.au/news/news169.html.

Parkes, G. (1996). Death and detachment; Montaigne, Zen, Heidegger and the rest. In J. Malpas & R. C. Solomon (Eds), *Death and philosophy* (pp. 164–180). London: Routledge.

Rinpoche, S. (2002). *The Tibetan book of living and dying* (10th Anniversary Edition Revised and Updated). San Francisco, CA: Harper Collins Publishers.

Schrader, M. P. & Wann, D. L. (1999). High-risk recreation: The relationship between participant characteristics and degree of involvement. *Journal of Sport Behaviour*, *22*(3), 426–431.

Slanger, E. & Rudestam, K. E. (1997). Motivation and disinhibition in high risk sports: Sensation seeking and self-efficacy. *Journal of Research in Personality*, *31*, 355–374.

Soll, I. (1996). On the purported insignificance of death: Whistling before the dark. In J. Malpass & R. C. Solomon (Eds), *Death and philosophy* (pp. 22–38). London: Routledge.

Templar, D. I. (1970). The construction and validation of a death anxiety scale. *The Journal of General Psychology, 82,* 165–177.

Todhunter, A. (2000). *Dangerous games: Ice climbing, storm kayaking, and other adventures from the extreme edge of sports.* New York: Doubleday.

Wicks, R. (1996). Death and enlightenment. In J. Malpas & R. C. Solomon (Eds), *Death and philosophy* (pp. 71–82). London: Routledge.

Young, J. (1996). Death and authenticity. In J. Malpas & R. C. Solomon (Eds), *Death and philosophy* (pp. 112–119). London: Routledge.

7   The 'no fear' hypothesis

Fear, or, more accurately, 'no fear' or fearlessness has, like risk-taking and death, been evoked to explain the extreme sports experience. It is not always clear whether the attribution 'no fear' refers to being generally fearless or whether exhibiting 'no fear' is context specific. It might be the environment implicit with a specific activity, for example water for surfing or cliffs for BASE jumping. On the other hand, purported fearlessness might refer to some other aspect inherent within a specific activity such as falling for extreme skiing or drowning in waterfall kayaking. The 'no fear' attitude might also signify a relationship to potential pain or even the possibility of death. Whatever it is, the 'no fear' aspect of extreme sports has strong appeal.

At one level the 'no fear' notion makes sense. After all, just imagine sitting in a kayak perched on the lip of a waterfall approaching the size of Niagara, waiting to guide your craft into the current and over the top, or standing with your toes dangling over the edge of a bridge or cliff waiting to leap into thin air. Such situations would scare most of us. One only has to reflect on the feelings of fear created by hurtling around a roller coaster ride where pain or death are not likely to appreciate the potential feelings involved in extreme sports. Thus anybody willing to voluntarily, for leisure, partake in an activity that might trigger such fears, would have to be fearless, otherwise they would surely just freeze or panic.

Furthermore, participants keep going back for more even after experiencing a serious injury. There are numerous cases where an injury has resulted in long term hospitalisation. However, despite being carried from the scene on stretchers, being considered lucky to be alive and receiving numerous broken bones, most participants continue with their chosen activity. In some cases participants have been reported to 'chuckle' about their near death experiences (Greenberg, 1977, p. 18). Is this evidence of fearlessness?

The 'no fear' notion might be more a function of non-participant naïvety and misinterpretations of the real experience as alluded to in the following quote:

> The basic drives behind these kinds of sports are based on fear and life – it's these philosophies that often get misinterpreted. If you can face your fears

you get a new dimension on life, new possibilities. The second is that life's sweet, explore it and treasure it.

(Co-researcher, mid 30s)

An extreme whitewater expedition kayaker and medical doctor Jessie Stone indicated, extreme sports might actually help fear management and extend to other aspects of life (Stone, 2003a, 2003b).

The role and experience of fear is complex. It is not just marketing and general opinion that has considered extreme sport participation as indicative of an inappropriate relationship to fear. Academic research has also expressed a similar view. Extreme sport activities have been considered as the undertakings of those, otherwise known as adrenaline junkies, who actively search for (and perhaps are addicted to) the effects of adrenaline, which we create in response to fear. This of course presents a quandary and potentially calls into question the relationship to 'no fear' and suggests an unhealthy addiction to the effects of fear.

This chapter builds upon our critique of the 'risk hypothesis' and the 'death-wish hypothesis' by examining the role of fear in understanding extreme sport participation. That is, our aim is to question these common assumptions and provide a basis for the phenomenological investigation of the extreme sport experience. We will consider what has been written about the relationship between extreme sports and fear in order to explore where the 'truth' might lie, or, in phenomenological terms, the explication of the lifeworld of the extreme sportsperson. To begin this process, we define fear or fearlessness and reflect upon how these constructs might relate to extreme sports. The following section explores fear itself in order to determine what fearlessness might entail.

Fear: an overview

Fear, like death, is one of those unmentionable elements of human experience. In society, we go to great extremes to obviate situations associated with fear, and mastery in the face of intense danger is reframed as bravery. Fear and its related manifestations are generally perceived to be unwanted states deliberately inflicted on us by others, or as a consequence of the natural environment and our own limitations. As individuals, we all experience some degree of fear, or *angst*, to use the German term. Other terms include apprehension, scare, hysteria and panic. Fear, in human terms, has been described as an emotional response to a stimulus that human beings strive to obviate, avoid or escape from. The most likely responses to a source of fear are flight, fight or freeze. The capacity to experience fear and the behavioural arousal that correlates with it emerge from a 'FEAR circuit' in the brain and its relationship to a multitude of neurological, biochemical, hormonal and other physiological mechanisms. A fearful event is accompanied by the excretion of adrenaline from the adrenal glands and the neurones in the brain.

The experiential and physiological responses of fear include the startle response, trembling, increased heart rate, increased blood pressure, cold sweats, apprehensive worry, nervousness, tension, a feeling that safety is threatened, excessive vigilance and fidgeting, gastrointestinal disturbances, increased defecation and increased and shallow respiration. Adrenaline also causes an increase in blood sugar levels that ready the body for flight or fight. The precise mechanisms depend on the level and intensity of the fear felt and the ensuing flight, fight or freeze characteristics. For example, intense fear is most often characterised by flight while low or mild levels of fear are typically characterised by freezing. Intense levels of fear also impair cognitive ability.

Research has explored fear as both an innate biological component of humanness and a learned behaviour. Biological understandings include the role of genetics, and the structure of the brain and nervous system. Contemporary research on fear suggests that the fear response is based upon the amygdala regions of the brain. From an evolutionary perspective, the amygdala represents a primitive region of the brain responsible for the fight or flight response. The fear response is, in part, regulated by a central autonomic–interoceptive network which, in turn, recognises a neural substrate of conscious fear processing (Fullana et al., 2016). This response underpins the person's experience of fear. Research has also pointed to the role of cognitive processes associated with the fear response and the mediating role of learning.

Behaviourists propose that some fears are innate reactions to specific stimuli, which may include sudden loss of support and pain. However, while pain may be effective in generating or creating fear, it does not in itself constitute fear. For example, while fear may trigger an analgesic influence over pain, fear can often be experienced without a relationship to pain. Fearful reactions to stimuli other than these innate responses may be a result of classical conditioning. Needless to say, the original behaviourist explanations of fear were simplistic compared to current theories. For example, Gray (1987) observed that human beings seem to have an innate fear of snakes but such fear does not manifest itself until the age of two. For Gray this was evidence of either a maturation process or learning.

Innate fear can be broken down to cover four principles: novelty (e.g. strangers, unfamiliarity), intensity (e.g. light, sounds and other pain-inducing stimuli), stimuli arising from social interactions (e.g. threatening behaviours) and evolutionary dangers (e.g. darkness, dead or mutilated bodies, situations that may cause death). For humans, the 'novelty' and 'intensity' fears may diminish within a few years of birth due to a familiarisation process often called habituation. Such fears are evolutionarily determined but, as previously noted, may not mature for some time after birth. Earlier fears are more abstract whereas fears that develop later in life are more specific to particular stimuli. Any fear that does not fit within these categories is either a learnt or an augmented disposition towards a fearful stimulus.

Learnt fears can cover a range of contexts. For example, the fear of psychological annihilation is, according to Rowe (2002), our greatest fear, even greater than the fear of physical death. Often, fear is caused by the struggle between fitting in with the group and remaining an individual or the balance between security and freedom. Where freedom is required to explore and determine who we are, freedom is also characterised by uncertainty and great danger. Freedom is potentially frightening as it involves the need to balance choice and security.

When thinking of extreme sport, it is useful to distinguish between anxiety and terror which emerge from the 'FEAR circuit'. Both anxiety and terror can be activated by external and internal stimuli. Anxieties might include such constructs as the fear of heights or fear of pain. Terror is considered to be the more sudden intense form of fear. General anxiety is a more continual and consistent fear that tends to gnaw away, destroying any sense of security. Panic can be considered an extreme and groundless fear that manifests in flight.

Response patterns related to fear are also continually modulated through direct emotional or cognitive learning. Learning can aid the effective channelling of fears to ensure contextually appropriate responses. However, fearful events can trigger long-term responses such as avoidance of similar situations, intense dreams of terror that seem to re-enact the event or even taking drugs to drown out the fear. For example, chronic fearful anxiety may eventually be accompanied by post-traumatic stress disorder or obsessive-compulsive behaviours and rituals. Equally, the onset of fear responses without apparent reason can themselves trigger fear responses which might trigger a cycle where we end up being afraid of fear itself.

Fear in some of its manifestations should not be considered innately negative. A low level of anxiety can actually be motivating. For example, anxiety about the need to protect oneself could lead to an action that effectively provides protection. However, the motivation effect works best when a person also has the required skills and abilities to reduce the anxiety in question.

Our intention is to explore the phenomenon of fear from a stance which might lead to an understanding of fearlessness within a context more often associated with fear. Fear then is both innate and learned and defined in terms of degrees and responses. Some fears, such as the fear of death or pain, are manifest at birth and possibly augmented through learning. Anxiety, terror, panic, guilt and fear itself are all potential manifestations triggered by similar internal or external stimuli. From this brief overview of fear it is easy to see why the idea that extreme sports participants must have 'no fear' is so powerful. Extreme sports seem to epitomise an activity that flies in the face of everything we know about human beings and fear. This leads to the assumption that the only way an athlete can undertake an extreme sport is if they do not have normal fear responses or circuits, they must have 'no fear'.

One way of understanding how fearlessness might manifest is to explore the physiological responses associated with an activity. Let us imagine what it might be like to jump off a cliff with a parachute. From a biological perspective, your heart starts to race, your mouth gets dry and you will start to experience uncomfortable changes in blood pressure, as your body produces a massive surge of adrenaline, noradrenalin and growth hormone. Your hypothalamus secretes hormones which eventually facilitates the release of adrenocorticotropin and cortisol. People next to you will notice that you are breathing much faster and you will feel butterflies in your stomach as a result of the blood draining into areas that are required to prepare you for flight or fight. The whole experience feels unpleasant and outside of your control. It happens almost instantaneously as you wrestle with the decision to jump or not to jump, thus overcoming your fear of falling to your death.

While this biologically based explanation might be accurate it tells us little about the experience or meaning of the phenomenon. In fact it cannot even inform the aims of the chapter which is to explore whether extreme sports people are fearless and crazy. Further, if this is the kind of experience the extreme sports participants have, then it is reasonable to ask, given all this potential negative physiological and emotional experience, why would anyone undertake an extreme sport? Perhaps, after all, participants of extreme sports are fearless. If someone is fearless in a given situation, one would expect that they would report an absence of fear and that the associated physiological and emotional responses to fear (e.g. heart rate increases) would not be evident. Thus, extreme sport participants, who face a real possibility of dying every time they participate, would claim fearlessness and indicate a lack of a physiological or experiential relationship to fear, or at least a much-reduced physiological and experiential relationship. For some theorists and researchers, participation in extreme sports does involve a much reduced sense of fear.

Psychoanalysis

One approach that has been used to investigate extreme sports has drawn upon psychoanalytic concepts. We use the terms 'psychoanalysis' and 'psychodynamic' interchangeably, as they both rely on reference to unconscious processes. From this perspective, purported fear stems from unconscious and pathological origins, rooted in childhood fantasies and issues. For example, a study undertaken with a single deep diver asserted that motivations for diving were based on preoedipal, oedipal, sadomasochistic attachments and bisexual conflicts (Hunt, 1996). The study postulated that the diver's career was based on a desire for recognition which may have resulted from feelings of deprivation resulting from his father's inattention. These issues were not considered conscious processes, but as hypotheses to explain unconscious processes. In this vein, Hunt suggested the anxiety experienced by the diver 'may reflect preoedipally rooted castration concerns' which were later strengthened through 'oedipal conflicts and related aggressive fantasies' (Hunt, 1996, p. 598). In Hunt's opinion the diver's relationship with his father may have resulted in what she termed 'sadomasochistic paternal attachment' which initiated problems in negotiating later oedipal conflicts. These terms are used to delineate unconscious processes and refer to aspects of human subjectivity which are otherwise not as accessible as more overt processes.

While the suggestion from this study has been generalised beyond the original case study, Hunt's analysis needs to be considered in the context of a clinical case report, and her knowledge of the diver, who was engaged in a particularly dangerous aspect of diving. In her quest to provide an explanation for his involvement in such extreme activity, she questioned whether the person lacked 'an appropriate sense of fear' and had an inappropriate love of pain. Participation in the extreme sport of deep diving was considered, amongst other sex-related struggles, to be a reflection of the struggle 'for power over frightening phallic women' which in more common language, refers to the diver challenging his own fears in the context of feeling quite vulnerable in a particular interpersonal context. Certainly, Hunt extends her ideas to suggest a strong masculine focus in deep sea diving which, in turn, is used to explain the lack of involvement of women in deep sea diving at that time. However, she goes on to observe that people are different and that to explain extreme sport experience in such terms may be an over-simplification. Furthermore, she recognises that deep diving is most often conflict and injury free and an immensely creative endeavour.

Psychoanalysis was founded upon the discovery of the unconscious, and the foundation that we were influenced by unconscious processes. In fact, it is a misnomer to think of psychodynamic theory as a single theory, and, as in many complex fields of human endeavour, there are multiple perspectives incorporated under the general rubric of psychodynamic theory. There have been some rather crass interpretations of psychoanalytic theory, in which objects are said to be associated with some kind of sexual significance, such as a snake being imbued with some characteristics of the penis (Gray, 1987). While this process has been used to explain what are seen as innate or instinctual fears, the theoretical foundations of such interpretations are fraught with problems and do not represent current psychodynamic ideas. It might also be that Hunt's interpretations have fallen into the trap of drawing upon predefined concepts rather than following the dictum of staying close to the original experience.

Stress-seeking

Stress is most commonly understood as both a psychological and biological response to some kind of threat, real or imagined. Fear is a key component of such a response. That is, stress induces both fear and anxiety, where fear is a response to a particular object, for instance, fear of a precipice, while anxiety is a more generalised response. Biological manifestations of stress include increased heart rate, increase in breathing, and a decrease in digestive activity and the release of glucose. The bodily response is based upon both sensory input and processing and the person's memories of related experiences.

Rather than actively seeking an external construct called risk, some people might seek situations deemed to be stressful through sports culturally considered 'risk sports'. Thus, in contrast to the perception that participants must be fearless or not have an effective appreciation of fear, this view suggests that fear is definitely experienced and is a constant companion when engaging in such activities. Houston (1968), the leader of many Himalayan expeditions, wrote that climbers are continually psychologically burdened by the fear of falling, which we have seen is considered one of humanity's fundamental fears. The implication is that the climber actively searches for experiences designed to induce fear.

As we argued at the beginning of this chapter, fear is one of the great unmentionable aspects of being human. Adults are supposed to control their intense emotions, and fear is supposed to be curtailed at the very least. Whilst children are permitted an element of uncensored emotion, similar exposure of reactions in the face of fear by adult men and women is at the very least a matter of embarrassment and a demonstration of non-normal behaviour. Fear, according to our cultural norms, is not something we should seek out.

Excitement is an essential element of the human experience and the role of leisure or play is to enable participants to achieve this state. This is contrary to those theorists who suggest that participants are motivated by the desire for a release from work tensions or the desire to attain something not achieved in work (Greenberg, 1977). Leisure and play are not merely relief from the tensions of everyday life or the antecedent of work; they are essential for human well-being. Arguably, play in dangerous environments is a search for intensity that is associated with fear. In this guise fear becomes excitement, an expression that does not require intense reflection, foresight and knowledge.

> In a society in which the propensies of the serious and threatening type of excitement have diminished, the compensatory function of play-excitement has increased. With the help of this type of excitement, the mimetic sphere offers again and again the chance, as it were, for a new 'refreshment of the soul' in the otherwise even tenor in the ordinary social life.
>
> (Elias & Dunning, 1986, p. 72)

The focus of this theory is on play pursuits that mimic or imitate dangerous activities, not necessarily on those that have an actual relationship to loss of life. As Elias and Dunning put it, 'mimetic excitement is socially and personally without danger' (1986, p. 80), whereas extreme sports could lead to a very real threat to life. So, in contrast to the views on the relationship between drama and reality attributed to Aristotle, extreme sports are not imitating any real situations that might trigger a sympathetic response called fear. Rather, they allow participants to truly experience fear itself. Furthermore, extreme sports often require extensive knowledge and foresight. That is, extreme sports participants do not search for tension that mimics fear, as theories of play might suggest, in an attempt to arouse emotions normally avoided. On the contrary, the role of fear, and in particular the fear of impending danger, is an essential element of the extreme sport experience. Extreme sports are most definitely non-mimetic. Still, this argument does touch on one very interesting proposition: that the raising of tensions and the feelings associated with fear or excitement are essential for mental health. The position being argued is that we should not fear fear but embrace it as part of being human. We may postulate that the relationship between participation and fear is an important element of the motivation to engage in extreme sports.

Whilst the experience of fear may be part of life, it may also be the case that experienced extreme sports participants do not feel the tension associated with fear or anxiety. It is plausible that continued exposure to extraordinary stress such as extreme sports becomes a routine experience. The activity may become normal and only those who cannot imagine how it is possible to be comfortable in such experiences consider it to be stress seeking. This hypothesis leads to two different propositions. The first is that participants are not searching for the experience of fear and the second is that the experience of fear may dissipate or give way to other experiences as one gets used to engaging in certain activities. Reflecting back on the conditions leading to a sense of fear, the thought that fear subsides makes sense. Psychologists refer to this as the process of extinction. After all, the experience of extreme fear is said to immobilise emotional, mental and physical abilities which clearly is not the case in athletes engaging in extreme sport.

Anxiety

Research on anxiety in extreme sport people may help shed some light on their relationship to fear. While in recent years some work has been undertaken that investigates anxiety and competitive adventure sports, the results have tended to focus on the anxiety as a function of competition rather than the activity. In general, even in this population, results do not mirror findings from traditional sports. With regards to extreme sports as defined in this book, Ogilvie (1974) found, over four decades ago, that those who participated in parachuting and race car driving had exceptionally low anxiety levels. Robinson (1985) found that in general, elite climbers had low levels of anxiety in both life and climbing. However, approximately a third of those tested reported a degree of anxiety whilst thinking about climbing, indicating that whilst in general life their anxiety might be low, the thought of climbing did induce an anxious state for one third of participants. However, his report does not indicate anything about the nature, difficulty or intensity of the climb being considered.

Himalayan climbers have been found to be less tense than the general population (Breivik, 1996). Breivik argued that the participants in his study were more inclined to be courageous on a continuum spanning fearlessness, courage and overconfidence. Courageous people are those people who undertake an activity even though they feel apprehensive and worried, and as a result they feel better. Overconfident people feel little worry before a dangerous situation but have greater feelings of fear preceding further similar situations. Another study on expedition climbers found that anxiety was experienced but climbers were skilled at coping with these psychologically stressful situations (Magni, Rupolo, Simini, De Leo & Rampazzo, 1985). A study carried out using a battery of tests on parachute athletes which included physiological, perceived arousal and personality comparisons, found that increases in heart rate and arousal for experienced parachutists were only slightly lower than for novices (Breivik, Roth & Jorgensen, 1998). Further, experienced parachutists were better informed about their arousal states.

Essentially these studies suggest that whilst extreme sport participants may feel generally less anxious, they do feel heightened anxiety or fear whilst participating in their sports. Extreme sport participation has been associated with a range of responses eloquently articulated by Schultheis as 'possessed by something between panic and euphoria, dread and ecstasy' (Schultheis, 1996, p. 7). In the words of one BASE jumper:

> You can't even begin to try to make somebody who hasn't done it understand how frightening, how exciting, how peaceful and beautiful that sensation is.
>
> (Co-researcher, mid 30s)

However, participants are still able to function effectively, thus the debilitating effects of fear do not seem to take hold in the same way as traditional anxiety-evoking situations. In fact extreme sport participants demonstrate a capacity to transform fear into a more productive state. This state may be associated with increased productivity and focus:

> ... when people judge themselves capable of handling an activity, they perform with assurance, approach threatening tasks nonanxiously, experience little in the way of stress, and are able to direct all effort to the task in hand.
>
> (Slanger & Rudestam, 1997, p. 366)

In the study that compared extreme sports with other sports, self-efficacy was the only distinguishing factor between people labelled as high-risk and those labelled as extreme (Slanger and Rudestam, 1997). However, far from approaching the task nonanxiously and without stress, some participants actually report that they feel extreme levels of stress or fear – they are just able to overcome it. This is a point poetically described by the great waterfall kayaker Corran Addison as he recalled preparing, and eventually succeeding, to kayak over a 30 metre waterfall in France. Addison described how immediately before the event he was focused on how often he needed to urinate:

> delivering the testimonial to those about that I was paralysed with fear... it is one thing to be paralysed with fear, but the unfortunate result of such a condition is the very real possibility of permanent paralysis ... It takes a very special mind to be able to put that fear aside.
>
> (Addison, 2003, p. 2)

So what have we learnt so far?

Research drawing upon psychoanalytic theory claims that the extreme sport experience characterises an activity where fear is either inhibited, not appropriately felt, or somehow explained away. However, research in stress seeking seems to discount this view. The indications are that participation in leisure activities where death is the most likely outcome of a mismanaged mistake or accident involves the experience of fear, but more than that, fear is actively sought. Critics of this perspective point out that the experience of intense fear may more accurately reflect the feelings of non-participants. That is, extreme sport participants develop the capacity to respond to potentially frightening situations in a manner quite different from those who do not participate in such activities, who may well be overwhelmed by a fear response. Research on the experience of anxiety indicates that whilst participants may generally be less fearful than most people in their day-to-day lives, participation facilitates fear. However, unlike many people in situations where acute fear is endured, extreme sports participants are not immobilised. Far from assuming the typical notion of flight, fight or freeze associated with the rush of adrenaline it would seem that participants are able to remain calm and focused on their performance. Participants know that fear is a constant companion that requires great psychological skill to overcome, and furthermore, that to freeze in the face of fear would be to invite injury or worse.

For those dedicated to extreme sports, the adrenaline junky stereotype is considered detrimental to their chosen engagement. This view is succinctly expressed by a BASE jumper:

> The trouble with BASE as it gets more well known is it starts to attract extremists, people who want that edge thing, that sort of high risk adrenaline, are coming across and they're dying.
>
> (Co-researcher, mid 30s)

Perhaps the most appropriate way of summing up what we have learnt so far is through the words of the same BASE jumper:

> All these clichés you hear, the classic saying like fear not death, it is your destiny, unless you're living on the edge you're taking up too much space, that's all ridiculous ... The most logical thing, the only natural thing, the most normal thing to be saying at a time like that is I'm scared, I hope I don't wet my pants! Oh God! Oh please, let me do this. They're the things we say. If you want the truth, if you want a true slogan for these kinds of sports it is Oh please – don't let me die!
>
> (Co-researcher, mid 30s)

The same BASE jumper goes on to explain that a decision to jump is made by balancing the natural state of fear with knowledge based on personal capabilities, technical expertise and environmental awareness. It is only when these considerations are effectively balanced that the magic alluded to above can be released.

Fear emerges as an important construct in our effort to better understand the extreme sport experience. Participants are clear about the intense feelings that are experienced during the preparation and pre-activity stage. Further, those who claim 'no fear' are most often considered, by experienced extreme sport participants, to be a danger to themselves and others. As one would expect, the human body prepares for the typical responses to fear: to run, fight or hide. However, the response is not one of flight, fight or freeze. An extreme sport participant accepts the inevitability of fear and is able to move through it in order to participate effectively.

Extreme sport experiences are unlikely to become less fear-inducing with expertise, rather contrary to the everyday experience of fear, the extreme sport participant overcomes the fear barrier to perform successfully despite the natural desire to react to fear by flight, fight, or freeze. It is the person's ability to move through the fear that enables the extreme sport experience. Furthermore, the experience is not brought about outside of one's control but is deliberately approached as if fear is the doorway to something more. By passing through this doorway, the experience that is the extreme sport experience is gained.

Reflections on fear and life

Within the phenomenological tradition, and, more specifically, existentialism, fear is central to the idea of living authentically, and the fear of death is regarded by Heidegger as being fundamental to recognising the temporality of our existence. For Heidegger (1996), fear consists of three interlinked elements: the object of fear, the act of fearing, and why it is that we are afraid. The object of fear is the thing which threatens us or has the potential of causing harm. The nearness of that threat determines the intensity of fear. But the question arises for extreme sports: what is the object which is fearsome? The immediate response is death, as this is a potential and, as previously argued, a possibility to be confronted. The outcome of such an experience is uncertain; it is only by experiencing it that the outcome can be known. Still, the aim of this chapter is to show that fear is a part of the extreme sport experience and that without fear, the extreme sport experience would not be the same.

For those adopting a traditional phenomenological approach, the concept of anxiety or more correctly, *angst*, may help shed light on this question (Heidegger, 1996), especially when the object of the feeling is uncertainty linked to death (May, 1983). The terms, fear and *angst* differ in that *angst* is an ontological inevitability whereas fear is more intense and situational. *Angst* or a more pervasive sense of apprehension is not to be confused with anxiety about certain events but considered in terms of a direct link to death. Thus angst is not anxiety as typically defined in English but a more powerful emotion that may be closer to dread (May, 1983). The essential understanding of *angst* is that:

It is an experience of threat which carries both anguish and dread, indeed the most painful and basic threat which any being can suffer, for it is the threat of loss of being itself.

(May, 1983, p. 111)

In the previous chapter we disputed the death-wish myth, nevertheless the potentiality of death is real. The notion of angst provides a link between the potential of death and the human experience, however, fear in the context of the extreme sports person is about constructive information which lies at the core of his or her expertise. Fear is no longer a simple and crude reaction or something that induces an immediate flight, fight or freeze response. Fear is highly nuanced and for the extreme sport participant such responses are not considered undesirable but have a capacity to provide cues and information that the activity should be taken seriously and the sports person is an active agent in negotiating the demands of the task.

In contrast to the Western traditions in which we avoid all things associated with fear and train our children to avoid fear laden situations there are traditions in which fear is not considered a troublesome emotion. For example, the Dalai Lama describes three kinds of fear: virtuous, non-virtuous and neutral. A virtuous fear is exemplified by the fear of evil; an example of the non-virtuous might be a shrinking aversion to an internal or external stimulus. The Dalai Lama considers fear as one of the emotions that needs to be effectively surmounted on the journey to enlightenment (Goleman, 2003). The ability to let go of the need to control is the essence of mental health. Fear is related to the need to control uncertainties. For Buddhism, the only way to deal with uncertainty is to accept that fear is a part of life and to unlearn that which has been learnt, perhaps even that which has been learnt through evolutionary tendencies (Goleman, 2003). Thus, a person is asked to surrender to uncertainty. In the extreme sport experience the outcome is uncertain. Death may result but then so might other experiences, such as elation. A major component of a fear state, whether anxiety, terror or fear itself, is uncertainty. This uncertainty triggers helplessness and a feeling of being manipulated by forces that we cannot control, which contradicts our learnt striving for control and therefore security. A BASE jumper described this challenge as follows:

I was seriously challenged and a couple of times I did think maybe all those people are right I am going to die, but I didn't. At the end of the day I had an epiphany because I did not die but I really enjoyed it. An environment that I never imagined existed was opened up to me. I realised that all that stuff that I had feared, like everybody else, was fundamentally wrong 'and I don't do that so I'm not crazy'. You know it's one of those self-validations.

(Co-researcher, 40s)

He thus explicates at least two components of the experience of fear, that is, the fear of death, the potential for elation and the fact that in this instance fear was transformational. A similar theme of transformation resulting from responding to fear is evident in the following:

> We do these things for a number of reasons but one of the most powerful reasons for me is overcoming my own personal fears. That gives you so much more of an insight into your being into your potential and into your capacity.
>
> (Co-researcher, 30s)

This BASE jumper clearly articulates the transformational potential of responding to fear as information which guides rational decision making in a manner that is perhaps counterintuitive to Western norms.

Fear is connected to both internal and external realities. For some people, the greatest reality is the internal reality and the greatest fear is external chaos. For these people the unknown, uncontrollable external forces provide the greatest influence. For others, the more significant reality is their sense of external reality and the greatest fear is represented by an internal state of abandonment or rejection. Being left alone with personal internal forces provides the greatest challenge. Extreme sports, it could be argued, involve both internal and external forces.

Fear has been interpreted as a positive contribution to personal growth and the development of authenticity. The activity does not necessarily have to be as extreme as BASE jumping or waterfall kayaking to facilitate these outcomes. For instance, fear for whitewater rafting participants helped cement a sense of self:

> Their concerns carry an undercurrent of fear of rafting – that this is something they might die doing. Such fears contribute to a perception of the experience as extraordinary and set the stage for a rise of intensification that extends and renews the self.
>
> (Arnould & Price, 1993, p. 29)

This relationship between fear, self-awareness and personal transformation has been well described in the literature. The challenge is not just about relating to experiences that might be fearful in new ways but also about transcending contemporary society's aversion to fear. A successful society is one which tends to 'insulate itself from both environmental (e.g. cold, dark, hunger) and societal/psychological (e.g. confrontation, alien cultures) fear' (Ewert, 1986, p. 45). Arguably, contemporary Western society is characterised by constant and endemic fear. Paradoxically, by facing and overcoming fear a person gains self-knowledge and personal growth (Ewert, 1986). We may speculate that the extreme sports person seeks this experience: the approach of the potential of non-being and the potential for life-fulfilment.

For Heidegger (1996) the greatest edge is the threat of physical death. By approaching threat and moving through the accompanying fear, a person moves towards authenticity. As we have seen, the outcome of an extreme sport experience is not certain death, but a potential that death may occur. Thus the sensation of fear is the fear of possible death, fear of an unknown ending where life or death may result but, if approached and successfully traversed, fulfilment and wonder await.

Summary

Contrary to the 'no fear' hypothesis, the extreme sport experience involves intense fear. However, rather than let fear take control, extreme sport participants continue to participate in their chosen activity. They accept that control of the future is not always possible. They face these intense and nuanced fears, move through them and commit to informed action. By taking action based on knowledge about self, task and the environment, in the face of their experiential understanding of intense fear, participants move towards a potentially greater understanding of self. Participants who exercise agency in the face of fear report experiencing something that can only be described as magical. That is, by facing our greatest 'true' fears whether they are of death, uncertainty or something else, and taking action despite these fears, we transcend the ordinary. Or to put it another way, by not answering this call to adventure in order to avoid such intense fears, we perhaps experience life as potentially less meaningful and filled with fear.

So, as this part of our journey of understanding draws to a close, it seems appropriate to briefly review some of the most important points reviewed in the last three chapters covering risk, death and fear. The relationship between extreme sports and risk is misunderstood. This was very evident in the voices of extreme sports participants. In our discussion of death and fear it was evident that traditional notions were very limited in informing our understanding of the extreme port experience. In fact it would be more accurate to think of notions of both death and fear as providing a type of gateway to a sense of elation and personal transformation that can only be understood by reconceptualising the meaning of both death and of fear in the life of the extreme sports person. The more able one is to experientially come to terms with the reality of one's own death, the more able one is to live one's own unique life. Accepting and confronting fear offers the potential for extraordinary experiences. However, the relationship to fear and death are also connected in that the fear which extreme sport participants experience and move through is for all intents and purposes a fear that derives from the potential of death.

If these arguments are accepted, then extreme sport participants should be describing something extraordinary and something life-changing. Perhaps the reader has already observed that throughout the previous three chapters the quotes from participants have invariably hinted at something wondrous which will be described in the chapters following.

References

Addison, C. (2003). Fear. Retrieved 20 August 2004 from www.eruditium.org/pete/fear. html.

Arnould, E. J. & Price, L. L. (1993). River magic: Extraordinary experience and the extended service encounter. *Journal of Consumer Research, 20,* 24–45.

Breivik, G. (1996). Personality, sensation seeking and risk taking among Everest climbers. *International Journal of Sport Psychology, 27,* 308–320.

Breivik, G., Roth, W. T. & Jorgensen, P. E. (1998). Personality, psychological states and heart rate in novice and expert parachutists. *Personality and Individual Differences, 25,* 365–380.

Elias, N. & Dunning, E. (1986). Quest for excitement in leisure. In N. Elias & E. Dunning (Eds), *Quest for excitement: Sport and leisure in the civilizing process* (pp. 63–90). Oxford: Basil Blackwell.

Ewert, A. (1986). Fear: uses and abuses in outdoor adventure activities. *The Underseas Journal, First Quarter,* 44–48.

Fullana, M., Harrison, B., Soriano-Mas, C., Vervliet, B., Cardoner, N., Àvila-Parcet, A. & Radua, J. (2016). Neural signatures of human fear conditioning: An updated and extended meta-analysis of fMRI studies. *Molecular Psychiatry, 21,* 500–508.

Goleman, D. (Ed.) (2003). *Destructive emotions and how we can overcome them: A dialogue with the Dalai Lama.* London: Bloomsbury.

Gray, J. A. (1987). *The psychology of fear and stress* (2nd ed.). Cambridge: Cambridge University Press.

Greenberg, P. F. (1977). The thrill seekers. *Human Behaviour, 6,* 16–21.

Heidegger, M. (1996). *Being and time: A translation of Sein and Zeit.* (J. Stambaugh, Trans.). Albany, NY: State University of New York.

Houston, C. S. (1968). The last blue mountain. In S. Z. Klausner (Ed.), *Why man takes chances* (pp. 48–58). New York: Doubleday.

Hunt, J. C. (1996). Diving the wreck: Risk and injury in sport scuba diving. *Psychoanalytic Quarterly, LXV,* 591–622.

Magni, G., Rupolo, G., Simini, G., De Leo, D. & Rampazzo, M. (1985). Aspects of the psychology and personality of high altitude mountain climbers. *International Journal of Sport Psychology, 16,* 12–19.

May, R. (1983). *The discovery of being: Writings in existential psychology.* New York: W. W. Norton & Company.

Ogilvie, B. C. (1974). The sweet psychic jolt of danger. *Psychology Today, 8*(5), 88–94.

Robinson, D. W. (1985). Stress seeking: Selected behavioural characteristics of elite rock climbers. *Journal of Sport Psychology, 7,* 400–404.

Rowe, D. (2002). *Beyond fear* (2nd ed.). London: Harper Collins Publishers.

Schultheis, R. (1996). *Bone games: Extreme sports, shamanism, Zen, and the search for transcendence.* New York: Breakaway Books.

Slanger, E. & Rudestam, K. E. (1997). Motivation and disinhibition in high risk sports: Sensation seeking and self-efficacy. *Journal of Research in Personality, 31,* 355–374.

Stone, J. (2003a). Inner city whitewater: Jessie Stone's kayaking camp hits its line. *Paddler Magazine, 24.* Retrieved November 2003 from www.paddlermagazine.com/issues/2003_2/article_213.shtml.

Stone, J. (2003b). Spotlight on Jessie Stone. *Discover Boating.* Online November 2003.

8 Experience of transformation

The extreme sports experience may well be described as a profound experience of transformation (Brymer, 2009, 2012, 2013). This chapter begins by examining the typical attributes of extreme sports participants that relate to this concept in order to position a more comprehensive explication of the lived experience of extreme sports people. This critical assessment of previous work is set against the words and viewpoints of those who participate, as we begin to explore the lived experience. Reflections from participants are explicated and mapped out against the relevant literature to gain an understanding of a theme emerging from the data; that is, the experience of transformation. This construct has previously been referred to as 'awakening' (Welwood, 2014).

Extreme sports exist in a context. To consider the extreme sport experience as purely *modern* and *Western* tends to negate the experiences of peoples across the millennia who have undertaken activities out of the ordinary. This includes those travellers who have ascended the highest mountains for the sake of religious ceremony. For example, the remains of human sacrifices have been found on mountains in the Andes as high as 22,000 feet. In pre-historic times Indigenous American medicine men climbed mountains for vision quests (Schultheis, 1996). In one example an eagle trap was found by the first Westerners to climb Blanca, the fourth highest peak in Colorado. Buddhist and Taoist monks search out the high mountains in the Himalayas to gain powers, as these places were considered the connection between heaven and earth. The prowess of our forebears is illustrated by reports of Chinese attempts to destroy carvings situated high up in the Tibetan mountainside. The Chinese authorities could not achieve this without highly technical abseiling devices to reach areas that holy men had reached with apparent ease. In Japan the Shugendo monks have been climbing the highest mountains in search of spiritual enlightenment for more than 1,500 years. Furthermore, those climbing to the roof of the world are most likely do so only with the guidance of skilled and determined guides from the Sherpa community. Buddhist and Hindu sadhus and shamans have been spotted as high up as 22,500 feet in the Himalayas, and at one time a mystic was even found asleep covered with snow in the middle of a blizzard, shoeless and wearing only thin trousers, shirt and three-button jacket (Schultheis, 1996). More recently, shoeless African mystics have been reported on the summit of Mount Kenya in areas supposedly only reachable by Western mountaineers equipped with ice axes and crampons (Schultheis, 1996). Even from a modern perspective, an exclusively Western outlook on extreme sports negates examples such as the first Japanese all-woman team to reach the summit of Everest in 1976. Mountain climbing has been traced to the BC era and the first deliberate attempt to summit high mountains traced to the 1790s by Western scientists attempting to 'discover' the world beyond familiar borders. The first mountaineering guidebook on the Alps was published in 1860.

Surfing, which had spiritual connotations, was banned by the Calvinists as far back as 1838 though the indications are that surfing was part of Hawaiian life as far back as AD 400. The Pentecost Islanders, ancient Hopis and Aztecs were reportedly jumping off structures of perhaps 100 feet or higher before Westerners 'discovered' their lands. Leonardo da Vinci is credited as the first designer of useable parachutes in the mid fifteenth century and the Chinese the first to use a parachute device hundreds of years BC. The first recorded parachute jump was witnessed in 1797. Records of the first BASE jump have been traced back to 1615 when Fausto Verancio was supposed to have jumped from a bridge in Venice with a parachute. However, despite these examples there is a body of literature that attributes extreme sports to particular modern, Western groups and sub-cultures.

Epitomising the ideal Western male

It is commonly assumed that the extreme sport participant epitomises modern Western male characteristics. The implicit message is if you undertake an extreme sport you will automatically transform to an idealised version of Western male adulthood, presumably as a caterpillar transforms to a butterfly. The association is often one of acceptable rebellion, peer position, masculinity adventurousness, and natural leadership where all too often women are relegated to being attracted to extreme sportsmen by 'their youthful virility, independence and spirit of adventure' (Pollay, 2001, p. 72).

This relationship is culturally ingrained as epitomised by modern marketing which reflects dominant values. This is associated with extreme sport products, products on the periphery of extreme sports and also products with no distinct extreme sport connection. Even products, such as drinks, tobacco and alcohol, with no discernible connection at all to extreme sports have associated themselves with the extreme sport experience (Pollay, 2001). Close-up images of solo extreme sport participants wearing mirrored sunglasses engaging in glamorous and exciting activities have been developed to associate the product with 'positive' masculine attributes.

The image of the extreme sport experience as one that projects peculiarly Western adult male attributes has also been noted by theorists and researchers (Groves, 1987; Wheaton, 2003). For example, extreme sports have been presented as a means for Western male blue-collar workers to demonstrate individualisation, competition and success. White-collar workers could achieve these characteristics at work, blue-collar workers had to find this image through extreme sports. Whilst it may be that the balance of participation is still in favour of males, this is more likely a response to societal expectations rather than a response to the extreme sports themselves. That is, thought patterns that associate extreme sports with 'masculine' attributes may not be considering the total picture. Women have been pioneers in extreme sports. For example Olsen (2001) traced female high-level mountaineers to 1799. Similarly, the first woman parachutist undertook a 3,000 foot jump in 1799 and landed safely in the Tivoli gardens of Paris. The assumption that extreme sports portray certain predetermined attributes required for the modern Western adult male is little more than a self-fulfilling prophecy.

The continual push to portray extreme sports as a legitimate way of living out individualised, competitive and independent attributes without referring to the level of experience or knowledge required is in part responsible for the impression that extreme sports are deadly activities. This recurrent emphasis on the idealised representation contributes to the incidence of accidents and deaths. Because the knowledge and experience required for participation is overshadowed by these unfortunate projections, inexperienced participants may be skipping essential steps and dying as a result (Bachmann & Moldofsky, 1999). Breashears (1999), a veteran Everest mountaineer, supports this argument when he reported that even as a well-respected, experienced climber in his midtwenties, he realised that he was too young and inexperienced to climb Everest. The projection of extreme sports as the epitome of modern Western male attributes is just that, a projection.

Extreme sports are more gender neutral than appreciated and actually provide a potential to merge traditional male and female norms:

> Young men have been able to access something traditionally defined as feminine, that is, to value that which comes out of the state of being while keeping a capacity for action, traditionally coded as masculine. The opposite is also true for young women. Youths of both sexes have sought a harmonious fusion with nature.
>
> (Midol & Broyer, 1995, p. 208)

Attitudes, body shape and body movements challenge the norms associated with men and women and the views of the traditional patriarchal society. This notion is supported by the writings of those reflecting on extreme sports:

> There is no such thing as a glass ceiling in the mountains; male-dominated though mountaineering may be, I found no resistance to my quick rise to the top other than an occasional ice shelf.
>
> (Yakutchik, 1995, p. 1)

While the assumption that extreme sports promote the acquisition of idealised Western masculine characteristics is well ingrained in contemporary society, these assumptions do not actually reflect the lived experience.

Neotribes and transformation

The last few decades have been witness to an enormous increase in extreme sport participation and a decrease in traditional sport participation. Some theorists and researchers link this change to identification with certain sub-culture or neotribe norms. Neotribe or sub-cultural identification has been considered in terms of role identity, social identity and self-categorisation. Identity characteristics for both role identity and social identity are usually explicitly stated by the culture in question, though sometimes they are implicitly determined. Self-categorisation suggests that individuals choose different social group identities for different contexts. Specific cultural norms are identified as central in determining group identity. The norms and values of chosen groups are readily accepted.

As with the hypothesised process of transformation into an idealised modern Western male, extreme sports are said to be a function of youth sub-cultures. Participation is either about being identified as a person who enjoys taking risks or about hedonism and social uniqueness, depending on the generational label being characterised. Often, the assumption is that participants will outgrow the need to participate as they become adults. This is challenged in the current research which focuses on people over the age of thirty.

In examining extreme sports and transformation of identity, researchers and theorists have posited a focus on pre-determined identity formation. However, on careful examination these assumptions do not portray the lived experience of participants. This is epitomised by a BASE jumper who noted that not only does the identity 'extreme sport' participant not fit, but even being identified as a BASE jumper is just a convenience:

> I just think it's a convenient label we have to put on things but if you look at a community of BASE jumpers then it will be different for all of them what they get out of it and I don't classify it as an extreme sport.
>
> (Co-researcher, mid 30s)

And following an enquiry as to whether she would prefer a different title:

> I don't care what anyone else labels it – it only matters what it means to me. Now I want people to understand that it's a valid worthwhile thing to do and that you're cheating yourself when you label it as crazy as everyone does. To just say 'oh that's crazy' is an indication that they are constantly judging and prejudicing and cheating themselves of a whole world of other possibilities and a whole other way of thinking about things. So I would like to see it understood better but a label is meaningless.
>
> (Co-researcher, mid 30s)

Opposing perspective

Other perspectives on extreme sport activities reveal an identity at odds with the personal qualities encouraged by modern Western countries. Rather than identifying with certain cultural norms, participation in extreme sports is supposed to express attributes of unpredictability and opposition to safe, predictable and boring societal regimes. In Western societies 'the confrontation between self and uncertainty [and] the need to act, reflect, and appreciate our actions' has been reduced (Holyfield, 1999, p. 25). The implication is that in contemporary Western societies the extreme sport experience is about living a life that is not constrained by a desire for control, and instead embraces uncertainty. The 'what' of the transformation takes its form from an association with a like-minded 'deviant' group. The extreme sport experience is characterised by a deviant social attitude and set of attributes. However, other writers have contradicted this perspective and emphasised mainstream values such as healthy competition, personal drive and individual excellence.

Whichever of these two explanations one subscribes to, the perception reflects a peculiarly Western perspective, where extreme sports participants are motivated by values that are either pro mainstream society (individuality, competition, independence and achievement) or by a rejection of mainstream values. In the latter case, either from a desire to portray an image of excitement, bohemianism and unpredictability or a desire to identify with and attain attributes of a particular sub-group.

Despite the contention held by many the relationship between extreme sports and the transformations experienced by participants may be more complex. Extreme sport participants most often report that experiences of transformation were unanticipated and unexpected. For example, in a study of the whitewater rafting experience participants reported enduring and positive life changes as a result of participation (Arnould, Price & Otnes, 1999). These life changes were unplanned and occurred when the initial hedonistic intentions were transcended and the experience transformed the participants' relationships to themselves and the world.

Participant reports indicate that not only do motivations evolve, but individual lived experience is changed as a result of participation. That is, *'Life'* is transformed, not just viewpoints on participation. In contrast to current perspectives where an understanding of transformation is often limited to predefined constructs, such as self-esteem and self-efficacy, experiences of transformation are deep and extensive, filtering across all aspects of life and even influencing perspectives on what it means to be human.

Self-constructs

The interaction between lived identity and social environment has been an area of study. Individuals who perceive a social threat to 'self' experience diminished positive affect, decreased self-esteem and increased hostility (Heatherton & Vohs, 2000). Nevertheless, extreme sport participants invariably report that social perception does not influence their decisions. Research on the relationship between activity and an improved sense of self is limited and might only relate to a person's sporting identity. A study on rock climbers, for example, found that regular climbing did not change perceived competence or self-esteem (Iso-Ahola & Graefe, 1988). The study found that specific climbs could positively affect self-esteem if accompanied by perceived competence. However, the converse is also true: negative experiences can reduce self-esteem. It does not require an extreme activity to enhance self-esteem and therefore there would appear to be no direct relationship to self-esteem and participation at an extreme level.

However, participants in extreme sports consistently report a life transformation which goes well beyond their involvement in a specific activity. For example, Cathie Cush, a deep sea diver, considered that just one extreme sport experience was significant in changing her perspective on life:

> It was also certainly a tremendous sense of accomplishment, and a boost to self-esteem. I could have a client screaming at me, and I would think, 'Buddy, I've been places that would make you cry'. And even to this day, I feel I carry that with me.
>
> (Cush cited in Terwilliger, 1998, p. 1E)

Self-efficacy is the belief that one has the personal capabilities to successfully complete a task. Research suggests that self-efficacy might be one construct that differs in extreme sport participants. Greater self-belief enables the participant to focus on the task at hand without interference from fear or anxiety.

> They set themselves challenges that hold their interest and they approach threatening tasks nonanxiously. Instead of being disturbed by thoughts concerning their own capabilities, they can direct all effort to the task at hand.
>
> (Slanger & Rudestam, 1997, p. 356)

The experience of fear and sense of self efficacy are interrelated. According to common stereotypes, participants should feel 'no fear' yet, as already argued, participants generally report intense fear. Furthermore, it is not uncommon for participants to also experience thoughts and feelings of inadequacy whilst participating. For example, an extreme kayaker noted:

> People always say you must have an amazing positive mental attitude to know you are going to make it, but although I think I'm gonna make it, I never actually feel like I'm gonna make it.
>
> (Co-researcher, late 30s)

He later elaborated on his 'nagging doubts':

> I sometimes wish I had a more positive mental attitude because it wouldn't make any difference to whether I ran the fall or I didn't but I'd like to feel positive on the way down.
>
> (Co-researcher, late 30s)

The Everest guide Pemba Nuru Sherpa expressed the feeling as 'I felt only five per cent hope getting back alive and 95 per cent certainty I would die' (Sherpa, 2003, p. 88). Similar self-doubts were experienced by many extreme sport participants interviewed. It might be that self-efficacy has a ceiling where continued development in the sport does not correlate with continual increases in self-efficacy. Self-efficacy does not fully explain involvement in extreme sports where death is a potential outcome.

In summary, many researchers and theorists have recognised the potential for personal transformation and the contribution of extreme sports to an enhanced sense of self, yet it would seem that research is at best contradictory and at worst on the wrong track. Something which remains undefined influences a participant's understanding of self, perhaps best expressed by the following quote from a professional extreme kayaker: 'kayaking has changed my life, it has taught me who I am. Going to rivers changes who you are in a positive way' (Luden cited in Heath, 2002, p. 1).

Notions of deep and enduring transformations have been observed in many other contexts. In most cases transformations are considered instant, unexpected and permanent. A BASE enthusiast (a committed and experienced medical practitioner) who was persuaded to take part in a single event as an adult of twenty-eight years, despite initially thinking that undertaking such activities was crazy and tantamount to a death wish, put it this way:

> A whole 'environment' that I never imagined existed was opened to me. My life has been radically altered by that choice, by that day.... I just went to work and this guy said 'hey do you want to do this on the weekend' and I didn't know that my life was about to be turned totally on its head on the weekend.
>
> (Co-researcher, late 40s)

Participation in extreme sports is not an external pull to identify with a group or an activity in order to enhance an external or internal construction about self. Rather, the extreme sport experience transforms the lived world of participants in another, unique, way. Participants are clear that the extreme sport experience is transformational spilling over to many aspects of life. For some extreme sport activities (e.g. BASE), the actual 'active' element of the experience may only last a few seconds – however, the essential nature of the experience is more lasting. This is not just in terms of thinking about the experience or building up towards the experience, which in itself is reported to be enduring, but also how life is transformed. Participation is transformational and extends beyond the self and includes relationships with others and the world. A surfer described this as equating to the sense of awe experienced while surfing a wave the size of a three storey building:

> That's what I mean when I say 'that buzz'. I mean I might die in bed. I'll probably try and remember those things and I'll just go 'yes, I'm

ready to go, see you later', because nothing can upset you when you think of those things. I think it just makes you a better person, makes you more content, makes you realise more what life is all about and the pleasures in life.

(Co-researcher, mid 50s)

Although this quote reflected his experience of surfing big waves in general he exemplified the benefits through this story about one particular wave and the transformation that resulted. He claimed that the inner changes provided strength to negotiate life challenges described as the 'worst moments of my whole life' (co-researcher, mid 50s). In the interview his face lit up as he described that wave and he seemed to become lighter in appearance, almost as if he had only surfed the wave the day before. It was only after sharing this story that he revealed that the event took place fifteen years prior to our interview. Bane (1996) wrote:

Extreme sports change people who participate in them. While a bungee jumper might feel a certain rush of immortality, the other extreme sports offer something far less tangible – and far more rewarding.

(Bane, 1996, p. 9)

So to sum up the argument thus far, the extreme sport experience is more than the momentary action of for example jumping off a cliff with a parachute, as the reported experience of transformation is intrinsic to the experience. The experience includes pre and post aspects to the 'active' element of the experience but the process of transformation is often dynamic, ongoing and lasting. Furthermore, these experiences of transformation seem to be instant and unexpected, leading to the realisation that the experience may not be about a deliberate search for a socio-culturally or psychologically pre-determined ideal.

Transformation as experience

The lived experience of extreme sport participants sets them apart from the non-participant. Participants describe an experience that radically alters meaningfulness, manageability and comprehensibility and enhances their perceived intra- and interpersonal capabilities and sense of confidence in their relationship with others and the world around them. That is, part of transformation is linked to positive changes in social interactions and their ability to 'do'. Participants report increased self-confidence. One of the foremost extreme climbers of our time, Lynn Hill, explained that confidence should not be confused with egotism. For Hill, such a self-centred approach would be counterproductive and perhaps even deadly. Hill considered every climb provided an opportunity for personal growth and 'provides a very meaningful experience' (Hill cited in Olsen, 2001). An extreme skier put it this way:

I think that skiing has given me incredible confidence in myself, it's been invaluable for that. I really really like who I am as a person and it's because I like who I am as a skier and I've grown to have so much confidence in myself as a person.

(Co-researcher, mid 30s)

Thus, part of the experience of transformation refers to positive changes in a participant's ability to perform and interact. However, this change is not about constructs such as self-esteem, self-efficacy or self-mastery which are drawn from a reductionistic psychology. For a BASE jumper participant, the experience is essentially an emergent experience of being 'self-possessed' (co-researcher, mid 30s).

The extreme sport experience has been described as providing freedom from anxiety and the tendency towards excessive self-consciousness and concern for appearances such as waistlines and weight. This freedom resulting from hurtling towards the potential of death alters the participant's values and priorities. In one study, climbers were said to:

overcome some of their own inner obstacles, among these, fear – of heights, of loss of control, of death.

(Roberts, 1994, p. 4)

In particular, Roberts cited a forty-two-year-old climber who considered that climbing helped with overcoming his fear of death. Co-researchers in our study also considered that fears outside of the extreme sport experience become insignificant, not that such fears were not felt, just that the power of fear is reduced and re-categorised and considered as important information.

Other fears are generally insignificant. The ones that plague most people every day, like speaking up, being themselves, looking foolish, people won't like me, all of those fears just seem insignificant and ridiculous.

(Co-researcher, mid 30s)

A BASE jumper in his late forties felt that this sense of transformation had ramifications that were part of a general struggle to be authentic. The extreme sport experience facilitated the realisation of his own potential, capacity and meaningfulness. He described transformation as a process: instead of fear determining his choice and restricting his freedoms, he reframed the relationship:

You have choice and you have freedom to have choice and that can be physical, emotional or mental.

(Co-researcher, late 40s)

Another BASE jumper considered that she had transcended the fear of death. Essentially, the experience of fear is still present but it has lost its power to constrain action, thus it becomes a transformational process. Participants report more positive perceptions on self and experiencing life as having endless achievable possibilities.

A changed view on life and living

The extreme sport experience transforms participant views on life and relationships with others. Sometimes this is about becoming less judgemental about life and others. At other times, it is about becoming more open or aware. For example, Guy Cotter, the extreme mountaineer, noted that mountaineering had taught him about life, death and spirituality. He appreciated that what he once judged in terms of right and wrong he now welcomed as different perspectives. He reported that mountaineering had removed the normal insulation from reality experienced in everyday life and instilled a more measured appreciation of the meaning of life and death. Being so close to death enabled Cotter to appreciate even the simple things in life more acutely, from a different perspective and with fresh eyes (Spence, 2001).

A BASE jumper and co-researcher in this study recalled that before BASE he was engrossed in his professional life as a successful emergency medical professional, on a defined career path representing an ideal for many.

> I can only compare myself now with what I used to be when I was not an adventurer and was a more closed, arrogant, limited, unbalanced person and you know the worst part was I didn't even know I was unbalanced.
>
> (Co-researcher, late 40s)

Later he likened the changes to getting off the treadmill of a pre-determined, socially desirable pathway. Following his extreme sport experiences, he opined that he responded to patients with greater awareness and in a more human way.

> Pretty well every aspect I handle differently now, for example when I practice medicine now I'm a lot more aware of a patient not just as 'bed four's got a stroke' or whatever. I'm much more aware that Mrs so and so is a lady who's got a lot of other things and just happens to have a stroke right now.
>
> (Co-researcher, late 40s)

Other participants described similar experiences whereby life was deemed to have 'no limits'. The extreme sport experience facilitates a life liberated from externally and internally imposed limitations. A female BASE jumper expressed this view by noting that the extreme sport experience taught her that her possibilities were endless and that the absolutes she had previously imposed on herself were not absolutes but self-inflicted constraints which prevented her realising her potential. She recognised this as liberation from 'holistic gravity' or in other terms, from all those aspects of life that pulled her down.

The experience of transformation might also be seen as realising a link between transcendence of externally and internally imposed limitations and reframing the power of fear. Jacobs (1998) a double PhD (health psychology and education) and kayak explorer describes how extreme sports facilitated changes for him:

> I had changed. I found myself to be more forgiving and more patient; reflection replaced reaction more often than before. My hard logic more readily made room for intuitive considerations, something I had seldom given much notice. I no longer thought of truth as something definite and unyielding but as something woven into both sides of an issue.
>
> (Jacobs, 1998, p. 17)

Later, Jacobs wondered whether the intense fear he had to face as a result of the experience had triggered deep concentration and subsequently released some profound abilities, which he termed primal awareness. We will return to his fascinating story later.

Another typical response is that participation at such an extreme level teaches humility (Ahluwalia, 2003; Breashears, 1999; Muir, 2003; Spence, 2001). Bane (1996) described his experiences as:

> I came to risk sports looking for Indiana Jones, or, at least, someone like him … I have never met anyone who has stood, however precariously, on the flanks of a great mountain, or who has been, however briefly, to the dark world at the edge of the abyss, and not come back changed. Changed how? More humble, perhaps, more aware of the fragility of life.
>
> (Bane, 1996, p. 232)

A BASE jumper and co-researcher in this project put it this way:

> Well for me it's about accepting that you're mortal and that you're very vulnerable and that you're like a piece of dust really or a leaf in the wind.
>
> (Co-researcher, late 30s)

However, rather than the reality of her own mortality defeating her, she noted that being like a 'leaf in the wind' empowered her to become self-possessed and to make a difference.

> When you accept that, then the power of one day becomes more than just some sort of paying lip service to an idea. … while you're like a leaf in the wind you can also make a difference and you can also explore parts of your self that you had no concept of even being there.
>
> (Co-researcher, late 30s)

These two quotes exemplify the dynamic of transformation – for example the effect of accepting death, connotations of releasing control or surrendering during the 'active' aspect of the event and exploring parts of the self that may have been hidden from awareness. We will develop these themes further in the chapters following.

Laird Hamilton, an internationally renowned pioneer of extreme surfing, considered that he developed an appreciation of life and living through his experiences of the natural world as something greater than humanity, a realisation that changed him emotionally, physically, cognitively and spiritually (Williams, Hamilton & Kachmer, 2001). Jacobs (1998) extended his earlier perceptions on his transformation to include an appreciation of profound and spiritual changes that even awakened hitherto unappreciated skills as a horse whisperer. Reaching the highest point on Earth is also a prolific instigator of spiritual transformation (Ahluwalia, 2003; Benegas, 2003; Chiow, 2003; Weare, 2003).

Feelings of deep psychological wellbeing and meaningfulness have been reported as a connection with a core self, as realised by a co-researcher whilst reflecting on how extreme sport participation facilitated his connection to knowledge about his own core self:

> Finding my own truth, my own being, my own core and honouring that because that's the essence of finding your own meaningfulness. It's my concept of spirituality which is very much linked to my emotional and mental health.
>
> (Co-researcher, mid 40s)

In summary, the extreme sport experience enables participants to break through personal barriers and develop understanding of their own resourcefulness and emotional, cognitive, physical and spiritual capabilities and wellbeing. Phenomenologically, the horizons of their world are expanded. The breakthroughs described appear to trigger profound changes in personal philosophy or views on life and reality. Extreme sport participants report enduring changes, perhaps stemming from a greater understanding of their own human potential.

Lived experience involves unanticipated responses with life-changing implications. The changes often occur instantaneously but are strengthened through continual participation. Participants learn that fear does not have to control them and that life is for living. They report learning humility that allows for something greater than a limited anthropocentric sense of self. This transcendence of a previous sense of being and life transforms their understanding and capabilities in multiple aspects of life, including a more sensitive apprehension of their relationship with others. Broadly, a previous self is transcended and life takes on a new and deeper meaningfulness. Thus participants undergo a type of re-birth that enables a process of intra-personal transformation, inter-personal transformation and even extra-personal changes.

The transformational benefits of extraordinary experiences that take place in the natural world, akin to extreme sports, have been previously documented. Extraordinary experiences are necessarily unique and differ from flow experiences (absorption, involvement and joy), from peak experiences (intense joy) and peak performance (superior functioning). Extraordinary experiences require neither extra effort nor an independent relational model but are necessarily outside the ordinary. Typically, these experiences are described as involving intense emotional experiences that often result in life changes. Often, these changes are recalled, as if in the present, years later and the lessons learnt transfer into other aspects of life. In these instances, nature is seen as immeasurably powerful and the human as intensely vulnerable. The relationship between the extreme sportsperson and nature 'activates a link between people and natural forces' that transforms both existentially and socially (Arnould et al., 1999, p. 38). Transformation resulting from participation in extreme sports requires that participants be actively and physically involved. In contrast to the contemporary emphasis on risk reduction, the activity necessarily entails some degree of overt danger and uncertainty of outcome. The intense emotional and cognitive arousal experienced in such activities acts as a stimulus for expanded awareness of self and others. Participation in extreme sport, where the unexpected is always present, allows for expanded awareness of self that facilitates and develops awareness of others and more immediate, authentic and open interactions. The extreme sport experience changes attitudes and values. The quality of the experience becomes the point of judgement for all aspects of the person's life.

A phenomenological perspective

There is a dearth of phenomenological literature exploring the human dimensions of personal transformation. Yet, as Hanna (1993a, 1993b) argued, the phenomenological method itself, as outlined by Husserl and Heidegger, might provide insights into such experiences of transformation. The practice of phenomenological reduction enriched Husserl's psychic life and triggered a personal transformation that he reportedly compared to a 'religious conversion' (Husserl cited in Hanna, 1993b, p. 41). Whilst differences in the descriptions of the phenomenological reduction by these two philosophers have been widely documented, Heidegger also seemed to have experienced transformation (Hanna, 1993b; Zimmerman, 1986). Though neither Zimmerman nor Hanna specifically detailed whether Heidegger's changes involved re-birth, humility, nonjudgement and so on, they did describe them as profound and transcendent and resulting from deliberately courting or entering the 'transpersonal realms' (Hanna, 1993b, p. 41). Heidegger's experience of transformation was akin to an experience of personal enlightenment.

An implication of Hanna's (1993b) thesis is that the transformation resulting from the extreme sport experience might be similar to the transcendental understanding of the phenomenological reduction and therefore akin to reaching transpersonal realms. Even though a description of the changed self was not proffered by either Husserl or Heidegger, the end result was a profound change in their understanding of consciousness (for Husserl) and Being (for Heidegger) and in their existential understandings (Hanna, 1993a). To return 'to the things themselves' also requires a way of knowing beyond thinking which is often described as 'seeing' (Husserl, 1977); a way of knowing prior to thought (Merleau-Ponty, 1999).

Often the experience includes bliss, transcendence, freedom (or liberation), self-knowledge, consciousness, being, ultimate reality and an element of truth. Experiences such as the phenomenological reduction alters perceptions on what was considered to be 'reality' and as such results in deep personal transformations (Hanna, 1993b). In Husserl's case the process triggered an opening 'to a possible self-experience that can be perfected, and perhaps enriched, without limit' (Husserl, 1977, p. 29). If extreme sports can result in transformations similar to this, then the descriptions of participants should reflect this similarity. Such a discussion is for a later chapter. For now it is sufficient to note the similarities. At this stage, we wish to point to the similarities between experiences of transformation as reflected in the writings of the founders of the phenomenological movement and the experiences of extreme sports persons.

Heidegger's concept of the 'fourfold' might be relevant to understanding transformation in the context of extreme sports where death is a real potentiality. The fourfold involves four components, earth, sky, divinity and mortals. Extreme sports expose people to awe-inspiring aspects of nature, always in juxtaposition of earth and sky, and appreciation of forces larger than the self. As noted in the previous chapter on death these experiences are necessarily coupled with an awareness of one's own mortality. A greater awareness of the reality of imminent death gained by participating in activities that are potentially life threatening highlights the preciousness of each moment, opens a door to individual potential and enhances connection with humanity. Death awareness provides meaning to individual lives. We speculate that extreme sports are transformational possibly for their experiential realisation of the fourfold.

Philosophical writings from Buddhist, Hindu and Taoist traditions all note the potential of deep transformations that manifest themselves as core personality or lifeworld changes. In many traditions, transformations are deliberately sought through involvement in activities that are potentially lethal, the aim being to collapse the walls of ignorance, pride and ego. To reach this point a person must become fully, profoundly, self-aware. One needs to detach oneself from the external world and focus on the internal world (Campbell, 1993). We argue that the extreme sport experience, with its unknowns and potential dangers, initiates a focus on the internal and contributes to an experience of positive transformation.

Summary

The aim of this chapter was to explore the structure of the transformative aspects of the extreme sport experience. We have argued that participants' understanding or knowledge about themselves changes as a direct result of participating in their chosen extreme sport. The experience is likely to be strengthened through continued involvement in the chosen activity. Life and sense of self is experienced as changed, often instantaneously. Participants report a range of responses including positive capabilities, humility, meaningfulness and spirituality that facilitates greater appreciation of sense of place bounded by land and sky. This experience of transcendence of a previous sense of self transforms participants in personal and interpersonal aspects of life. The experience results in positive, personal and life-enriching transformations which result in participants becoming more aware and capable in the personal, interpersonal and extra-personal spheres.

Similar processes of transformation have been described in phenomenological practice, wisdom philosophy, and other fields. Such writings have extended human possibilities and indicated that certain transformations are often accompanied by more positive relationships to death and the fear of death – concepts already considered in the context of extreme sports. However, a change in one's relationship to death cannot be the entire phenomenological experience; it is just a point along the journey. Such transformative experiences are accompanied by changes in a participant's relationship to self. We are left with the key to our quest, that is, to discover the essence of the extreme sports experience. Does it lie with the sense of transformation described in this chapter or does it lie in the process of becoming who we are?

References

Ahluwalia, H. P. S. (2003). Major (ret) H. P. S. Ahluwalia. In C. Gee, G. Weare & M. Gee (Eds), *Everest: Reflections from the top* (p. 3). London: Rider.

Arnould, E. J., Price, L. L. & Otnes, C. (1999). Making consumption magic. *Journal of Contemporary Ethnography, 28*(1), 33–68.

Bachmann, H. & Moldofsky, L. (1999). Switzerland's river of tears: The tragic deaths of 21 young adventurers raise the questions about regulation of 'extreme' sports. *Time International, 154*(5), 40.

Bane, M. (1996). *Over the edge: A regular guy's odyssey in extreme sports*. New York: Macmillan.

Benegas, W. (2003). Willie Benegas. In C. Gee, G. Weare & M. Gee (Eds), *Everest: Reflections from the top* (p. 10). London: Rider.

Breashears, D. (1999). *High exposure: An enduring passion for Everest and unforgiving places*. New York: Simon & Schuster.

Brymer, E. (2009). Extreme sports as a facilitator of ecocentricity and positive life changes. *World Leisure Journal, 51*(1), 47–53.

Brymer, E. (2012). Transforming adventures: Why extreme sports should be included in adventure programming. In B. Martin & M. Wagstaff (Eds), *Controversial issues in adventure programming* (pp. 165–174). Champaign, IL: Human Kinetics.

Brymer, E. (2013). Extreme sports as transformational experiences. In Y. Reisinger (Ed.), *Transformational tourism* (pp. 111–124). Wallingford: CABI.

Campbell, J. (1993). *The hero with a thousand faces*. London: Fontana Press.

Chiow, K. S. (2003). Khoo Swee Chiow. In C. Gee, G. Weare & M. Gee (Eds), *Everest: Reflections from the top* (p. 27). London: Rider.

Groves, D. (1987). Why do some athletes choose high-risk sports? *The Physician and Sports Medicine, 15*(2), 186–193.

Hanna, F. J. (1993a). Rigorous intuition: Consciousness, being, and the phenomenological method. *The Journal of Transpersonal Psychology*, *25*(2), 181–197.

Hanna, F. J. (1993b). The transpersonal consequences of Husserl's phenomenological method. *Humanistic Psychologist*, *21*, 41–57.

Heath, J. (2002). First descents: When life is more scary than kayaking. Retrieved 3 November 2016 from http://coloradowhitewater.org/spray/HTML_mar2002/1d.htm.

Heatherton, T. F. & Vohs, K. D. (2000). Interpersonal evaluations following threats to self: Role of self-esteem. *Journal of Personality and Social Psychology*, *78*, 725–736.

Holyfield, L. (1999). Manufacturing adventure. *Journal of Contemporary Ethnography*, *28*(1), 3–32.

Husserl, E. (1977). *Cartesian meditations: An introduction to phenomenology*. (D. Cairns, Trans.). The Hague: Martinus Nujhoff.

Iso-Ahola, S. E. & Graefe, A. R. (1988). Perceived competence as a mediator of the relationship between high risk sports participation and self-esteem. *Journal of Leisure Research*, *21*(1), 32–39.

Jacobs, D. T. (1998). *Primal awareness*. Rochester, VT: Inner Traditions.

Merleau-Ponty, M. (1999). *Phenomenology of perception*. (C. Smith, Trans.). London: Routledge & Keegan Paul.

Midol, N. & Broyer, G. (1995). Toward an anthropological analysis of new sport cultures: The case of whiz sports in France. *Sociology of Sport Journal*, *12*, 204–212.

Muir, J. (2003). Jon Muir. In C. Gee, G. Weare & M. Gee (Eds), *Everest: Reflections from the top* (p. 77). London: Rider.

Olsen, M. (2001). *Women who risk: Profiles of women in extreme sports*. New York: Hatherleigh Press.

Pollay, R. W. (2001). Export 'A' ads are extremely expert, eh? *Tobacco Control*, *10*, 71–74.

Roberts, P. (1994). Risk. *Psychology Today*, *27*(6), 50–56.

Schultheis, R. (1996). *Bone games: Extreme sports, shamanism, Zen, and the search for transcendence*. New York: Breakaway Books.

Sherpa, P. N. (2003). Pemba Nuru Sherpa. In C. Gee, G. Weare & M. Gee (Eds), *Everest: Reflections from the Top* (p. 88). London: Rider.

Slanger, E. & Rudestam, K. E. (1997). Motivation and disinhibition in high risk sports: Sensation seeking and self-efficacy. *Journal of Research in Personality*, *31*, 355–374.

Spence, A. (2001, April). Into the mountains. *North & South*, 52–62.

Terwilliger, C. (1998, 28 March). Type 'T' personality. *The Denver Post*, pp. 1E, 4–5E.

Weare, G. (2003). Introduction. In C. Gee, G. Weare & M. Gee (Eds), *Everest: Reflections from the top* (pp. xii–xvii). London: Rider.

Welwood, J. (2014). *Toward a psychology of awakening: Buddhism, psychotherapy, and the path of personal and spiritual transformation*. Boston, MA; London: Shambala.

Wheaton, B. (2003). *Lifestyle sports magazines and the discourse of sporting masculinities*. Paper presented at the Leisure and Visual Culture, Roehampton University, Surrey.

Williams, B., Hamilton, L. & Kachmer, J. (Writers). (2001). *Laird* (Directors: T. Monaghan & B. Williams). USA: Blue Field Entertainment and Laird Hamilton.

Yakutchik, M. (1995). A grand lesson: For a first time mountaineer, life's limitations vanish into thin air. *Women's Sport and Fitness*, *17*(1), 82–83.

Zimmerman, M. E. (1986). *Eclipse of the self: The development of Heidegger's concept of authenticity* (Revised ed.). Athens, OH: Ohio University Press.

9   Becoming who you are

This chapter explores the extreme sport experience in terms of the experiential given-ness of the self, where given-ness refers to the taken-for-granted world of immediate experience and self is described as 'becoming who you already are'. The chapter builds upon the previous chapter, which focused upon an important aspect of the lived experience of extreme sport, which we conceptualised in terms of a process of transformation. We have sought to gain a greater understanding of participants' experiential selves as they emerge through the extreme sport experience. The closeness and imminent potentiality of death and the context of the environment appears to facilitate a unique window into participants' very being.

For many involved in extreme sports, participation in their chosen sport is often central to their lives. Indeed it would seem that their involvement is so important that participants continue despite disapproval from family and others. Participants consider that not participating in their chosen activity is akin to eliciting an inner death, presumably more intense than an outer death. This is well expressed in a quote from a forty-seven-year-old Korean climber who stated 'it is better to die in the Mountains than be hit by a car' (Gangully, Macintyre & Randolph, 2001, p. 74).

Participants report that gaining a deeper understanding of personal resource-fulness and spiritual, emotional, cognitive and physical knowledge and capabilities stem from a connection to a deeper self. For example, Breashears, a well-respected Everest mountaineer observed:

> People tell themselves that Everest is a dangerous place. For some people that makes the mountain more appealing. Only a few of the people heading towards camp IV that late afternoon really understood the indifference Everest holds toward human life. You can climb the mountain a thousand times, and it will never know your name. Realizing your anonymity, accepting it in all its terrible consequences, is the key to a mountaineer's humility, key to a climber's self-awareness.
>
> (Breashears, 1999, p. 259)

The notion that extreme sport participation might facilitate the realisation of a deeper sense of self has been explored in the past. We begin this chapter by investigating what is already known about this experience from non-phenomenological studies in order to lay the foundations for a more nuanced phenomenological explication.

Self as constructed renewal

Sense of self lies at the centre of who we are. There are at least two ways we can think about identity: identity as according with perceived stereotypes of the group we identify with, or identity emerging out of our own experience and reflections. Extreme sports participants have most often been presented as an ideal vehicle for constructing a new preconceived intrapersonal as well as inter-personal sense of self based on the attainment of idealised stereotypical con-structs. The emergent self, which some writers refer to as a 'new self', applies both within the extreme sport context and in everyday life. This recognition has been part of the discourse in the extreme sport literature for almost three decades and extreme sports are said to 'provide a well-defined context for personal change, as well as a clear-cut means to organize a new, and sometimes central identity' (Celsi, Rose & Leigh, 1993, p. 11).

For Celsi et al. the development of a deep central identity is best explained through the 'dramatic framework' as it is the foundation of a Western mindset and of identity formation.

> in Western society the dramatic framework is a fundamental cultural lens through which individuals frame their perceptions, seek their self-identities, and engage in vicarious or actual behaviours.
>
> (Celsi et al., 1993, p. 11)

Extreme sport participants are social actors influenced by mass media, social specialisation and technology. A new, more idealised, version of identity is created that replaces a current identity viewed by the participant as non-ideal and circumstantially determined. For others the process of personal identity develop-ment comes about through self-extension which enables self-renewal. Extreme sports, according to this view, are a medium for image re-design either as a deliberate intent to cultivate an image that is different from the one currently embodied or to develop an extreme sport identity based on the attributes of the extreme sport 'group'.

The importance of camaraderie associated with belonging to a group are con-sistent with findings in whitewater rafting (Holyfield, 1999). Involvement with others in adventurous experiences facilitates meaningful experiences with others and develops special bonds, often called *communitas* or 'the sense of community that transcends typical social norms and conventions' (Shoham, Rose & Kahle, 2000, p. 12). However, this process is governed by a ceiling effect which sug-gests that this argument may not be appropriate for activities where a misman-aged mistake or accident would most likely result in death. Furthermore, there are an ever-increasing number of disparate extreme sport activities, not necessarily a uniform group, and just because a lot of people undertake an extreme sport does not mean that an identity or culture is being formed. It may just be that a lot of people are participating in similar activities.

Rite of passage and sense of self

One theory associated with the extreme sport experience is the notion of a rite of passage from youth to adult. This is an active process designed to cement an adult identity. In bygone times a specific ceremony or rite determined the readiness of an individual to pass into adulthood. As has been documented elsewhere, an example is the ceremonial process of jumping off tall structures with ropes tied to the ankles or, among the Maasai, a young male would enter adulthood only after undertaking an elaborate ceremony that included killing a lion. In contemporary society extreme sports have been proffered as an equivalent rite of passage. Rites of passage ceremonies are generally characterised as non-voluntary, involving separation, transition and reintegration.

Another theory that has been proposed is the pilgrimage. Pilgrimages share a similar structure to a rite of passage but in a pilgrimage, participation is voluntary and not necessarily linked to the transition between youth and adult. However, whether we are talking about rites of passage or pilgrimages, the focus is still on personal experience and reintegration as cultural citizens. This is unlikely to be the way extreme sport participants view their involvement because, as has already been argued, the external perception about the extreme identity is often vastly different from a participant's own point of view. Furthermore, the change which results from participation, unlike changes associated with pilgrimages or rites of passage, is often unexpected and unplanned.

Living in relationship to nature

Identity formation has also been associated with a sense of self as relating to nature. The traditional perspective is that extreme sports epitomise the desire to conquer nature or battle against nature. As humans we have become so insulated from the natural world that it is seen as something to fear and therefore control. The extreme sport experience is portrayed as the ultimate hand-to-hand fight, where an individual's battle against nature somehow adds importance and value to their life:

> The clash occurring between the body and nature is like seeking the ultimate truth of western individualism, it is seen as the only partner of any value, the only speaker worthy of respect.
>
> (Le Breton, 2000, p. 2)

But Le Breton's thesis is contradictory because in the same context he also writes about the importance of being in 'perfect harmony with the world' (Le Breton, 2000, p. 2). Still, there is at least one intriguing point here: Le Breton's perception that nature is the only partner of any value may be significant, but perhaps not as a partner for conquering but a partner in our journey to learn more about ourselves.

The relationship may not be as initially perceived, it is not about conquering but about the journey. The notion of the natural world being a thing to conquer may be more a reflection of how a naïve non-participant understands the relationship rather than an element of the extreme sport experience. A person does not construct an identity through mastering the environment. Houston (1968) was quite clear about his views on attempts to conquer the natural environment:

> Mountaineering is more of a quest for self-fulfilment than a victory over others or over nature. The true mountaineer knows that he has not conquered a mountain by standing on its summit for a few fleeting moments. Only when the right men are in the right places at the right time are the big mountains climbed; never are they conquered.
>
> (Houston, 1968, p. 57)

Compare those words with the following from a whitewater kayaker recalling a trip in Russia:

> You cannot conquer a river. How can you defeat something that is never the same twice, that is unaware of your presence? To the river, we are so much flotsam, and if we forget that the results can be decidedly final.
>
> (Guilar, 1999, chap. 11)

Similarly, big waves pay no attention to the surfers riding them and by implication would not even know that a competition is occurring (Page, 2003). The experience is more of a dance and should the dance turn to competition or fight then the likely result is death. A more appropriate understanding of the relationship between person and nature is one that emphasises harmony *with* the environment, where the participant needs to adapt to the environment:

> It is not about going out there and conquering something – proving that you are somehow stronger than other people or the rock you're about to climb. It is much more about interacting with your environment.
>
> (Hill cited in Olsen, 2001, p. 59)

It is only by achieving an harmonious relationship with the rock that an extreme climber can progress at all.

> Climbing is a sport that involves you and the rock. The rock is a totally natural formation that's been there for maybe millions of years. When you're on the rock, you have no choice but to adapt to what is there. It may not be what you'd hoped was there or what you think should be there. The rock is indifferent to gender, size or whatever you think it should be.
>
> (Hill cited in Olsen, 2001, p. 64)

The skills required are 'more like water – strong but soft' (Hill cited in Olsen, 2001, p. 67). The climber yields, adapts and is in harmony with the rock and the activity.

The environment is considered to be sentient and permission for successful interaction is granted only when a participant appreciates and understands the subtleties of their relationship with the environment. This is likened to interacting with other human beings, though one could argue with the potential for a more deadly outcome. The nature–human relationship is more about interacting and blending with the environment:

> Snow and mountains are perceived as living entities, at once dangerous and benevolent. In their return to an intimate dialogue with mythical characters, skiers experience a phantasmagorical relationship that is also real. One must blend with the environment, become one with it.
>
> (Midol & Broyer, 1995, p. 207)

We should not confuse the experience with an aesthetic or romanticised appreciation or blending with the natural world in which, a naïve perception might presume, the beauty instils a sense of wonder and integration. Such an experience can be obtained by easier routes, or even vehicles. Rather, the beauty of the environment is a secondary concern for the extreme sport participant. An extreme skier specifically noted that whilst the aesthetics were a welcome bonus they were not the essence:

> For me the beauty of the mountains and the environment is the bonus, but that's not why I'm out there.
>
> (Co-researcher, early 40s)

This is echoed by a solo climber who expressed the view that:

> Part of climbing is being up in the mountains enjoying the scenery or whatever although I think most people don't climb because of that; they climb because of the fulfilment they get from the action of doing it.
>
> (Co-researcher, late 40s)

An experienced Himalayan expedition climber observed:

> The aim is not to conquer, for mountain climbing is not a conflict between man and nature. The aim is to transcend a previous self by dancing a 'ballet' on the crags and precipices and eventually, at very long last, to emerge exhilarated and addicted.
>
> (Houston, 1968, p. 49)

The partnership with the natural environment is about being in harmony with self and the environment. Perspectives that propose metaphors about conquering and battling with nature miss the very essence of the relationship. Nature is far too powerful to be conquered. The relationship is all engaging where the participant experiences being part of something more powerful than him or herself.

> Imagine being caught in a cosmic washing machine in the agitate cycle. Imagine being lifted out of your crib by your mommy and shaken hard while your daddy turns the full force of a fire hose on your body. Make that an icy fire hose – the water temperature is just above freezing; my wetsuit feels more like a T-shirt.
>
> You cannot 'fight' the river. You are in it, a part of it, being acted on by not just what you can see on the surface, but surging raging currents below the surface. They pull you in contradictory directions, shove your legs apart and together. The river is unimaginably strong and you are so very, very small.
>
> (Bane, 1996, p. 107)

Thus, the natural environment reveals the powerlessness of being human. However, this does not automatically result in the participant withdrawing. Participants report an appreciation of powerlessness which, if effectively used, enables the appearance of an extra 'something' to emerge from deep within. This is akin to surrendering control. The natural world might be acting as a facilitator to a realisation that the natural world is immensely powerful and humans are comparatively powerless. A participant foregoes any attempt to control natural forces but at the same time, some type of control is maintained in order to participate effectively.

> You really have to accept that you have a measure of control, but you don't have control. The mountain could fluff you out in a second.
>
> (Co-researcher, late 30s)

Living in relationship to nature moves beyond being in control when one is in an environment that is uncontrollable. The natural world, when experienced in its raw sense, where there is an acceptance of the reality of potential and imminent death, facilitates deep learning about one's self and one's capabilities. For an extreme skier and co-researcher, the relationship between being able to remain cool and mentally and physically, and emotionally in control was considered empowering:

> It's really empowering, it makes you feel like there's nothing you can't do. If there are avalanches coming down around you and you're on something where if you fall you die but you still manage to keep your head together you feel really really good about yourself. It's very empowering, these experiences make me feel so charged and so proud of myself and in control of my life despite all these out of control things that were going on around me.
>
> (Co-researcher, mid 30s)

A New Zealand mountain guide and owner of an international guiding company, Guy Cotter emphasised the point by differentiating traditional sports with extreme sports:

> in Mountaineering, it *really* matters whether you make the correct decision or not. That's the beauty of sports like this.... Going into the Mountains and actually making a decision and doing something that's going to be the difference between you living and dying, on a daily basis – it's empowering for the soul.
>
> (Cotter cited in Spence, 2001, p. 54)

The words of many are echoed by Cotter who further asserted that an extreme mountaineer cannot allow the ego to make decisions, as each decision must be based on realistic appraisals of activity skills and personal capabilities (cited in Spence, 2001). The alternative would likely be death. He considered that whilst participation teaches humility, this has to be balanced with self-discipline, otherwise a summit would never be reached.

Laird Hamilton, a pioneer in extreme surfing, developed a deeper appreciation for life through a realisation that the natural world is greater and more powerful than humanity. Extreme surfing elicited a deeper knowledge of his inner self; a realisation that changed him emotionally, physically, cognitively and spiritually (Williams, Hamilton & Kachmer, 2001). This is reflected in the words of extreme sports athletes from all disciplines. The natural world plays a role akin to that of a facilitator or mentor:

> If ever there was a mountain that can temper human arrogance and teach humility, it's Everest. Whatever name you want to give it, the Nepali Sagarmatha, or the Tibetan Chomolungma – the Mother Goddess – or the British surveyor general's name, Everest, the mountain is a massive living presence that changes every day. With the terrible winds of 1986, it seems that Everest was intent on showing us how fragile we truly are.
>
> (Breashears, 1999, p. 171)

> And I was certain that in exploring the terrain of the mountain, we were really exploring a far more mysterious terrain – the landscape of our souls.
>
> (Breashears, 1999, p. 242)

The experiential giveness of the self, revealed through the nature–human relationship has been shown to be one where the immense power of nature acts as a pointer to our inner beings.

> It's all about learning to adapt totally to the environment you're in. I think it provides the perfect opportunity for learning about what makes you tick. When you're that involved in the external world, you can really explore your inner nature.
>
> (Hill cited in Olsen, 2001, p. 66)

Bachar, a free-solo climber, was insistent that the experience was about looking within:

> I can't understand why people play baseball when they could be climbing. It's so many things, not just one. Outdoors ... beautiful, with unbelievable exposures ... mentally challenging ... gives you the chance to face fear and overcome it ... And it's so natural ... little boys are always climbing trees aren't they? ... But the real reward is being able to look within, to learn about myself.
>
> (John Bachar cited in Boga, 1988, p. 16)

Those who participate in extreme sports consider the concept of fighting or conquering the environment, at best, an unfortunate misunderstanding. After all, how can a person conquer a mountain that does not even know that they, a small insignificant human, exist? How can one defeat a river that is never the same? One cannot compete with nature when nature does not even know that a competition is taking place. The experience is more akin to respect for the natural world and a realisation that nature is both destructive and regenerative. The very terrible power, uncertainty and potential of death, where the structure and laws of civilisation are no longer apparent, facilitates the discovery of what lies deep within. The natural world is seen to be a great teacher about living as a human. Let us once again return to the words of Lynn Hill the extreme climber:

> I guess the whole 'extreme' movement is somehow an attempt to try to recreate the 1960s ... maybe some people think that there's something to be gained by 'defying' nature the way the young people in the 1960s defied authority. I'm not sure. I just know that that's not the way I do things.
>
> (Hill cited in Olsen, 2001, p. 60)

And perhaps herein lies the assumption of most 'extreme' sport research which deals with the formation of identity. Theorists assume that because one group battles human authority, others must therefore become a homogenous group battling nature's authority. Another example of people (expert and non-expert alike) transferring their own perceptions onto others, as suggested in a previous chapter. The aim of phenomenology is to search beyond the preconceived and to explore and make explicit that which lies beyond the horizon. Extreme sport participants find nature as experienced, raw and untouched, as still deeply embedded in human mythology, and experience a spiritual awakening through contact with nature. Participants are those who desire to reach wild and untamed places and experience a depth of human spirit.

Living authentically

In critiquing the idea that the extreme sport experience is about conquering nature, a deeper, more meaningful, position emerged. The experience clearly touches something deep within each participant's being that enables improved personal knowledge and enhanced personal capabilities. Breashears (1999) observed this inner knowledge in himself and others when reflecting on the otherworldly adventure of engaging with Everest:

> I recognized something very familiar about this scene; yet I also felt an acute sense of displacement. I've always looked to the sky, the snow, the clouds for that light. I've climbed to the highest reaches of the planet in search of it. But when I looked closely into Bruce Herod's eyes, facing his own camera lens, I saw what I might have known all along, and it is this: The risk inherent in climbing such mountains carries its own reward, deep and abiding, because it provides as profound a sense of self-knowledge as anything else on earth.
>
> (Breashears, 1999, p. 304)

Usher (2000), when documenting the lives of free divers (those who descend to depth of up to 800 feet without oxygen) noted that:

> You are in another world, where there is no gravitational force, no colour, no noise ... one does not descend in apnea to look around but to look into oneself. It is a long jump into the soul.
>
> (Usher, 2000, p. 1)

The changes involved in extreme sports result from a deep internal process. Essentially, the extreme sport experience transforms a participant, though not through working towards an external (social or cultural) perception of identity or towards some constructed perception of an ideal self, but by touching something within.

Extreme sport as living the dream

The connection with a deep self in extreme sports can take the form of realising deeply felt dreams: 'it was something I always knew I'd do ... before I knew I would do it, I didn't even know what form it was' (Ted cited in Welser, 1997, p. 26). For some this is expressed in terms of actual dreams and for others the realisation of a personal destiny. Co-researchers for this book observed even on the first attempt at their chosen sport, it was as if something inside of them knew that the activity was right for them. For example, an extreme kayaker reported that he knew he had an affinity for water from an early age. However, whilst he tried swimming, surfing, windsurfing and other water-based activities, it was only when he discovered kayaking, and in particular kayaking down waterfalls, that something clicked inside.

A BASE jumper reported strong feelings and dreams about flying at an early age. While she did not attempt BASE jumping until the age of thirty-three, she felt an instant connection to the activity, a connection she did not get with similar sports such as sky-diving or bungee jumping. The connections reported was as if they had found their natural environment, not unlike indigenous people from many indigenous tribes who report a relationship with a totem animal.

The intense experiential nature of extreme sports involves both body and feelings enabling the realisation of an inner being, as if the participant is coming home. Once the chosen activity is 'found', further understandings of self are challenged. A participant initially learns about their nature through participating and extends this learning to develop better emotional and physical capabilities. This process may be less about learning something new and more about realising an inner potential that has always been there, waiting to be set free – perhaps even a primal understanding of what it means to be human living in a natural world.

Listening to one's body

Extreme sports people often talk about trusting intuition and gut feelings and how these aspects are essential to effective participation. The first person to climb Everest solo and without oxygen, Rheinhold Messner (1998), described relying on instinct for his successful ascent. The extreme climber Lynn Hill maintained that she had to listen to her inner voice, rely on her own intuition and instincts, live in the moment, remain focused and rely on her own ability, even in team-based expeditions. Co-researchers interviewed for this project reiterated the importance of trusting one's intuition. An extreme kayaker described the process of choosing the route down a waterfall as 'an instant gut feeling' and a big wave surfer observed that participation was dependent on gut feelings about the environment and about his own self-readiness. A solo climber observed that ignoring such inner 'feelings' would inevitably result in death:

> I think the fool is the person who ignores what their body is telling them to do. That's the person who ends up dying. If you're going to solo, you have to listen to your body … Your fear is the thing that keeps you alive. So it's a good thing, if you don't ignore it.
>
> (Mike cited in Soden, 2003, p. 254)

Thus, the consensus is that successful participation in extreme sports necessitates listening to and trusting one's inner knowledge, one's inner experience.

On being alone

The lived experience of being alone is consistent with the fact that most extreme sports are undertaken solo. Even when participating in expeditions, each participant is inevitably 'alone' and dependent on their own physical, emotional and cognitive abilities. There is little that team members can do to rescue a waterfall kayaker heading offline half way down a 30 metre waterfall or to rescue a proximity pilot heading towards a cliff at 200 miles per hour (over 300 kph). Most often, the participant is required to undertake their own rescue and trust their own decisions. Thus, even when part of a team, each member is required to be fully self-sufficient and confident in their own skills. An extreme kayaker voiced the following:

> There are some very strange physical situations as well at the top of the waterfall that make you feel like you are totally alone, apart from the fact that you usually are totally alone because nobody has got any interest in sitting at the top of a fall when they can't see the bottom. You are just the only person left sitting up there. As soon as you say you're ready to go everybody leaves you.
>
> (Co-researcher, mid 30s)

Participants frequently speak about the power of solitude. Lynn Hill, the extreme climber previously cited, accepted that climbing is a distinctly personal activity where each participant focuses only on the essentials and has to be continually aware of what their body is doing. Others reiterate this point:

> It's always a mental exercise. If it's really cold and snowing hard, you can't waste time and energy thinking about how miserable you are. You need to focus and mentally walk through what you're trying to do. You can't go moaning about the fact that there's no one to help you.
>
> (Lignell cited in Olsen, 2001, p. 104)

Participants need to balance self-confidence and self-belief in order to participate in an extreme sport in the first place. Acceptance of personal responsibility for the consequence of actions is a major element of the extreme sport experience. A BASE jumper described his experience by reflecting that participating in extreme sports was a personal call to be himself, realise his potential, fulfil his own destiny and discover what lies within. In this instance the participant had spent time reading and exploring the experience from a scientific and mythological point of view in an attempt to investigate what he considered to be a profound medium that helped him discover what he saw as his own core self. The extreme sport experience emerges as presenting participants with an amazing gift, the gift of discovering a deep sense of authenticity that had previously been dormant and hidden.

> Re-establish that connection with a really fundamental core part of your being and yourself. You really learn so much about yourself when you do any adventure sport.
>
> (Co-researcher, early 40s)

Phenomenological perspectives on selfhood

Let us for a moment briefly revisit the argument presented in the chapter on death. We asserted that extreme sport participation allowed an experiential relationship to death and that this relationship enabled an experience of living life to its fullest. The phenomenological concept of being-towards-death was presented as one piece of evidence to support this argument. In making this claim we suggested that by experientially confronting and accepting the inevitability of death, the Heideggerian concept of authenticity emerges (Heidegger, 1996). Heidegger posited that each *Dasein* (individual Being) had the potential to connect with and be itself. Truly being-towards-death provides the space to receive the call to live authentically. According to Heidegger, the typical *Dasein* lives an inauthentic life caught up in a 'they-self', pre-determined by the 'they' of its world and resplendent in an illusion, or what Heidegger terms 'lostness'. To put it simply, a person wrapped up in mundane and predetermined rules, tasks and standards inevitably leads an inauthentic life. However, it is possible to reconnect with an authentic life by connecting with a deeper sense of self, a self beyond all psychological, biological or anthropological definitions.

Essentially, Heidegger posited a summoning 'call' to return to the authentic self (as opposed to the 'they-self'), a call without words or explanations. In Heidegger's words, 'the call of conscience has the character of summoning *Dasein* to its ownmost potentiality-of-being-a-self' (Heidegger, 1996, p. 249). However, the potential of becoming this 'self' depends on *Dasein's* ability to hear the call:

> Losing itself in the publicness of the 'they' and its idle talk, it *fails to hear* its own self in listening to the they-self. If *Da-sein* is to be brought back from this lostness of failing to hear itself, and if this is to be done through itself, it must first be able to find itself, to find itself as something that has failed to hear itself and continues to do so in *listening* to the they. This listening must be stopped, that is, the possibility of another kind of hearing that interrupts that listening must be given by the *Da-sein* itself.
>
> (Heidegger, 1996, p. 250)

In Heidegger's view the 'they' listening is interrupted by the silent unambiguous call to conscience. Returning to Breashears:

> The stresses of high-altitude climbing reveal your true character; they unmask who you really are. You no longer have the social graces to hide behind, to play roles. You are the essence of what you are.
>
> (Breashears, 1999, p. 247)

Authentic self is a self which is already understood by *Dasein* but which has been lost in a world swamped by the experiences of the they-self (Burston, 1998). The call removes *Dasein* from its lostness in the they-self. However, Heidegger was quick to note that this was not an inwardly directed analytic dissection of an inner life. Once the call is answered, the authentic self is realised with a 'worldly' orientation (Heidegger, 1996, p. 253). The authentic self is summoned to its potentiality-of-being or, in other terms, to live out its potential. An authentic being-towards-death enables the realisation of authentic self. Those who are more daring, who 'catch the scent of death', who give up the struggle and let things be, are said to reach deeper fulfilment.

We argue that the extreme sport experience, being one where death is experienced as real, triggers the call to authentic self and authentic living free from social ties and expectations. However, authentic self is not an idealised or willed version of self as, say, a more macho, indestructible being that masters his or her environment. It is more than that; it is a self that is already part of each being and each being has its own authentic self. By listening to and honouring that authentic self, one is able to live an authentic life. In Heideggerian terms 'in order to gain everything, one must give up everything' (Zimmerman, 1986, p. 292). The idea that extreme sports promote an authentic life does not imply selfishness. Living an authentic self allows authentic relationships with others.

The emergence of an authentic self also forces one to rethink the idea that human beings are the centre of life. The natural world is repositioned as more than an enemy, resource or plaything since authentic being transcends anthropocentrism. The natural world cannot by anything other than the lifeworld – the lifeworld is thus meaningfully co-constituted through our consciousness of its qualitative and flowing given-ness. Authentic being thus points to the intentional relationship inherent in consciousness as we are intrinsically meaning-making within a meaning-giving world (Todres, Galvin & Dahlberg, 2007). The natural world is us and, by extension, we are the natural world. It is only recently that Judeo-Christian Western culture adopted an alienated and hostile stance to nature. Traditional wisdom makes no such separation; each of us is at home in the natural world as we are perhaps at home in our own skin. Life does not orient itself around humanity. The natural world is not outside of being; it is at the very core of being and human beings understand themselves by being engulfed in the natural world (Bourgeois, 2002). Humanity cannot be separated from nature. The experience of being part of the natural world cannot be willed but must come about by the self being released to authenticity. Each of us is presented with an opportunity to get back in touch with a 'self' that is beyond our social self and outside of our tendency for anthropocentrism. We argue that the extreme sport experience is one way of achieving a connection with nature which in turn reveals who we are, a becoming of what we already are.

Summary

Extreme sports participants accept a range of deeply personal challenges. Closeness to death and their relationship with the environment facilitates understanding of themselves not otherwise available. We have argued that the extreme sport experience might be an overt expression of a participant's sense of being, enabling a deeper understanding of a participant's core or authentic self. Thus, participation in extreme sports can be the key both to realising deeply felt dreams and becoming more aware of one's core self, perhaps akin to the

Heideggerian call to realising and living an authentic life. By searching out, accepting and honouring that call, participants gain insights into the personal and interpersonal realms, where humility and humbleness mix with confidence, trust, personal responsibility, meaningfulness and wellbeing.

Human beings are inseparable from the physical world. Despite naïve perceptions that human beings are unique amongst animals, we are embedded as part of nature. This is not in the sense of nature as playing field or resource but in the sense of nature-as-family, nature-as-self and nature-as-unity, where there is no relationship as there is no separation. This unity facilitates a deep sense of being and even extraordinary states of awareness and consciousness. To fight nature is to fight oneself; to understand nature is to understand oneself. We can only really know our true selves by returning to 'wildness' and confronting death. One of the challenges of authenticity is the degree to which we make decisions and are responsible for our own lives. Decision making lies at the heart of human freedom, the topic of the chapter following.

References

Bane, M. (1996). *Over the edge: A regular guy's odyssey in extreme sports.* New York: Macmillan.

Boga, S. (1988). *Risk: An exploration into the lives of athletes on the edge.* Berkeley, CA: North Atlantic Books.

Bourgeois, P. (2002). Maurice Merleau-Ponty, philosophy as phenomenology. In A. Tymieniecka (Ed.), *Phenomenology world-wide: foundations – expanding dynamics – life-engagements: A guide for research and study* (pp. 342–383). Dordrecht, the Netherlands: Kluwer Academic Publishers.

Breashears, D. (1999). *High exposure: An enduring passion for Everest and unforgiving places.* New York: Simon & Schuster Inc.

Burston, D. (1998). Laing and Heidegger on alienation. *The Journal of Humanistic Psychology, 38*(4), 80–95.

Celsi, R. L., Rose, R. L. & Leigh, T. W. (1993). An exploration of high-risk leisure consumption through skydiving. *Journal of Consumer Research, 20,* 1–23.

Gangully, M., Macintyre, D. & Randolph, N. (2001). Asia answers the call of the wild: Affluence, fashion and daring have created a new breed of adventurer. *Time International, 158*(7/8), 73.

Guilar, L. (1999). *Dancing with the bear: An online book of a kayaking adventure in Russia.* Retrieved 3 November 2016 from www2.isu.edu/outdoor/dwbstart.htm.

Heidegger, M. (1996). *Being and time: A translation of Sein and Zeit.* (J. Stambaugh, Trans.). Albany, NY: State University of New York.

Holyfield, L. (1999). Manufacturing adventure. *Journal of Contemporary Ethnography, 28*(1), 3–32.

Houston, C. S. (1968). The last blue mountain. In S. Z. Klausner (Ed.), *Why man takes chances* (pp. 48–58). New York: Doubleday.

Le Breton, D. (2000). Playing symbolically with death in extreme sports. *Body and Society, 6*(1), 1–11.

Messner, R. (1998). *Free spirit: a climber's life.* (J. Neate, Trans.). Seattle, WA: The Mountaineers.

Midol, N. & Broyer, G. (1995). Toward an anthropological analysis of new sport cultures: The case of whiz sports in France. *Sociology of Sport Journal, 12*, 204–212.

Olsen, M. (2001). *Women who risk: Profiles of women in extreme sports.* New York: Hatherleigh Press.

Page, G. (2003). Vintage days in the big waves of life. In R. E. Rinehart & S. Sydnor (Eds), *To the extreme: Alternative sports, inside and out* (pp. 307–314). New York: State University of New York Press.

Shoham, A., Rose, G. M. & Kahle, L. R. (2000). Practitioners of risky sports: A quantitative examination. *Journal of Business Research, 47*, 237–251.

Soden, G. (2003). *Falling: How our greatest fear became our greatest thrill – a history.* New York: W. W. Norton & Company.

Spence, A. (2001, April). Into the mountains. *North & South, 52*–62.

Todres L., Galvin, K. & Dahlberg, K. (2007). Lifeworld-led healthcare: Revisiting a humanising philosophy that integrates emerging trends. *Medical Health Care Philosophy, 10*(1), 53–63.

Usher, R. (2000). Depth chargers: Divers without air tanks are reaching limits once thought too dangerous for submarines. *Time Europe, 155*(4).

Welser, H. T. (1997). *Finding life: The meanings of climbing to dedicated climbers.* Masters dissertation, Miami University, Oxford, Ohio.

Williams, B., Hamilton, L. & Kachmer, J. (Writers). (2001). *Laird* (Directors: T. Monaghan & B. Williams). USA: Blue Field Entertainment and Laird Hamilton.

Zimmerman, M. E. (1986). *Eclipse of the self: The development of Heidegger's concept of authenticity* (Revised ed.). Athens, OH: Ohio University Press.

10 Experience of freedom

The self lies at the core of the phenomenological explication of the lifeworld of the extreme sports person. But the self is always intentional. In this chapter, we explore extreme sport participation as a search for sense of freedom. Once again, the lived experience of extreme sports participants will guide our understanding of the phenomenon. Few studies have explicitly researched the relationship between extreme sport participation and sense of freedom and those that have, have drawn upon a focus on the socio-cultural explanations where freedom is freedom from normative constraints. We base our assertions on participants' lived experience, and themes explicated in the previous chapters, which we termed 'transformation' and 'becoming who you are'. The reader will sense a certain coherence between these three themes: a process of achieving a sense of transformation, becoming who you are, and ultimately, gaining a sense of freedom in the context of engaging in activities which may be associated with loss of life in the event of an error.

The explication of sense of freedom will once again consider elements of the socio-cultural but this time the critique will articulate the relationship itself. This exploration of sense of freedom will begin by exploring the socio-cultural dimension, not as conformity or opposition, but reframed as sense of freedom.

Freedom as a socio-cultural reframe

Along with fear, and identity, freedom is embedded in a particular socio-cultural context. That is, participation in extreme sport stands in opposition to work responsibilities, which are often construed as alienating and acting as a route to disempowerment for workers due to an imbalance in power relations. In contrast, extreme sports are seen as an active means to free a participant from unidimensional thought and behaviour patterns. At one level this is understood by practitioners as freedom from normal social constraints. The nature of freedom in this context is best reflected by its opposite, that modern society enslaves the individual through comfort, reason and democracy which lead to the justification for submitting to domination. Welser (1997) argued that climbing, as an instance of extreme sports, becomes an experience of freedom from domination, freedom to live by one's own rules, freedom from extrinsic projections and freedom from society's control.

Thus, extreme sports provide an opportunity for participants to free themselves from the rules, restrictions and limitations enforced in the everyday social world. Yakutchik (1995) phrased this as 'a place to color outside the lines' (Yakutchik, 1995, p. 1). The experience is all about 'looking for a sense of excitement and challenge that is missing from their everyday lives' (Bower, 1995, p. 21). By extension, extreme sports participants are freeing themselves from boredom and routine. Theorists have recognised that 'what people do and how much money they make just doesn't matter' (Celsi, Rose & Leigh, 1993, p. 12). That is, what happens in everyday life has little significance when participating at the extreme.

Extreme sports have been described as providing an 'aesthetic liberation of life' (Midol & Broyer, 1995, p. 209) that transgresses both traditional sporting rules and those regulations imposed by traditional societal norms. In extreme sports rules are rare and those rules that do exist are most often invented on the spur of the moment with no link to end results. Olsen quoted a climber who left gymnastics for climbing, even though she enjoyed the movements of gymnastics, because of the monotony and routine: 'climbing let me use my gymnastic skills, but in a way that offered much more freedom and spontaneity' (Hill in Olsen, 2001, p. 58). Those involved in extreme sports are not searching for idealised attributes found within mainstream society or in opposition to mainstream society. Neither are they in pursuit of characteristics attributed to supposed subcultures. Instead the desire is to be free from mainstream demands and assumptions. The lack of restrictions in how extreme sports are undertaken facilitates a sense of freedom and an opportunity to explore personal boundaries. Not even age restricts participation. Older people who participate in extreme sports tend to do so more often than their younger counterparts (Shoham, Rose & Kahle, 2000).

Experience as freedom from gender norms

A fundamental feature of the extreme sport experience is the absence of constraints apparent in normative socio-cultural life. Extreme sports are the essence of a free lifestyle, not just freedom from the restrictions of sporting norms and competitive rules. In this case being free signifies freedom from the constraints of a wider socio-cultural context including norms around gender and ageing. The perception that life is work is challenged, as participants achieve a new sense of freedom, emancipation and self-determination (Welser, 1997).

Extreme sports provide an opportunity for freedom from gender-based expectations. Participants describe a sense in which their body engages in actions liberated from gender. In fact the relationship between body, equipment and the environment is so complex that gender ceases to be significant. The writings on extreme sport describe that for both men and women movements are often energetic but 'fluid, gracious, imaginative, fanciful, and full of rhythm' (Midol &

Broyer, 1995, p. 208). Extreme sport participants describe new awareness of their own musculature quite divorced from the demands of the everyday world. The experience is often described as uncontrolled, fun and solitary or shared with a few (Midol & Broyer, 1995, p. 208).

An extreme climber explained that she was 'not limited by what other people thought a little girl was capable of' (Hill cited in Olsen, 2001, p. 58). Yakutchik (1995) reflected on similar perceptions in mountaineering:

> This is a place where men and women can be both strong and nurturing; where fierce independence walks hand in hand with cooperation. Here I understood what I could not comprehend at sea-level.
>
> (Yakutchik, 1995, p. 1)

Extreme sports provide an opportunity for equality not just because the body awareness, movements and psychological approach are different but also because the environment that is so essential for extreme sports does not judge (Laird Hamilton cited in Booth, 2003).

There is a faint dissenting voice amongst those who discuss the extreme sport experience as freedom. Those theorising from post-structural, post-Marxist or post-modern standpoints argue that as self is contextually and biologically based, the notion of freedom is no more than delusion (Kiewa, 2002a, 2002b). From this perspective the process is more akin to spontaneity and creativity, and an escape from an over-rationalised and bureaucratic society that has instilled feelings of alienation and constraint. Whilst heeding such opinions, it is important not to lose track of the experience of participants '40 seconds of pure happiness ... I am engulfed with optimism, screaming with the feelings of freedom and liberation. An addictive sensation. Birds feel similarly' (Zundar cited in Shoham et al., 2000, p. 1).

Yet there is a more deeply felt sense of deliberate and active freedom that lies beyond freedom from cultural or societal constraints. This aspect of freedom is recognised as an active physical freedom. A kayaker reflecting on freedom spoke about the importance of accepting responsibility for his own physical life, expressed as 'my responsibility is just for my life' (co-researcher, mid 30s).

Freedom is associated with the freedom of physical movement. A study on climbers who participate in free solo climbing, or climbing without ropes reported a sense of freedom of movement not found in other types of climbing because the climber was free to move without physical or equipment constraints (Wesler, 1997). An exponent of solo-climbing and co-researcher on this project expressed a similar feeling:

> so I was stuck on my own usually in mid-week here in Wales and that's when I started solo climbing. So I really started from necessity really plus it appealed to me but I found out that I had a great delight in doing it. I liked the feeling of the freedom of up there you know with no paraphernalia no slings or things or ropes and you just move freely. That sort of freedom was

really freedom of movement as opposed to what you'd think as freedom being in the mountains and the wide open spaces.

(Co-researcher, late 40s)

Even BASE jumping participants where the equipment is similar to skydiving perceived a difference in the freedom involved. In this case the comparison is made with the need for an aeroplane and other people:

> Again it's linked to the freedom thing. One way to describe it is to compare it to a skydiver. When you skydive you're reliant on that plane and you're relying on the pilot and you're stuffed in with a bunch of other people, so it's anything but peaceful. Lots of noise, lots of smells and things like that. Whereas on a BASE jump off a beautiful cliff there are no people and there is no wind because you're not going to jump if there is wind, so it's very very still, very quiet. You can take a few moments to become one with the environment and that's very peaceful. You sometimes sit at the top of cliffs for ages waiting for the right conditions, waiting for the wind to drop. There's nothing else to do but be there and be with yourself and be with what you're about to do. You've taken yourself out of your everyday existence where peace is quite hard to find and put yourself in an environment where it's easy to be peaceful.

(Co-researcher, early 40s)

This more intense feeling of freedom is often considered to be directly related to a participant being responsible for their imminent destiny and physical life. In the above quote there is also a corporeal relationship to the natural world and the intensity of peace. Participants indicate that the physical freedom felt in extreme sports is on a different level of consciousness to the freedom experienced by their less extreme cousins. This level of consciousness requires a deeper focus, a realisation of mortality responsive to the real potentiality of death, precision during the activity and enhanced awareness of surroundings. In Welser's (1997) study on climbers, the solo climber related this experience to an *Ultimate Freedom*. Freedom is a bodily feeling of freedom. Freedom for the extreme sports participant is more than an active and deliberate attempt to unknot the socio-cultural restraints; it is also an active and deliberate attempt to experience physical freedom. Where physical freedom is revealed as being beyond just the ability to physically move and encompasses a kinaesthetic sense of being free.

Another element to this freedom is linked to accepting personal responsibility. A BASE jumper interviewed during the course of this exploration, reflected on his own experience:

> I would have to take total personal responsibility for my actions. There was just me, my physical and mental abilities, my training, and 'a piece of nylon and string' to save my life. This satisfied another one of my dreams: to be

able to exist outside the confines/rules/protection/brain numbing existence that typifies modern society.

(Co-researcher, late 30s)

Freedom is more than solely an active and deliberate attempt to be free from socio-cultural norms or physically free but also freedom to accept responsibility for one's own actions and one's own physical destiny. Another BASE jumper expressed a similar opinion in that her active and deliberate accepting of responsibility for her own destiny was recognised as a total freedom. This freedom came from letting go of the need to attach experiences to external answers and an acceptance of inner experiences.

> I call it defying gravity and I define gravity as all the things that pull you down in life. Everyday life is often a hassle whereas BASE jumping is very free and very peaceful.

She then continued:

> People call it selfish and probably it is the ultimate selfishness because it's just you and nobody else can help you; there is no-one else to turn to, so you have total responsibility. There's a lot of freedom in that knowledge because you're not looking outside of yourself for the answers, they can only come from inside. For me that is freedom. It's that concept of commitment and taking responsibility. The powerful thing about it is that it is totally up to you, no one can help you and you are taking responsibility for your own life, totally.

(Co-researcher, mid 30s)

She elaborated upon her experience by explaining that it is always her decision and hers alone as to whether she will jump or not jump, based upon contingencies acting upon her at the time of the decision. She continued by defining freedom as a bodily expression directly linked to her chosen activity within her chosen environment and an expression of faith in her own capacities.

> The sensation is a great freedom. There's a physical sensation that feels very free, for example, we did one jump at night and it is like nothing else, you don't have a filter for that. You don't have anything to compare it to. Imagine just jumping into blackness. So the only thing you got to rely on is yourself.

(Co-researcher, mid 30s)

This experience of self-responsibility relates to being responsible for one's own life in terms of the 'life–death' relationship and also in terms of being-and-accepting-personal-responsibility for meaningfulness and fulfilment.

To accept and handle that responsibility and say yes I will, I will find my own meaningfulness and my own fulfilment. You know everybody gets an opportunity but not that many people actually take up the mantle.

(Co-researcher, early 40s)

Freedom from the need to be in control

Another element of freedom has to do with control. The relationship to control should not be confused with controlling the environment but rather that participants have to know what elements they are able to control and what elements they have to accept as uncontrollable. Nature is too powerful to attempt to control. For an extreme skier, the feeling is akin to straddling the edge of control:

When I'm skiing at my very best I feel like I'm on the very edge of complete destruction. I look totally in control. But it's like if you watch a downhill skier in slow motion, their skis are just wobbling all over the place but they're still hanging on. That's when I'm skiing at my best. How that looks is how I feel.

(Co-researcher, late 20s)

A significant part of the extreme sport experience is the need to accept the reality of a potentially fatal randomness that cannot be controlled. An extreme kayaker and co-researcher expressed the feeling as:

It is not a feeling of accomplishment but a feeling of freedom more than anything else, in particular a feeling that I had bitten off more than I could chew almost as soon as I'd done it. ... It still happens all the time now when I run waterfalls.

(Co-researcher, late 30s)

The experience is not about just seeing what happens but a managed non-control. The participant controls what can be controlled and then accepts the process, and perhaps even surrenders to the experience. Gonzales (2003) described the experience as a release from the desire to predict and anticipate and the ability to watch, be clear and calm and react decisively to stimuli.

I like to have a good knowledge of, or a good idea of what is gonna happen before it actually does. I wouldn't throw myself off a waterfall just to see if I'd come out at the bottom. I do believe I can get out of the bottom, but not a hundred per cent, there's always that nagging doubt. ... But I also like the attitude of living life where you deal with what goes wrong rather than living life in such a structured way that you know exactly what is going to happen, and nothing does go wrong.

He continued:

If I'm running a fall and I hit a rock, I like to bounce off the rock and the boat will spin around and I know that I'm dealing with a real situation. So it's not to see what happens but just maybe five per cent of me feels that I don't actually know what is going to happen.

(Co-researcher, late 30s)

Participants often speak about the paradox of both being in control and not in control. For example the following quote from the same extreme kayaker, describes an intense, real feeling of non-control over death:

I'm sitting at the top and the final goodbye is said and the last person walks away from the top of the fall. Often at that stage I stop talking to people, completely even if they're standing next to me talking and saying I've got quite a crowd gathered here today or something like that.... I am totally focused on the only thing I have to do and to survive and then the arm goes down, the signal to leave the eddy current. That's quite an amazing turning point because that's the last point at which I can say no. If I am going to die that was the last time that I had any control over it and it's a very very strange feeling to break out of that eddy current.

(Co-researcher, late 30s)

He provides some insights into the experience in his further description:

I can hear the sounds but they couldn't ask me anything about what they're saying. I'm totally inside. It's almost like going over in a barrel, it feels like my only job is to get out of the bottom of the waterfall alive and that's the real turning point. It's like the last person I have any responsibility to walks away from me and closes the door behind them and I'm on the river and I'm part of my kayak and I'm so happy that I've spent all the time designing that equipment and getting it all exactly how I want it. Everything fits perfectly; I've got all the wrinkles out of my wetsuit before I sat in the boat, that kind of thing.

(Co-researcher, late 30s)

Freedom as experienced in extreme sports is thus a sense of emancipation that is at once socio-cultural, physical, emotional and mental as epitomised by the following reflections from an extreme skier:

You feel so free out there, you don't worry about anything, you don't think about the bills you've got to pay or your life problems, you are just kind of free of thought. That's kind of what makes it all worthwhile, just for that five minutes of freedom.

(Binning cited by McCallum, 2001)

This quote highlights that an aspect of the extreme sport experience involves freedom from all thoughts and anxieties or fears and a sense of physical freedom, with connotations of surrendering to the experience. This does not mean a sub-mission or fateful acceptance but an experience more akin to deliberate relaxa-tion into the experience.

Experience of freedom as mental quietness

Freedom may be seen as, essentially, a state of play, freedom from the perceived influence of the other, which may include mental attitudes characterised by intru-sive and unwelcome thoughts and sense of responsibility. Participants in extreme sport described experiencing freedom from everyday thoughts. The focus required whilst undertaking an extreme sport leaves no room for any other thoughts or distractions.

> On the one hand, it puts a tremendous amount of stress on you, because you couldn't make a mistake. But because you were so focused on doing what you were doing, everything else goes away ... you're doing something so primal, your focus is just getting there and back alive.
>
> (Cush cited in Terwilliger, 1998, p. 3)

A climbing participant and co-researcher reflected that the intensity of the extreme climb forced absolute concentration: 'You really had to concentrate so then you'd lose track of other things' (co-researcher, mid 40s). The extreme kayaker Corran Addison, who once held the waterfall kayaking record for descending a 31 metre waterfall in France, maintained that his focus is always so intensely on the activity that all other thoughts are excluded (cited in Richard-son, 2001). Lynn Hill, an extreme climber, described the focus required to climb extreme climbs as one which frees a participant from thoughts about all other aspects of life. This has often been described as a calmness that results from climbing beyond ego. A BASE jumper explained this notion as 'letting go of attachment':

> To step off you have to let go for an instant of your attachment to every-thing, your attachment to your life, your attachment to things, you just have to let go of that.
>
> (Co-researcher, late 30s)

The sense of freedom described in this section is often associated with a state of complete relaxation and mental release of thoughts that were extraneous to the immediate present. On occasion the experience has been likened to meditation where everything else is stripped away except the focus on the task. Participants describe moving into a tranquil or thoughtless state of mind akin to letting go of the need to ruminate or control. The focus required to participate frees the mind from unnecessary mental activity.

Freedom as the release of fear

In a previous chapter on fear we demonstrated that fear is part of the extreme sport experience. However, a sense of freedom from fear is attained as exemplified by Addison (2003) the extreme kayaker. He was clear that intense fear was experienced in the lead-up to kayaking over waterfalls. However, as soon as the decision to descend is made and the first stroke takes him from the safety of the eddy, fear dissipates:

> And while the fear remains, when I finally look up, ready to take that first stroke, it simply vanishes. It must be gone so that the body is loose and can function efficiently, quickly and naturally.
>
> (Addison, 2003, p. 1)

Fear is transcended in the active phase even though fear is initially intense. Thus, fear loses its power. The fear of fear is overcome. Through action fear is transcended and the power of fear is dissipated.

> Fear mounts and swallows him in a rush. He falls into his fear and soon wants nothing more than to let the paddle slip from his fingers, lower his head into his hands and, and close his eyes. He will stop paddling and disappear beneath the surface of the waves. At the very bottom of his fear his mind grows quiet. He cannot hear the wind or feel the spray against his face. He feels nothing but a blessed warmth.
>
> (Todhunter, 2000, p. 34)

Some extreme athletes describe the process as intentional. One participant recounted her inner struggle with fear before climbing a mountain which she described as a metaphor for her life.

> The trick I think is to be able to control the fears and then if you've got full control over that then you don't feel hyped up with adrenaline but you are feeling relaxed.
>
> (Co-researcher, late 30s)

For another BASE jumper the experience is described as turning fear into elation:

> You know we learn all these complex systems of fear as we get older and that's part of society's rules. So the real reward of doing something like BASE jumping which initially you fear, like it's scary. The real personal reward is overcoming that fear, going right through it and turning it into elation, turning it into this incredibly exhilarating experience, this absolute celebration of living.
>
> (Co-researcher, early 40s)

In climbing, the moves required to climb a particular route are the same whether the climber uses rope or not or whether the climb is close to the ground or 2,000 feet up. A fundamental characteristic of rope free solo climbing at high levels is the ability to perform without interference from the physiological or psychological outcomes of fear. The challenge is to move through fear. As described above the reward is elation and a 'celebration of living'. The relationship to freedom, fear and the activity was described by an extreme mountaineer as follows:

> It comes back to pushing yourself physically past what you thought you could do to even get to the top. Then to be able to stand at the top and look at all of your fears as represented by one fear; the fear of dying. And then to be able to just act regardless of those fears is very powerful.
>
> (Co-researcher, early 40s)

A BASE jumper describes a process of self-discovery that comes about as a result of freedom from fear

> All of a sudden you see you're not this body, you're not these thoughts and you're not that part of you that's constantly chattering away about the things you can't do. You're none of those things; you're so much more than that. Everything else is stripped away so we don't have any of the things that distract us.
>
> (Co-researcher, mid 30s)

She reflects further upon her experience as she articulated the lived experience of freedom realised through BASE jumping:

> When you continue to drive yourself past the point where you thought you could not physically take one more step or go any further or you're terrified but you keep going then all of a sudden you know the world keeps getting bigger. Your possibilities are bigger because you taught yourself that those absolutes that you were putting on yourself were not absolutes at all; they were just false. It's a false feeling, the fact that we think we're bound by a particular area. We're not, but you can't get that on an intellectual level.
>
> (Co-researcher, mid 30s)

As mentioned above moving through fear is often associated with the sense of 'letting go', or surrendering to the experience as identified by a solo climber and co-researcher.

> The greatest fear comes the night before when my mind is in overdrive but I seem to be very calm when it actually comes to do it. There seems to be like an inner turmoil where one part of my mind says 'don't do this it's crazy you might kill yourself' and the other part says 'no I'm gonna do it'. It seems to me that when the part of me that's trying to keep me alive gives up

and says 'well you are gonna do it anyway' and it more or less joins forces with the other part, it keeps me calm because subconsciously you probably realise that's the way you are gonna do it, as safely as possible.

(Co-researcher, late 60s)

Participants reach a state that is akin to letting go of the security of attachments, perhaps even to life itself, and the desire to maintain physical, mental and emotional control.

In summary, an element of the extreme sport experience is freedom from norms, or socio-cultural control. On closer inspection there is also freedom to be responsible for one's own destiny. The experience of freedom is reportedly both an aversive experience of being-free-from and a positive experience of being-free-to. While in the socio-cultural context freedom might reflect an active desire to move towards a becoming-free an element of the experience requires a high degree of focus which facilitates being-free. Participants describe being physically free to move, mentally free from unwanted noise and free from the chains of fear, often considered to reflect total relaxation. Freedom is about letting go and surrendering the need to control and experiencing self in relation to, and in a sense, at one with the environment. The following section explores a phenomenological perspective on the meaning of freedom.

Phenomenology and freedom

Freedom represents an important element of phenomenological and existential philosophy. Sartre (1956), describes a humanity that is wholly free in that each of us is able to choose or create our own self, determined by our own free choice. Human beings determine themselves in terms of what they are. For Sartre, to be human is to be free, not just as freedom in doing and self-determination but also as freedom in being or the choice to be who we are. Sartre (1956) proposed that limits on a person's freedom are in themselves not limitations but result from being free.

An inevitable implication of Sartre's position is the immense burden derived from individual responsibility for one's life and one's death. Thus, to be human is to have unlimited freedom and, as such, no imposed direction or security. According to Sartre, even not to choose is to choose. The realisation or awareness of this freedom is unavoidably overwhelming because it means a person becomes aware of the reality of infinite responsibility and the knowledge that any decision logically excludes the actualisation of all other potentialities. The essence of Sartrean freedom was a total freedom, and awareness of such a freedom often came suddenly and without warning (Sartre, 1976, 1981).

There is a fundamental connection to freedom and authenticity in Sartre's early work where authenticity and consciousness combine to create freedom. Sartre's phenomenological insights on freedom fit with exploration of the extreme sport experience to the extent that the participant searches for a freedom to do with their life as they wish; a life lived under total personal responsibility.

In his later writings Sartre reflected this juxtaposition and noted a struggle between freedom and responsibility. This is reflected in the explication of the extreme sport experience as the choices made about participation and the level of participation.

Contrary to Sartre's view, Merleau-Ponty (1999) recognised that freedom is limited in essence by a person's embodied abilities. Thus, he rejected certain elements of Sartrean freedom whilst accepting the fundamentals of the pre-reflective and the body. That is, freedom is limited by our physical capacities.

> That mountains are tall for us, and that where they are passable and where not is not up to us but is a function of our embodied capacities. That the shape and physical capacities of the body is reflected in what we see is a powerful argument against Sartre's over-estimation of human freedom.
>
> (Dreyfus, 1996, p. 1)

The importance of freedom from Merleau-Ponty's perspective is that freedom relates to physical action. Freedom is still an element of human nature but limited by embodied realities. Embodied freedom as conceived in extreme sports is about going beyond perceived physical limitations. Participants have the capacity to experience physical potentials beyond those experienced elsewhere, and, as will become clear in the next chapter, this is indeed the case.

Following from an existential phenomenological perspective, participants choosing to extend self-imposed physical limitations realise additional, unexpected potentialities. This of course brings the story neatly to Merleau-Ponty's second notion – that of motivation. A truly skilful action does not require 'thought' or goals to act and in certain situations, thoughtless action equates to more effective motion. Dreyfus suggests 'one does not need a goal or intention to act. One's body is simply solicited by the situation to get into equilibrium with it' (Dreyfus, 1996, p. 5). The motion or action is purposeful without a person entertaining a purpose for the action. This contributes to our understanding of what happens in the extreme sport experience. Participation involves action requiring a focus that triggers freedom from thought and the influence of fear.

The notion of human freedom is also central to Ricoeur and Heidegger. From Ricoeur we learn that freedom entails awareness that a person is free to choose their own destiny but what prevents the realisation of each person's freedom is fear, perhaps fear of death but more specifically fear of being an individual (Ricoeur, 1966). Freedom also seems to be a freedom to exercise a certain capacity described as free will. Heidegger explored his notions of freedom in some of his early lectures. It was also the fundamental root to *Being and Time* (McNeill, 2003; Nichols, 2000). Heidegger posited a positive freedom which is more than just the absence of constraint or freedom-from. In Heidegger's terms, authentic *Dasein* is freedom for grasping and choosing itself. Freedom entails being free from the 'they' and accepting the reality of the abyss, of being free in the face of one's own death. Freedom is more than being free to do what one wants; it is about choice based on a primordial freedom. For Heidegger the common ordinary freedom as choice is only possible if the primordial freedom or the connection to or '*revealing* of historically "grounded" truth' is first experienced (Nichols, 2000, p. 14). Without such an intimate connection freedom becomes negative freedom which is at best enslavement and at worst dangerous. From this we might infer that the extreme sport experience enables a perception of 'truth' as primordial freedom leading to positive freedom as choice.

Phenomenology as philosophy has focused on positive freedom in the form of freedom-for or freedom-to action revealing itself in personal choice. That is, whether one follows the extreme freedom of Sartre or the bodily freedom of Merleau-Ponty the underlying concept is that freedom indicates action. However, reports from extreme sports participants indicate freedom-in-action, a freedom that seems to be born from 'freedom-as' or 'freedom-for', a freedom that entails a thoughtlessness and deep defusing of fears that does not seem to result from conscious will or action but seems to be experienced engagement with and letting go, a surrendering to the experience.

Summary

An essential piece of the extreme sport jigsaw of experience is sense of freedom, a multifaceted experience. Freedom is described as freedom from social, cultural and other elements that determine a participant's life. However, more than this, the sense of freedom is described as being free to accept personal responsibility. Freedom is more than mental and physical release from constraints, but encompasses movement and desires. The experience also equates to liberation from thought and fear. In order to explore this sense of freedom we turned to phenomenology and existentialism. An investigation of these realms suggests that the extreme sport experience touches aspects of human existence beyond that experienced in everyday living.

References

Addison, C. (2003). Fear. Retrieved 20 August 2004 from www.eruditium.org/pete/fear.html.

Booth, D. (2003). Expression sessions: Surfing, style, and prestige. In R. E. Rinehart & S. Sydnor (Eds), *To the extreme: Alternative sports, inside and out* (pp. 315–333). New York: State University of New York Press.

Bower, J. (1995). Going over the top (extreme sports). *Women's Sport and Fitness, 17*(7), 21–24.

Celsi, R. L., Rose, R. L. & Leigh, T. W. (1993). An exploration of high-risk leisure consumption through skydiving. *Journal of Consumer Research, 20*, 1–23.

Dreyfus, H. L. (1996). The current relevance of Merleau-Ponty's phenomenology of embodiment. *The Electronic Journal of Analytic Philosophy, 4*(Spring), 1–16. Available at http://ejap.louisiana.edu/EJAP/1996.spring/dreyfus.1996.spring.abs.html.

Gonzales, L. (2003). *Deep survival: Who lives, who dies, and why* (1st ed.). New York: W. W. Norton & Company.

Kiewa, J. (2002a). *Rockclimbing as oppressive resistance.* Paper presented at the Annual Conference of the Leisure Studies Association, Preston, UK.

Kiewa, J. (2002b). Traditional climbing: Metaphor of resistance or metanarrative of oppression? *Leisure Studies, 21*(2), 145–161.

McCallum, K. (2001, November). Personal Communication. Interview with an extreme skier.

McNeill, W. (2003). Review of Martin Heidegger's 'The essence of human freedom: An introduction to philosophy and the essence of truth'. *Notre Dame Philosophical Reviews, 01*(05), 1538–1617.

Merleau-Ponty, M. (1999). *Phenomenology of perception.* (C. Smith, Trans.). London: Routledge & Keegan Paul.

Midol, N. & Broyer, G. (1995). Toward an anthropological analysis of new sport cultures: The case of whiz sports in France. *Sociology of Sport Journal, 12,* 204–212.

Nichols, C. M. (2000). *Primordial freedom: The authentic truth of dasein in Heidegger's 'Being and Time'.* Paper presented at the Thinking Fundamentals, IWM junior visiting fellows conferences, Vienna.

Olsen, M. (2001). *Women who risk: Profiles of women in extreme sports.* New York: Hatherleigh Press.

Richardson, J. (2001). Kayak terror. *Extreme Features.* Retrieved 31 November 2002 from www.bluemanna.com.au.

Ricoeur, P. (1966). *Freedom and nature: The voluntary and the involuntary.* (E. V. Kohak, Trans.). Evanston, IL: Northwestern University Press.

Sartre, J.-P. (1956). *Being and nothingness: An essay on phenomenological ontology.* (E. B. Hazel, Trans.). New York: Philosophical Library.

Sartre, J.-P. (1976). The flies. In *No exit and three other plays.* New York: Vintage International.

Sartre, J.-P. (1981). *Three plays: Altona; Men without shadows; The flies.* Harmondsworth, Middlesex: Penguin Books.

Shoham, A., Rose, G. M. & Kahle, L. R. (2000). Practitioners of risky sports: A quantitative examination. *Journal of Business Research, 47*(3), 237–251.

Terwilliger, C. (1998, 28 March). Type 'T' personality. *The Denver Post,* pp. 1E, 4–5E.

Todhunter, A. (2000). *Dangerous games: Ice climbing, storm kayaking, and other adventures from the extreme edge of sports.* New York: Doubleday.

Welser, H. T. (1997). *Finding life: The meanings of climbing to dedicated climbers.* Masters dissertation, Miami University, Oxford, Ohio.

Yakutchik, M. (1995). A grand lesson: For a first time mountaineer, life's limitations vanish into thin air. *Women's Sport and Fitness, 17*(1), 82–83.

11 Evoking the ineffable

We now turn to a contradiction. Elements of the extreme sport experience are best understood as ineffable. The limitation of our descriptions lies in the fact that the extreme sport experience cannot be fully appreciated by common language or words. From a phenomenological perspective aspects of the experience may best be understood in terms of 'the sacred', that which is beyond words. We have chosen to refer to such experience as 'ineffable'. The notion of the ineffable is not new in phenomenology, but has been described in the journal *Phenomenology and Pedagogy* as an entity in its own right rather than just the lack of words or linguistic capacity to describe experiences. It is argued that the ineffable is an experiential fact which may be expressed in a variety of ways. That is, just as darkness is an event in itself and not merely the absence of light, the ineffable is its own entity. Phenomenologically, the ineffable is an everyday bodily, rich and unspoken experience. The experience of dance, for example, has been referred to by participants, yet without our own experience of dance and an appreciation of both its internal and its external aspects, dance might become just empty movement. In simple terms the phenomenologist needs to give voice to what others may describe as the 'wow' factor.

To return to the central point of this introduction, we claim that certain elements of the extreme sports experience are ineffable, not because the experience is an 'unreflected' or 'pre-reflective' experience but because a full understanding of the experience is beyond words. Thus, words become truly metaphorical, they point to the experience and the way we hear these words is dependent on our own understandings. Care should be taken not to confuse our understanding of the words with the experience or to reduce the experience to words. As Abrahams (1986) warned, we need to be careful when reporting experiences to avoid, as far as possible, the danger of reducing experiences to a merely typical or representative experience, for to do so would lose the spirit that resides within the many awesome experiences described. The challenge with giving voice to the ineffable is the fact that it refers not simply to some kind of cognitive process but is deeply reflective of a sensory awareness. Thus there is a demand for metaphors as we seek to give expression to the ineffable aspect of the extreme sport experience.

The ineffable or unnameable speaks volumes but perhaps tests our readiness to listen. The inexpressible component often exists in what has been termed timelessness. An experience of the ineffable involves a response characterised by a complexity of feeling or atmosphere. Some events remain pure experience. Part of the difficulty lies with the use of language. Words by their very nature imply separation and yet experiences might well be integrative. The process of naming might be restrictive, as we learn from some of the great religions in their taboo regarding naming the deity. Nevertheless we seek to explore and give meaning to the ineffable aspects of the extreme sport experience. From a phenomenological perspective this requires that we move beyond the Cartesian tradition and accept that language might only ever point to an experience. It is also important that language is used carefully and is respectful of the voices of co-researchers so that we do not detract from the emergent meanings of the ineffable through our words.

The aim of this chapter is to point to an experience and to relay the thoughts of others in such a way that the ineffable can be understood, or at least recognised. This chapter is not purely about relaying the metaphors that explore the experience but also about relaying the words that might further explore the metaphors. To do this is to attempt to write the private experiences of meanings and feelings *as if* they are a public experience, without losing their 'truth'. The aim is to provide a synthesis of the extreme sport experience in the full knowledge that it will necessarily remain an incomplete description.

Inadequacy of words

Without exception those interviewed were clear that words were inadequate tools for exploring core elements of their experience. Participants considered that the only way to know the experience was to engage with the experience. The extreme sport experience is immersed in and becomes part of a way of being in the world where notions of dualism are challenged at their most profound level. Possibilities become endless, thus pointing to the inadequacy of words. For those directly describing their experience for this project, a typical response was that words were inadequate to fully explore the experience.

> There are no words because it is a complete sensation, it's a sensation that's taking in all your senses and then some that you didn't know you had. It's more of a self-discovery [encompassing] spiritual, esoteric activity. It's another form of expression that's so outside any normal type of activity yet you can get results from it that are so outside anything you'd expect from any normal activity.
>
> (Co-researcher, late 30s)

This quote represents a typical expression by extreme sport participants who shared the view that not only were words inadequate but finding an appropriate simile was impossible. For example, a sexual orgasm was deemed a poor comparison. For a big wave surfer, whilst the sexual experience and the big wave experience were similar but different, the big wave surfing experience would take priority.

> It's just better than sex, better than any shit like that. It's just very very hard to describe. Unless they're surfers and they've been in a barrel, a really good barrel you've got no chance in hell of describing it to them. I know what I'm talking about but they wouldn't, they'd just go; 'look at you you idiot' and they'd say 'what the hell are you on?' I don't know what 'drug-goes' get but this has got to be better than that you know.
>
> (Co-researcher, mid 50s)

Thus, according to participants, elements of the experience are beyond description by words, or at the very least by those words comprising the English language. In the same way that a ripple in a pond might be used to point towards the 'something' that created it, the effect of the expression of the ineffable experience on the extreme sports participant is used to point to the nature of the ineffable itself.

The extreme sport experience has been likened to an intimate dance with nature. Participants often described this experience as if being 'connected' to the natural world. This point underlies the care required when interpreting the voices of others. For some, the word 'connected' may bring to mind the experience of being chained and the desire to fight or escape; and for others still, perhaps the way in which a leopard is connected to the forest or a bird to the sky.

On occasion, extreme sport participants were not able to put their reflections into words.

> It's just three hours of AAAAAARRRRR, and when I get back to the car that's my memory of going skiing, it's just this crazy wild ride for three hours in the day.
>
> (Co-researcher, mid 30s)

On deeper reflection this co-researcher described her experience as being 'as if every cell was twitching'. Similarly, an extreme surfer described his experience in terms of an 'aura':

> Well, imagine [you are really happy] that was like a two-foot aura around you, and you could see everyone's aura. A surfer, when he gets a barrel, would have an aura twenty foot around him. In the situations I've explained to you I'd have to say the aura is thirty foot around you, that's the buzz thing, that's what I mean when I say 'that buzz'. That's how strong that aura is and it will stay with you for as long as you care to remember it.
>
> (Co-researcher, mid 40s)

The use of the term 'aura' in the quote above suggests something that is ephemeral, filled with beauty and also out of the ordinary. An extreme kayaker considered the feeling to be like journeying through another world, like dropping through a door and back into the real world. He reported enhanced awareness of his beating heart and breathing intensity:

That makes me feel quite unusual and therefore alone, the silence and as I just said the [sense of] removal having all your senses removed from you so you turn inward on yourself and also this feeling that you might not make it and that's always in my mind that I might fly through the air. Out of the corner of my eye I can catch a glimpse of that other world that I want to be in but I might not emerge from the bottom of the fall.

(Co-researcher, late 30s)

The co-researcher described an incident that almost resulted in his death and the fact that the feeling of being alone and inner connection became even more intense as a result. He described the experience as an ultimate metaphor for life and for experiencing life rather than quivering on the edge.

Attempts to describe the experience often alluded to a powerful energy coming from the environment:

The place is still powerful, it has energy and it's giving back to you. For me I get an insight into the fact that we're interconnected and that while we can die, life and everything is connected. We're all part of this cycle, this sounds very esoteric I know and it's difficult to put into words, but with BASE jumping you can go places that other people can't go. You can stand on the edge of these huge cliffs and put your arms in the air where you're totally vulnerable and totally part of the environment, at the same time. So it gives an opportunity to experience places and a way of looking at things that we can't normally do because we're too restricted by fences and rules and our own fear.

(Co-researcher, early 30s)

This quote points to a dimension of the experience which can best be described as spiritual as the co-researcher realises the interconnectedness between herself and everything around her. At the same time she refers to a sense of vulnerability where anything could happen or wound her, but simultaneously she describes being part of something which is all-powerful.

Our co-researcher then described the personal insights which arise from her participation, which are profoundly spiritual:

The first time I BASE jumped it was one of those experiences that shatters the way that you looked at things in the past. We look at things through all these filters and we judge without even being aware of it, it's an unconscious thing, constantly, constantly filtering and judging. An experience like BASE jumping helps you shatter all of those things so you become inordinately humble but inordinately self-possessed and confident at the same time. All of a sudden you're totally connected to the environment, no longer an 'I'; you're not bound by the constraints of a physical body anymore. You lose the fear of death because death is just a death of the physical body and you know that you're not the physical body. The physical body is a vehicle or it's an expression of you at the moment but there's much more. When you get an insight into that it's a life-altering insight.

(Co-researcher, mid 30s)

The co-researcher gives voice to many aspects of the extreme sport experience. A significant theme in the above extract relates to connection, physical body and death. That is, she gives voice to the realisation, as in all the great spiritual traditions, that the 'sense of I' as physical body ceases to be significant. She points to something much larger. Descriptions of losing oneself through the action of participation are common. The inadequacy of words in delineating the notion of the ineffable is evident in the structures of participant's experience. The extract was one of many where participants evoke rich metaphors concerning their sense of self and transcending a physical sense of who one is.

Experience in time

The ineffable aspect of the experience was revealed in many instances as occurring immediately after a commitment to action. For example, extreme kayakers talk of this point in time as happening as soon as they peel out of the final eddy. For those involved in BASE jumping, the experience seems to come as soon as the active commitment to jump has been made and up to the point that the parachute is opened, for mountaineers it happens more gradually. BASE jumpers described feeling an intense fear whilst walking to the jump, whilst checking conditions at the edge and, whilst making the commitment to jump once the conditions are judged to be suitable. Commitment typically occurs a few moments before stepping off the edge. From this point, up until the time when the parachute opens, the component of the extreme sport experience we have termed the ineffable is experienced and a new sense of freedom and relaxation is felt.

The part that's intoxicating, the part that probably drives people back to it over and over again is the part between stepping off and opening the canopy. It's a time of complete and utter freedom.

(Co-researcher, early 40s)

Three stages can often be identified in the extreme sport experience: fear, followed by focus and then a sense of deep relaxation. These stages are correlated with moving from anticipation of the event to the actual extreme situation. However, on occasion the relaxation and focus stages can be reached without explicitly moving through an acute fear stage. For the big wave surfer, the experience begins whilst dropping into the wave. What follows is a synthesis of those characteristics that present themselves in the moment that is essentially ineffable – or rather, of those characteristics of the experience that can be described.

Intimacy and nature

Whilst the relationship between the extreme sport experience and the more-than-human (which of course includes humans) world has been considered, there is one further element that fits with the theme of this chapter; that is, a sense of mystery, often compared to animal prowess. The relation between intimacy and nature is described as unity between humans and the natural world where nature is felt as sentient and alive. For surfers, surfing big-tube waves is often portrayed as being in a 'room' that is alive and changing. When a surfer is properly attuned to the wave and becomes part of it by positioning the board exactly on the section of the wave that the wave allows, no feeling is more enjoyable.

Gonzales (2003) explored the notion that an intimate understanding of the energy and forces of nature seems to be forgotten in the modern world, as we become further removed from our awareness of our relationship with nature. Gonzales reported that those successfully participating at extreme levels have developed an intimate relationship to their chosen environment, a relationship in which the participant is able to tangibly feel energy and reciprocally absorbs the same energy when participating (Gonzales, 2003). Thus, the experience is more than an abstract, intimate understanding or detached knowledge but an engagement with the lifeworld of nature.

A primal thing

A sense of touching what has been described as a primal force or life energy is intrinsic to participants' experience of their chosen activities in the natural world. Participants report feeling more alive during participation than at any other time. Extreme sports are seen as enabling an experience of Being beyond that possible in everyday life. For example, Gadd and Rubenstein (2003) included a quote, amongst many, in which a participant describes the sensation as 'a direct tap into what I call the "life-force"' (Gadd & Rubenstein, 2003, p. 25). This has often been described as 'primal' state. The experience has been likened to being in touch with a primitive aspect of being human. Kremer portrayed the experience as tapping into the 'ultimate energy' (Kremer, 2003, p. 376). That is, the experience is described as a union with a universal primal awareness.

A co-researcher and BASE jumper interviewed for this book considered the experience to be an essential 'call of the wild' which was ignored at a cost. As previously discussed, the experience is often depicted as dealing with a primal force within oneself and the environment. Another co-researcher and extreme mountaineer spoke of connecting to a primal animal-like state as if connecting to all animals. Participants speak about an immensely powerful energy coming directly from the environment and connecting with the individual on an instinctual level.

Altered states

Altered states have been described as comprising enhanced sensory capacity and an experience of transcendence. The phrase 'extraordinary human experiences' has been coined to describe these states. This essential element of the experience occurs during that part of the activity related to feelings of relaxation. Doug Scott (2003), noted for the first ascent of the south-west face of Mount Everest in 1975, wrote about experiencing an intense calm in which awareness was heightened and he had a feeling of being lifted above his normal state.

The altered states described by participants include experiencing time, space, sensory capacity and relationships to the environment in non-ordinary ways. The extreme sport participant typically articulates feeling more alive than in everyday life. A BASE jumper described his sense of time altering as if time slowed down during the BASE jump experience as he slipped into being fully present in the moment. The few seconds that characterised the time between stepping off the cliff and the canopy opening were described as 'invigorating' as his senses took in more detail about colours, shapes and objects he was able to notice the tiniest of features. He described feeling as if the sky was simultaneously being sucked away and swallowing him up, as if he was motionless, while everything around him was moving. At the same time the experience is characterised by calm and a sense of oneness with the environment.

Altered states characterised by accentuated sensory acuity and clarity of perception are typical responses to extreme sport experience. An extreme mountaineer, and co-researcher, described the state as one where her senses and intuition are fully alive, awake and aware. Another mountaineer and co-researcher in this project described what he termed 'an animal nature' where:

> Things reel in slow motion and certainly my senses are never anything like as sharp as they are in those situations. You see things with incredible clarity and all your senses have an awareness, an alertness that you never gave them credit for in the past. You realise that your senses are not working to their full capacity or even coming close to it until you are in such a situation.
>
> (Co-researcher, mid 40s)

Thus, notions of certainty are changed as part of the ineffable. The extreme sport experience emerges as a medium for altered perceptions of space, time and clarity or enhanced state of sensual awareness and abilities to act. Time as 'normally' perceived seems to drop away and perceptions of time as being lost or slowing are experienced. Senses seem to grasp or take in more detail.

> I like to see the rock come by but I'm also fully aware of everything else that is going around me. It's the opposite of tunnel vision.
>
> (Co-researcher, late 30s)

A BASE jumper and co-researcher tried to explain the experience by referring to what might happen:

it's incredibly incredibly intense and mostly because if something goes wrong in a BASE jump you have to do something about it extremely quickly. So you're at this level of alertness that you're not in a normal life. You've got every central nervous system receptor ready to fire in case you've got to deal with a malfunction and in dealing with a malfunction you've only got seconds to sort it out or you die.

(Co-researcher, late 30s)

The extreme sport experience is multidimensional, including an enhanced, altered state of being that changes the participant's relationships with the environment. The experience is characterised by changes in relation to time and the ability of human senses to process and action information. Participants' relationship to time changes in two ways: first, a participant gets lost in the experience; second, the participant is able to fit more into a moment, or, in other words, participants are able to sense and do more in every moment of lived time, as the everyday perception of time slows down or perhaps because one's capabilities and relationship with the world of which we are part, are experienced as enhanced.

A BASE jumper co researcher described altered states as follows:

Very intoxicating and also important in helping us become more aware that we are not what we are in our everyday life. In our everyday life we are not particularly challenged or pushed, there is no necessity to reach those places in ourselves that are hard to reach and uncomfortable; uncomfortable to get there but infinitely worthwhile.

(Co-researcher, early 40s)

Extreme sports participants who regularly face the potential of death experience the activity as a celebration of being alive where senses are enhanced. By repeatedly facing the potential of death they reach awareness of life beyond the everyday.

Floating and flying

The lived experience of extreme sportspeople often include experiences described as floating or flying. The link might be obvious for some activities, for example BASE jumping has been described as:

the purest and most natural form of human flight. No aircraft, no motors, no man made devices, just my body and mind freefalling through space. For the first half a second your heart is in your throat but then it's just total relaxation.

(Co-researcher, mid 30s)

The experience was described as very different to skydiving and the best description the co-researcher quoted above could find was that the experience is 'pretty awe inspiring' (co-researcher, mid 30s). Many BASE jumpers and proximity flyers describe stepping off the mountain and flying like a bird. By its nature, the act of jumping off a cliff appears to trigger sensations of floating or flying. However, the notion has been described by other extreme sport athletes. A big wave surfer and co-researcher described this sensation as 'flying through the wave':

> Well if you can imagine a wave that breaks two hundred metres, there can be a stage along that line where you just stand there and you enjoy the moment and you're just literally flying along the wave with the air blowing up the face of the wave and under your board. It's almost making you weightless sometimes flying against your body and it's a sense of being.
>
> (Co-researcher, mid 40s)

The great pioneer of solo climbing, Reinhold Messner, who was the first person to ascend Everest without bottled oxygen, described feeling as free as a bird and experiencing blissful feelings as if an air balloon was carrying him (Messner, 1998). The extreme skier Andrea Binning elaborated on her reflections on extreme skiing with a description of floating:

> The feeling of putting in a good run, of being out there in the mountains. It's awesome. You feel like you're floating. You're kind of weightless. You feel like you can do anything, kind of indestructible, you just feel so good.
>
> (Binning cited in McCallum, 2001)

Those involved in extreme kayaking describe similar sensations:

> The feeling of flying is very natural. I'm flying very much from one hit to the next one rock or one lump of water to the next.
>
> (Co-researcher, mid 40s)

At some point, beginning with the commitment to undertake the activity, participants metaphorically leave this world for another. During this experience, senses are immensely enhanced and physical potentials are realised, often described as being like a particular animal. Such experiences are described as transcending human capabilities but also about connecting with an inner power. The experience is often described as relaxing and peaceful. A participant experiences 'being powerful' and 'alive' as if a primal element of their being is in direct contact with a universal life force. The experience involves becoming part of, or merging with, a natural environment to an extent that the concept of a separate 'I' identity might even disappear. During this experience, participants invariably reveal feeling conscious or more fully aware of 'non-material' potentials not experienced in other areas of their lives.

Extreme sports and the transpersonal

It is perhaps here that we will find the most enlightening phenomenological descriptions of experiences related to those we are investigating. This is not to suggest that the field of transpersonal studies is somehow uniform in its understanding of the phenomenological structure of transpersonal experiences, as this is clearly not the case. Daniels (2002), for instance, undertook a comparison of seven different descriptions of the transpersonal Self. Descriptions and understandings of the transpersonal realm range from a parsimonious differentiation between the material or bodily ego and the non-ego core. Comprehensive approaches to the transpersonal realm are based on extensive research recognising the self as inner core and universal. As phenomenology insists, even when exploring the ineffable, care should be taken to interrogate assumptions or preconceptions to ensure fidelity to the research method and the experience. Transpersonal studies, even those explicitly adopting a phenomenological approach, often base their descriptions on metaphysical or spiritual assumptions. As previously stated, the imperative is to stay close to the experience itself. Phenomenologically, if an element of the extreme sport experience is considered as transpersonal, then the phenomenological descriptions as outlined by participants should relate, at least in part, to the structure of transpersonal experience. Our findings concur with eight basic qualities which are said to characterise a phenomenological understanding of transpersonal awareness:

1   The experience has transformative power, often realised in a change in habits, inclinations, effects of emotions, preferences and understanding of life.
2   The experience involves a 'letting go' or surrendering sense of control and loss of fear.
3   Time is experienced as different from the everyday linear concept of time. There is a sense of stillness or even 'time standing still'. Thought patterns are entirely present-focused, neither past nor future oriented.
4   A dissolution of perceiver and perceived, there is often no sense of 'I'.
5   A deep sense of peace and stillness characterises the experience.
6   The experience includes flashes of insight as intuitive senses that might seem to come from an external source.
7   'An all-pervading aura of love and contentment for all that exists'. This may be experienced as intense inner energy, a desire to 'let it be', or total peace of mind.
8   The typical sense of space is altered to induce a radical extension of the normal perceptions of body-space.

(Valle & Mohs, 1998, p. 100)

Transpersonal experiences are often encased within near-death experiences involving intense emotions, whether painful or pleasant, and passions often beyond those normally felt. The experience is triggered by being in the present moment with an acute awareness of authenticity, often characterised by enhanced mental alertness. Passions are not the normal attachment-based passions but represent total passion about all aspects of life without clinging. These are described as a constant 'letting go' whilst still maintaining stillness of mind (Valle & Mohs, 1998). Relaxation in this context is not a dull state but an alert, receptive relaxation. Perceptions of time and space are altered as the experience is held constantly in the 'now'. The present now 'has a lived quality as well: it is a space we dwell in' (Varela, 1999, p. 119). The extreme sport experience is characterised by an extended 'now' and extended space.

Transpersonal experience often involves a deep connection to nature accompanied by absence of fear, and connection to what may be described as an inner or higher self or power. Transpersonal experiences involve a sense of surrender or letting go of the need to predict and control (Valle & Mohs, 1998). The phenomenological description of the experience of the ineffable is characterised by a deep sense of self-transformation with an ensuing loss of judgemental attitudes and a deep ability to engage with life. Transpersonal identity may be considered as beyond that which is traditionally associated with the existential or authentic self.

Husserl's (1977) transcendental phenomenology might provide some insights into the nature of the ineffable quality of the extreme sport experience. First, the transcendent nature of the phenomenological reduction implies that the ego is beyond the possibility of further reduction. Second, as Husserl recognised, human beings experience both unity and separateness; unity in the sense of transcendental empathy and separateness in the sense of individual core boundaries. Third, Husserl points out that the process of transcendental reduction needs to be experienced to be understood (Hanna, 1993; Spiegelberg, 1982).

Whilst much of the above might neatly describe the extreme sport experience, a glaring omission is the heightened abilities described by participants, the ability to 'see' and 'do' beyond that normally experienced. This absence is probably a result of research and theory being bound by the phenomenology of consciousness and not by bodily descriptions. Whilst the extreme sport experience undoubtedly shares some similarities with transpersonal experiences, they are not identical.

Ineffable experience is purported to be a central part of Buddhist philosophy. Buddhism recognises that some experiences are beyond the descriptive power of language. Language only becomes useful when meaningful communication occurs between those who share the experience. Often, ineffable experiences are characterised by seemingly greater-than-human powers and enhanced sensory abilities that are eventually revealed to have come from within. These experiences are characterised by feelings of unity and altered perceptions of time and space accompanied by descriptions of 'walking on air' or 'riding the wind', conceivably similar to floating and flying. This realisation of authenticity is often characterised by initial 'freedom from and transcendence of ordinary time and space' (Chihara, 1989, p. 211). Research shows that in a deeply relaxed meditative state, time seems to slow down as physical abilities speed up (Chihara, 1989).

The most powerful elements within many wisdom traditions are essentially ineffable, a point echoed by the great Christian mystic Meister Eckhart (cited in Caputo, 1978). Such experiences are often accompanied by feelings of bliss, peace, enhanced perceptions and unity that can be found at the very 'ground of our being' (Campbell, 1973, p. 151). These experiences may well comprise the release of seemingly superhuman powers, altered perceptions of time, unity and states of profoundly peaceful stillness (Watts, 2003). In some instances, these states are described in terms of letting go of the mind and attaining an awakened or enlightened state. Some exceptional experiences will transform us, should we choose to accept and identify with the experience. That is 'it only costs "not less than everything." But whatever that "everything" is to you, it will be given back a hundredfold' (White, 1993, p. 55).

Transpersonal states are considered non-ordinary but relatively common among people who are deeply connected to the more-than-human world. We see the merger of inner and outer worlds, the slowing of time. Austin (2000) reported dissolutions of self-in-time and self-in-space through disciplined participation in Kenshō (見性), a Zen practice of seeing with *shō* referring to 'nature, or essence' which in turn results in deep personal transformations. Being alone and meditating in the wilderness has been described as bringing about a state where 'the stones and leaves appeared more intricately patterned, the colours brighter' (Deikman, 2000, p. 76). The extreme sport experience was described as being more vivid and rich and essentially 'primitive' in nature, resulting from a shift away from the need to control and towards a more receptive, accepting mode. The return from an acquired nature to a basic nature releases our human capacity for experiencing altered states of consciousness. Thus, the extreme sport experience might not be about moving into non-ordinary or extra-ordinary states but, rather, participation removes the haze and mist from everyday states.

Summary

This chapter provides a synthesis between phenomenology and a description of the ineffable elements of the extreme sport experience. We have argued that elements of the extreme sports experience are ineffable, not because the experience is an 'unreflected' or 'pre-reflective' experience but because it is an experience characterised by intentionality where lived experience is beyond words. Thus, words symbolically point to an extraordinary experience and the way we hear these words is dependent on our own understandings. Care should be taken not to confuse the words with the experience or to reduce the experience to words. Of course, to attempt to describe the indescribable immediately reduces its intensity and power and creates defined, bound entities. It is unfortunate and yet inevitable that any description has the potential to violate all-encompassing and powerful experiences. Attempts to clarify certain events potentially results in the experience being lost: or, perhaps worse, being obliterated. Or as van Manen wrote, 'in the act of naming we cannot help but kill the things that we name' (van Manen, 2002, p. 239). Nevertheless, beyond the world of words is a distant shore that can be pointed to in an attempt to make explicit and outline some of the characteristics involved, characteristics of lived experience outside mundane experience. Senses are enhanced, time slows down and the seeming separateness of inner and outer worlds dissolves, evoking a glimpse into a world of multidimensional possibilities. It is to this degree that we have returned to the '*things themselves*!'

References

Abrahams, R. D. (1986). Ordinary and extraordinary experience. In V. Turner & E. M. Bruner (Eds), *The anthropology of experience* (pp. 45–72). Urbana, IL: University of Illinois Press.

Austin, J. H. (2000). Consciousness evolves when self dissolves. In J. Andresen & R. K. C. Forman (Eds), *Cognitive models and spiritual maps: Interdisciplinary explorations of religious experience* (pp. 209–230). Thorverton: Imprint Academic.

Campbell, J. (1973). *Myths to live by*. London: Souvenir Press.

Caputo, J. D. (1978). *The mystical element in Heidegger's thought*. Athens, OH: Ohio University Press.

Chihara, T. (1989). Zen meditation and time experience. *Psychologia, 32*, 211–220.

Daniels, M. (2002). The transpersonal self: 2. Comparing seven psychological theories. *Transpersonal Psychology Review, 6*(2), 4–21.

Deikman, A. J. (2000). A functional approach to mysticism. In J. Andresen & R. K. C. Forman (Eds), *Cognitive models and spiritual maps: Interdisciplinary explorations of religious experience* (pp. 75–92). Thorverton: Imprint Academic.

Gadd, W. & Rubenstein, B. (2003, 1 September). Why I go extreme. *New York Times*, pp. 24–25.

Gonzales, L. (2003). *Deep survival: Who lives, who dies, and why* (1st ed.). New York: W. W. Norton & Company.

Hanna, F. J. (1993). Rigorous intuition: Consciousness, being, and the phenomenological method. *The Journal of Transpersonal Psychology, 25*(2), 181–197.

Husserl, E. (1977). *Cartesian meditations: An introduction to phenomenology*. (D. Cairns, Trans.). The Hague: Martinus Nujhoff.

Kremer, K. (2003). May 27, 1998. In R. E. Rinehart & S. Sydnor (Eds), *To the extreme: alternative sports, inside and out* (pp. 373–380). New York: State University of New York Press.

McCallum, K. (2001, November). Personal Communication. Interview with an extreme skier].

Messner, R. (1998). *Free spirit: A climber's life*. (J. Neate, Trans.). Seattle, WA: The Mountaineers.

Scott, D. (2003). Foreword. In C. Gee, G. Weare & M. Gee (Eds), *Everest: Reflections from the top* (pp. ix–xi). London: Rider.

Spiegelberg, H. (1982). *The phenomenological movement* (3rd ed., with Karl Schuman (Ed.)). The Hague, Netherlands: Martinus Nijhoff Publishers.

Valle, R. & Mohs, M. (1998). Transpersonal awareness in phenomenological inquiry: Philosophy, reflections and recent research. In W. Braud & R. Anderson (Eds), *Transpersonal research methods for the social sciences: Honouring human experience*. (pp. 95–113). Thousand Oaks, CA: Sage.

van Manen, M. (2002). Writing in the dark. In M. van Manen (Ed.), *Writing in the dark: Phenomenological studies in interpretive inquiry* (pp. 237–253). London, ON: The Althouse Press.

Varela, F. J. (1999). Present-time consciousness. *Journal of Consciousness Studies, 6*(3), 111–140.

Watts, A. (2003). *Become what you are*. Boston, MA: Shambhala.

White, R. (1993). *Exceptional human experiences as a vehicle of grace: Parapsychology, faith, and the outlier mentality.* Paper presented at the Annual Conference of the Academy of Religion and Psychical Research Proceedings.

12 Returning to the lifeworld of the extreme sport experience

We set out to achieve three objectives. First, to provide a phenomenological understanding of the extreme sport experience. Second, to articulate the principles and application of the phenomenological method. And third, to demonstrate the phenomenological approach through its application to the extreme sport experience.

Three decades ago, Wertz (1987) argued that 'one of the most pressing questions for contemporary psychology is that of what research method will best provide access to the truly human' (p. 90). Arguably, this is an increasingly pertinent issue at a time where neuroscience is in the ascendency. The issue of an appropriate epistemology extends well beyond psychology to encompass all those disciplines involving human experience. Too often methodological arguments are reduced to qualitative versus quantitative research approaches. However, what we have argued is that this bifurcation is too simple and we need to reflect upon the paradigms and epistemologies which guide our methodological approaches. After all, some qualitative approaches might be based upon the same assumptions as traditional quantitative studies, in which the subjective experience becomes the object of study and which are thus driven by the same epistemological assumptions which underpin empirical approaches. This is most evident where qualitative approaches justify rigour by appealing to similar processes of determining reliability as identified in quantitative methodology, for example inter-rater agreement and triangulation. This is not a criticism of these approaches because they all have value but we wish to draw the distinction between such approaches and phenomenology. Our intention is not to present phenomenology as somehow superior to other ways of knowing but to argue that phenomenology has an important role in the human sciences, particularly when an experience is either not well understood or current understandings do not fit the lived experience of participants. In these instances phenomenology provides a perspective and paradigm to underpin authentic ways of knowing.

We have attempted to address this bifurcation of science, by providing an introduction to phenomenology, which, we argue, provides a relevant research methodology to better access that which makes us who we are. Phenomenological research investigates the phenomenon as concretely lived with the aim of explicating a renewed, rich description of embodied, experiential meanings.

Phenomenology, guided by specific principles, demands we engage with human experience differently. Essentially, phenomenology seeks to avoid the dualistic approach that emphasises separate constructs called subject and object and conceptualises reality as being co-constituted. However, we argued that even in the current climate of methodological fluidity driven by discourse informed by modern, postmodern and post-postmodern perspectives, phenomenology needs to be guided by key principles. These key principles include: the phenomenological attitude, non-duality, intentionality, *noema* and *noesis* and the lifeworld.

We described a process for undertaking phenomenological research and demonstrated this approach through an explication of the extreme sport experience. While our methodological approach was developed for the context of our interest in the extreme sport experience, it is not new. We built upon the work of contemporary phenomenologists who have informed our thinking and provided us with conceptual arguments to enable a scholarly understanding of the extreme sport experience. This approach, guided by the essential phenomenological principles, privileges the voice of the lifeworld of the men and woman who exercise volition in engaging in activities well beyond the boundaries of the mundane.

Husserl (1970) was preoccupied with what he considered to be a crisis in Western science which he observed as alienating the experiencing-self from the world of immediate experience. He called for a return to lived experience. His concerns assume more salience as we experience an increasingly urban and digital world. At the same time, and perhaps as a consequence, we are witnessing a surge of interest in extreme sports where individuals are deeply immersed in their experiences and engaged with their environment in a profoundly phenomenological sense. In the previous chapters we traced the extreme sport experience through a multitude of pre-reflective 'naïve' experiences to reveal and explicate dimensions of the extreme sport experience. We collaborated with a number of co-researchers from different extreme sport disciplines including: big wave surfing, BASE jumping, waterfall kayaking, extreme mountaineering, rope free climbing and extreme skiing. BASE jumping is considered to be the most extreme of the parachute sports where participants jump from solid structures such as cliffs, bridges or buildings. Extreme skiing typically requires skiing down sheer cliffs where a fall results in the skier tumbling out of control. Waterfall kayaking involves paddling over waterfalls that might be 30 metres tall. Big wave surfing takes surfers into waves over 20 feet tall, where even some of the most renowned surfers have died. Rope free climbers climb difficult cliffs without the aid of ropes or other protection. For all these activities the most likely result of a mismanaged mistake or accident is death. As one BASE jumper put it: 'There are no second chances' (co-researcher, early 70s).

Our findings challenge traditional explanations focusing on the motivation of risk-taking, and the death wish, or the notion of 'no fear' as representing a superficial understanding of the extreme sport experience. The notion that extreme sports are merely the domain of those with deficient or pathological personal attributes or personality traits does not stand up to scrutiny. Participants are not driven to risk life by psychological, biological or social forces. Contrary to common stereotypes, participants emphasise risk reduction, they report feelings of intense fear and a deep desire to celebrate life. Yet it is also clear that extreme sport participation has the potential to take life. Death and fear appear to provide a channel to experience the immediacy of life in the moment, with an intensity many would consider worth the risk of death. The previous four chapters gave direct voice to the experience as lived by extreme sport participants. The extreme sport experience has been demonstrated in our explication of four themes: experience of transformation, becoming who you are, sense of freedom and evoking the ineffable.

So what have we learned from our research exploring the journeys explicated in personal narratives of extreme sports people? We are able to draw several conclusions, each of which we will discuss in turn. First, the extreme sport experience represents, potentially, one of deep inner transformation. Second, we provided evidence that participants 'discover' inner capabilities including emotional, physical, mental and spiritual potential, which brings about a deep sense of self-integration. Third, in addition to deep relaxation the experience brings about a sense of inner freedom, enhanced sensory capacity and altered perception of time. Fourth, the experience touches on something that cannot be effectively expressed in words but involves a new sense of being in the world. Participants enter a realm beyond the everyday which has been described as the ultimate celebration and experience of life and living.

In our discussion on the philosophical and methodological aspects of phenomenology we suggested that an appropriate structure for scaffolding the phenomenological understanding of lived experiences comprises: lived space, lived time, lived other and lived body. In this chapter we synthesise our exploration of the extreme sport experience by exploring and integrating our phenomenological descriptions in terms of these four categories. As was noted in the early chapter on research methodology, illustrating the descriptions through the four separate notions does not imply that they are separate and distinct. Of course, in lived reality they are interdependent. Equally, we do not intend a hierarchy where one conception is seen as more important or relevant than another.

Lived space

Traditional notions of space are conceived in terms of measurable and dimensional space. Phenomenology considers space in terms of lived space which is felt space. Lived space may be experienced as more expansive than measured space or may be more confining than measured space. However, lived space is largely pre-verbal. Lived space refers us to the landscape in which we move. For the extreme sports person it is also the space in which he or she engages in their activity. Space comprises 'horizons of possibilities' each of which may be realised in the extreme sports person's activities.

At one level the extreme sport experience is about conventional conditions of space as outdoor space. It is about natural landscapes and aesthetic valuation. At this level the extreme sport experience is about fast flowing rivers, waves larger and more energetic than most of us can even imagine, and unassailable mountain sides. For co-researchers outdoor space was not something to be conquered or attacked but rather to engage with and move through. For extreme sports participants, such as the big wave surfer, space is both limitless and potentially life threatening. Being closed in upon by tonnes of water has very a different meaning than gliding with the wave.

> Well if you can imagine a wave that breaks two hundred metres, there can be a stage along that line where you just stand there and you enjoy the moment and you're just literally flying along the wave with the air blowing up the face of the wave and under your board. It's almost making you weightless sometimes flying against your body and it's a sense of being.
>
> (Co-researcher, mid 40s)

However, the extreme sport experience would seem to go beyond this. In the transcendent aspects of the extreme sports experience, lived space would seem to be about moving beyond the predictable and is experienced as a returning home to inner space. The experience is both about dwelling in inner space and stepping into the ineffable void, abyss and danger of external space.

> you know you're in this incredibly spectacular environment dealing with really really primal forces not only primal forces in the environment but primal forces within yourself. We have primitive parts of our being that are connected to primitive parts of every other being you know. We are part of everything that's around us at some deep deep deep unconscious level, connected to it. So to go mountaineering is to reinvigorate and re-establish that connection with a really fundamental core part of your being and yourself.
>
> (Co-researcher, mid 40s)

At some point in the experience, boundaries dissolve as attachment to the physical body is lost and both inner and outer space seem to be experienced as singular or unified space. Davis (1999) likened the experience as stemming from intimacy with self and a death-rebirth event. This process is experienced as if the material merges with the non-material; the initially perceived life-force of the external fuses with the initially perceived life-force of the internal to become one life-force.

Lived time

The notion of lived time (temporality) is located phenomenologically in past, present and future. As pointed out by Husserl, lived time cannot be reduced to a mathematical abstract view of time. In phenomenological language, all events are connected. Lived time refers to time as experienced, which in extreme sports, may include future-oriented activity bound by past experiences and training. However, in extreme sports the relationship to time changes. Time is no longer linear as experienced in everyday life. Time is most commonly experienced as slowing down. Many participants described their experiences by referring to events happening in slow motion. Past and future pass by as expected in the mundane experience of time but the now of time seems to hover for a while and immediate past and future slip by more sedately.

However, this is not as a response to boredom but an experience of living in a short moment of eternity, a moment that seems to have moved beyond the mould of past, present and future and is experienced in the present. Linear or measured time remains unaltered – as the video camera will adequately demonstrate, what is perceived to be an age in experiential time happens in an instant of worldly or measured time.

> it happened really really really really slowly but when I watched it on the video you know ... it must have been a matter of seconds but it felt to me like a good 5 minutes.
>
> (Co-researcher, mid 30s)

In other words, the mundane flow of consciousness is temporarily suspended and replaced with consciousness experienced as flow in harmony with the experience.

Lived other

The notion of 'the other' has a complex history within phenomenological thought. For instance 'the other' has been used to refer to an explicitly human-centric 'other'. However, from this study otherness emerges in relation to nature. This seemingly radical view accords with Merleau-Ponty who pointed to the potential for the other to refer to nature. Extreme sports participants provide a new and interesting perspective on the lived other where participants use metaphors such as 'dancing with nature' to describe their experience. In keeping with the concept of intentionality, the object of consciousness is revealed through an intimate relationship in which the 'partner' in the dance is the natural world. This is revealed in the following quote:

> It's about feeling at one with the whole world, the whole universe, it's about understanding why and you can't put it into words, you can't it's just you know, it's like forty-two, you know. You have to experience it to really know what it's about. I mean you can't describe to someone what an orgasm is like. I mean you can try to but unless you have it you'll never know
>
> (Co-researcher, late 30s)

The paradox is that even within this perspective humans might be seen as separate from nature. Extreme sport participants speak about relating to nature in an intimate manner. The relationship between the extreme sport participant and the natural world facilitates self and self-understanding. This was previously evidenced in the following:

in exploring the terrain of the mountain, we were really exploring a far more mysterious terrain – the landscape of our souls.

(Breashears, 1999, p. 242)

Participants describe integration with the world of nature revealing a sense of belonging to the world as it is calling towards the primordial Being. That is, there is a repositioning of the other from over-there to merge with the here (Langer, 1990). An aspect of this repositioning of the self-as-part-of-nature was often referred to as being experientially awakened to our primal self.

All of a sudden you're totally connected to the environment, no longer an 'I'.

(Co-researcher, mid 30s)

This concept has been recognised in phenomenological writings as restoring the 'squirrel self' which, according to Zimmerman restores our true humanity (Zimmerman, 1992, p. 269). The participant moves beyond the mental/material, internal/external duality and experiences connectedness, or as some might argue a 'merging'. Such a momentary integration passes beyond a naïve understanding of the relationship between self and natural world to a new ecocentric experience of self-in-relation to the world. This represents a profound example of the phenomenological critique of the subject–object dichotomy and the realisation of unity.

Lived body

Phenomenology strives to provide a perspective which is not dependent on the dualistic perspective that characterises so much of Western knowledge. The lived body within this context is something more primordial, than the body which lives in juxtaposition to the objects of nature. The lived body of extreme sportspeople is primordially expressive and meaning-giving, lives in relation to the objects of consciousness. The body is experiential as the person engaging in his or her sport is present in relation to the environment, whether that be water, rocks or a distant horizon. In contrast to an instrumental body in nature (earth, water or air), the lived body exists in relation to the quest. The participant's body is permeated with meaning, whether this refers to freedom, fear, being who we are or the ineffable. For some, there is no distinction between body and soul, or body and spirit. Participants' descriptions reveal the degree to which the lived body is part of the experience.

you're not bound by the constraints of a physical body anymore. You lose the fear of death because death is just a death of the physical body and you know that you're not the physical body. The physical body is a vehicle or it's an expression of you at the moment but there's much more. When you get an insight into that it's a life-altering insight.

(Co-researcher, early 40s)

Interestingly, the English language reflects assumptions of 'subject' and 'object'. However, many other languages have various terms to refer to the body and various levels of experiencing. For instance, the German word *Korper* refers to a body or the physical form of the body, while *Leib* refers to a body as it is lived and experienced. We can thus think of the *lived body* and *lived experience* of co-researchers in this project.

Corporeality or lived body is characterised by the notion that we are always bodily in the world. That is, the world is always experienced through our bodies. In extreme sport it is revealed that the experiences, as articulated, go beyond the everyday anthropomorphic structures as fear and mental chatter are suspended. Intentionality allows the person to look into what has been described as their authentic self or soul. Sensory ability and physical prowess are enhanced and even extended. Bodily energy is enhanced and wellbeing taken forward to the future. However, whilst this stance demonstrates an expansion of the conventional (by which we mean dualistic) notion of the body, the experience of extreme sport is also about moving beyond the conventional bodily experience to a primordial body experience and then to an experience of body in unity and harmony. The boundary role of skin disappears or merges with the external. That is, experience moves beyond 'human' experience to be released into openness for 'raw', primordial experience uncluttered by thought and emotion.

Accepting these arguments indicates that the extreme sport experience is about both external and inner extremes. The participant, or perhaps we should adapt White's (1993) term 'the outlier', by preparing and actively participating in external extreme environments, is 'given' the opportunity or presented with the 'gift' of being open to venture into the extremes where separateness between subject and object no longer hold. At some stage, the external and the internal are momentarily experienced as one; the closed system that is a person's perception of self is released to openness and what is inside rushes out as what is outside rushes in; the external and internal are in harmony, are essentially integrated. Integration transforms as awareness is expanded and previously assumed boundaries dissolve. Thus, the traditional phenomenological notions of lived space, lived time, lived other and body are expanded and perhaps even transcended.

Husserl originally wrote about transcendence, in terms of the 'transcendent', that which transcends our own consciousness, that is, that which is an object of consciousness. A more traditional understanding of transcendence is described as 'going out of the self towards that which is beyond it'. That is, transcendence in the phenomenological sense is also about moving beyond the psychological ego and into the transcendental ego or true self (Hanna, 1993a, 1993b). This is a state where core boundaries interpenetrated, a state that cannot be reached by rational efforts (Ramsay, 1998). In essence, transcendence is the ability to go beyond self-imposed limitations (Tymieniecka, 1988), beyond the domain of the psychological and cognitive.

In our book, we consider transcendence in the extreme sport experience as an inclusive or holistic level of consciousness, a way of being-in-the-world, in which participants experience a slowing down of time, letting be, surpassing one's limitations, accepting death, absorption, integration of dichotomies and loss of self-consciousness. Our understanding is akin to descriptions of transcendent awareness as including stillness and peace, absence of I-ness, transformed sense of space, intuitive seeing and a sense of presence. These experiences refer to phenomena which are arguably outside traditional descriptions of intentionality and perception. These experiences lie beyond cognitive understanding. Thus, the extreme sport experience taken to its core nature can be thought about in terms of transcendence. Transcendence of self may be understood in terms of a momentary peek into a participant's own essence, core or true self. Transcendence thus extends beyond naïve perceptions of existence in a material or mundane world. Transcendence in the experience of our co-researchers also emerges as a powerful process of transformation of self and one's place in the world.

We have explored phenomenology in a contemporary context. We hope that the ideas proposed contribute to new understandings of the extreme sport experience and its significance for participants. More importantly, however, it is our fervent hope that the ideas may also contribute to the understanding of a range of human activities, from a stance of curiosity in which assumptions of positivism are put aside and space provided for a refreshed perspective on lived experience. A number of examples that have come from our explication of the extreme sport experience that might be appreciated in other contexts stand out: the descriptions of instant and deep positive transformations; the descriptions of a more intimate relationship to nature, and the descriptions of connecting to a deep inner self. However, what is more exciting and perhaps most important are the descriptions outlined in Chapters 10 and 11, descriptions that offer a peek into a deeper human potential, descriptions that may challenge our own perceptions of reality if we can but stop, listen and open ourselves to other potentials. These descriptions point to something which is *more* and yet available to us all. They allude to a deeper learning of what it means to be human.

References

Breashears, D. (1999). *High exposure: An enduring passion for Everest and unforgiving places*. New York: Simon & Schuster.

Davis, J. (1999). *The diamond approach: An introduction to the teachings of A. H. Almaas*. Boston, MA: Shambhala.

Hanna, F. J. (1993a). Rigorous intuition: Consciousness, being, and the phenomenological method. *The Journal of Transpersonal Psychology, 25*(2), 181–197.

Hanna, F. J. (1993b). The transpersonal consequences of Husserl's phenomenological method. *Humanistic Psychologist, 21*, 41–57.

Husserl, E. (1970). *The crisis of European sciences and the transcendental phenomenology: An introduction to phenomenological philosophy*. Evanston, IL: Northwestern University Press.

Langer, M. (1990). Merleau-Ponty and deep ecology. In G. A. Johnson & M. B. Smith (Eds), *Ontology and alterity in Merleau-Ponty* (pp. 115–129). Evanston, IL: Northwestern University Press.

Ramsay, H. (1998). Transcendence and reason. *Ratio, XI*(1), 55–65.

Tymieniecka, A. (1988). *Logos and life: The three movements of the Soul.* Dordrecht: Kluwer Academic Publishers.

Wertz, F. J. (1987). Meaning and research methodology: Psychoanalysis as a human science. Methods. *Journal for the Human Sciences, 1*(2), 91–135.

White, R. (1993). *Exceptional human experiences as a vehicle of grace: Parapsychology, faith, and the outlier mentality.* Paper presented at the Annual Conference of the Academy of Religion and Psychical Research Proceedings.

Zimmerman, M. E. (1992). The blessing of otherness: Wilderness and the human condition. In M. Oelschlaeger (Ed.), *The wilderness condition: Essays on environment and civilization* (pp. 245–270). San Francisco, CA: Sierra Club Books.

Index

Taylor & Francis eBooks

Helping you to choose the right eBooks for your Library

Add Routledge titles to your library's digital collection today. Taylor and Francis ebooks contains over 50,000 titles in the Humanities, Social Sciences, Behavioural Sciences, Built Environment and Law.

Choose from a range of subject packages or create your own!

Benefits for you

>> Free MARC records
>> COUNTER-compliant usage statistics
>> Flexible purchase and pricing options
>> All titles DRM-free.

Benefits for your user

>> Off-site, anytime access via Athens or referring URL
>> Print or copy pages or chapters
>> Full content search
>> Bookmark, highlight and annotate text
>> Access to thousands of pages of quality research at the click of a button.

REQUEST YOUR FREE INSTITUTIONAL TRIAL TODAY

Free Trials Available
We offer free trials to qualifying academic, corporate and government customers.

eCollections – Choose from over 30 subject eCollections, including:

Archaeology	Language Learning
Architecture	Law
Asian Studies	Literature
Business & Management	Media & Communication
Classical Studies	Middle East Studies
Construction	Music
Creative & Media Arts	Philosophy
Criminology & Criminal Justice	Planning
Economics	Politics
Education	Psychology & Mental Health
Energy	Religion
Engineering	Security
English Language & Linguistics	Social Work
Environment & Sustainability	Sociology
Geography	Sport
Health Studies	Theatre & Performance
History	Tourism, Hospitality & Events

For more information, pricing enquiries or to order a free trial, please contact your local sales team:
www.tandfebooks.com/page/sales

Routledge
Taylor & Francis Group

The home of
Routledge books

www.tandfebooks.com